# IN PURSUIT OF PHYSICAL MEDIUMSHIP

# IN PURSUIT OF PHYSICAL MEDIUMSHIP

*A Psychic Autobiography*

**ROBIN FOY**

JANUS PUBLISHING COMPANY LTD
Cambridge, England

First published in Great Britain 1996
by Janus Publishing Company Ltd.
The Studio, High Green
Gt. Shelford
Cambridge CB22 5EG

www.januspublishing.co.uk

Reprinted 2007



British Library Cataloguing-in-Publication Data.
A catalogue record for this book
is available from the British Library.

ISBN 978-1-85756-662-8



Cover Design Harold King

Typeset in (10.5)pt New Baskerville
By Intype London Ltd

Printed & bound in Great Britain

# Contents

# FOREWORD

TODAY, SOME 22 years after I took my first steps into the field of psychic research, or more specifically into the area of physical mediumship and its remarkable phenomena, I am privileged to be one of four members of the Scole Experimental Group of the New Spiritual Science Foundation, where group members sitting twice a week are receiving wonderful physical phenomena, brought about by their dedicated commitment to, and full cooperation with, a marvellous 'team' of spirit souls who are using the group for the purposes of helping their pioneering scientific experiments with new energy-based methods of producing repeatable physical phenomena.

Physical phenomena is the term used to describe those psychic phenomena which are produced as a result of physical mediumship. They are very rare in the world today, and fall into the category of objective phenomena; that is to say, they are to all intents and purposes based on reality – everybody present is able to see, hear and feel such manifestations as they occur, and the phenomena themselves can be recorded on audio tape or photographed under favourable conditions for posterity, thus proving that the experience is not the result of over-active imagination.

At the time of writing, the group has been able to witness an astonishing 99 different types of physical phenomena, produced for us by our spirit friends, and that number is growing almost weekly. Many of these types are brand new forms of phenomena that have never been witnessed or produced before, and we are therefore obliged, on a regular basis, to provide new terminology for the phenomena we are witnessing. There have been quite incredible results with psychic photography, amongst other things, and during experiments, the spirit team are now providing their own lighting so that members of the Scole group can see much of these fantastic phenomena which are going on around them. This includes visits by solid spirit entities, who are also able to address us by means of independently generated energy voices emanating from their tangible forms.

Many people never have the chance throughout their entire lives to witness even a small part of the wonders which I have been fortunate enough to experience over the last two decades, although it is true to say that with the advent of the New Spiritual Science Foundation, started in 1994 as a partnership between the Scole group and the spirit world (and on the direct instructions of our spirit friends), men and women of science and letters, as well as the general public, are now able to witness these wonders for themselves at Scole.

This book charts my own progress within the world of physical psychic phenomena since I first became involved almost by chance many years ago, and shows how, through much experience, dedication to the task and sheer dogged persistence, I have finally managed to meet up with a group of friends who share my absolute dedication, and who, through their complete commitment to the task at hand, have together created the perfectly harmonious conditions required by the spirit people, within which it is possible for a resolute team of spirit beings to develop and demonstrate physical phenomena on a sustained basis.

To reach this privileged position, however, my journey has been an epic one, full of frustration, endless cul-de-sacs and setbacks. The overall concept might be likened to a game of snakes and ladders – just as I felt that one had reached the top of the board, I always seemed to land on that last big 'snake' which cast me down again to square one! As you might imagine therefore, I have experienced many high and low points along the way. Often, through sheer frustration, I have been tempted to give up my pursuit of physical mediumship altogether but always the task has proved greater than the man and I have once again picked up the reins, till finally all the essential criteria have come together to provide the superb phenomena we now enjoy.

The fact that I did persist with the effort throughout the difficult years to reach the wonderful level of success now enjoyed within the

Scole group, is in the main due to the influences of three people, who between them provided the motivation, inspiration, leadership and determination required to generate enough staying power for my efforts to continue regardless. The first of these, a discarnate person (spirit entity) pops up from time to time within the book and is the subject of a separate chapter in the latter part of the volume. I shall refrain from saying too much about him at the moment, since his role will become clearer as the story unfolds. He was a well-known man during his lifetime, and has proved to me many times over during the years that he still has the power to motivate and inspire from beyond the grave.

The second person to whom I owe so much was rather more alive when I knew him during the last twenty years of his life. You will find many references in this volume to the late Leslie Flint (1911–1994). I make no apologies for that, because without the substantial input to my quest as a direct result of his mediumship, I would never have pursued physical phenomena as vigorously as I did. Leslie Flint provided the essential inspiration, and for over 60 years he practised a highly developed and very rare form of physical mediumship known as the 'independent voice' where, through their mental manipulation of a physically created replica of the human voicebox, produced by spirit 'operators' in his seance room (using a substance known as 'ectoplasm'), spirit entities were able to converse directly with sitters in a voice which often bore a close resemblance to their earthly voice. This could be heard by everyone present and actually came from a point in mid-air.

Born into abject poverty, Leslie Flint was first urged to develop his mediumship so that he could be of service to humanity when, at the tender age of 17 years old, he attended a Spiritualist service for the first time. He was given remarkable and accurate personal evidence by the lady trance medium, who told him that he would himself one day become a famous medium, and that the information she was getting psychically was coming from a guide who dressed as an Arab, but was not really an Arab. Much confused, Leslie went on to join a circle where he first experienced a trance condition, but before long he decided not to continue with his development. Suddenly, and out of the blue, he received a letter from a lady in Munich, Germany – a total stranger to him, who explained that she had been given a message in her circle to write to him (the communicator supplied Leslie's name and address accurately) and to tell him from his guide (a man who dressed as an Arab but really was not an Arab) that he must not give up his development as a medium.

Well, of course, the rest is history. Finally convinced that he really should develop his mediumship, Leslie went on to join a wonderful circle composed of just the right harmonious combination of people to give him the development that he needed. When the independent voice first manifested, a voice spoke in Italian, and this communicator subsequently identified himself as the actor Rudolph Valentino. In his film roles, Valentino had played an Arab in *The Sheik* and *The Son of the Sheik.* Leslie's physical mediumship went on to blossom, and he gathered around him a wonderful group of souls who became regular communicators during his seances. Later on in his mediumship, the principal communicator at all his seances was a young Cockney lad known as 'Mickey', who had sold newspapers at Camden Town during his lifetime, until he was knocked down and killed by a horse and cart.

Leslie must have been the most tested of all mediums in modern times. He was 'boxed up, tied up, sealed up, gagged, bound and held, and still the voices came to speak their message of life eternal'. Although his seances were held in the dark, there were times when researchers were able to observe the production, existence and operation of the ectoplasmic voicebox through an infrared telescope, thereafter testifying to its reality. When most groups visited him for a sitting they would receive wonderful personal evidence from relatives, who would often address them directly. There would also be the occasional talks and messages from Leslie's guides and helpers.

Whenever I visited Leslie with our home circle members, things tended to be different. I was always very careful not to give the medium any personal information about sitters, or about our home circle, so that anything that might be volunteered by the communicators would be evidential. Invariably, the proportion of personal communicators would be smaller when our group sat, but there was usually a strong presence of guides and helpers from our own home circle, giving help and advice for the group, and the voices of these guides were almost identical to the trance and independent voices they used to speak to us in our own groups.

Many of the conversations we had with the various spirit communicators at Leslie's were extremely interesting in their own right, and I am therefore including several extracts from the many private sittings which we were able to enjoy at Leslie Flint's home – all of them previously unpublished, but between them giving a valuable insight into the unique mediumship of a remarkable man and explaining to readers some details of the complexities of physical communication between our two worlds. I still have in my possession today a complete set of cassette tapes which between them constitute a unique, historic and exact record of each and every one of the private group sittings I was privileged to attend in Leslie's seance rooms over the years and, as you might imagine, these have formed the basis of much of the accurate dialogue contained in this book.

My association with Leslie Flint continued until his death in 1994 and you will find that his sittings are the thread which neatly bind together the other events of this book. It is most appropriate that the book hangs together in this way, for without my access to Leslie's mediumship, none of these things would have happened to me, and if that were the case, I should be much the poorer for it today in having missed such significant experiences.

Apart from the above-mentioned Flint tapes, I have always considered it a vital requirement to keep an audio cassette record of all physical seances and sittings I have attended for my archives. It is so important to retain such a memory-jogger because I can virtually guarantee that nobody – even the legendary 'Memory Man' – can remember *absolutely* everything which takes place over a period of one-and-a-half to two hours in a lively seance room. That's one of the reasons we have to keep moving to larger premises, to house my massive and fast-growing library of cassette tapes! (Only joking, of course.)

Throughout the book, the reader will note that I have frequently used the terms 'evidence' and 'evidential' to describe certain phenomena or spirit messages I have witnessed, or been given by various mediums over the years. Perhaps I should clarify here the context in which I have used the two words. Just as in a court of law, an accumulation of 'evidence' is presented to prove a case; if the evidence given is vast in quantity, and accurate in its content, then a case can be said to be proven. Any excellent evidence, which constitutes proof in a case, can be said to be 'evidential'. With regard to the psychic matters in which I have been involved, the crucial issue at hand has been the survival of the human spirit after death, and the existence of an afterlife which, in a way, could be likened to a court case, argued for and against the issue. I have long had my own personal proof of survival, backed by a plethora of evidence obtained over the years from a veritable army of mental and physical mediums. The most 'evidential' items have involved a vast quantity of accurate information given by and through those mediums which they could not, under any circumstances, have known about beforehand, thus constituting my own proof of survival.

Returning to the more recent successes, my grateful thanks must also go to the other dedicated members of the Scole group whose concentrated efforts over the last two-and-a-half years have precipitated the amazing physical phenomena now taking place in the Scole cellar by courtesy of the spirit 'team', who utilise their own brand new energy-based spirit world technology to achieve such unique results.

Finally, it would not be appropriate for me to conclude this foreword without giving due thanks and acknowledgement to the third person who had directly enabled me to carry out this labour of love for so long by helping me to reach successfully the original goal of being a part of a group who could achieve some excellent physical phenomena on a sustained basis – my dear wife Sandra. Without her help and support, I would have given up long ago and today I cannot think of another single person who would have so patiently endured my eccentric behaviour during the years when this important quest was uppermost in my mind. She deserves a medal!

*Robin Foy 1996*

# HOW IT ALL BEGAN

THE ADVERT IN the personal column of the *Leicester Mercury*, a local evening newspaper, seemed to stand out from all the others, as if it were printed in bold type (although in reality, it was not). I was drawn like a magnet to the wording and felt that I really must reply to it:

'If you are interested in psychic research,' read its message, 'please write to box – *Leicester Mercury*, giving details of your interest. Suitable persons will be contacted ...'

The above advert appeared in the autumn of 1973. I replied to it, as I felt compelled to do, and I received a response from the advertiser at once, a gentleman by the name of Elmer Browne, who was a businessman with a furnishing fabrics shop in Hinckley, then living at Leicester Forest East. Elmer had for many years run a home circle for the development of physical phenomena, and having recently lost a few of his sitters, the advert had been placed to discover a few new sincere candidates for sitting regularly in that home circle. He was a good friend of Leslie Flint and of Bertha Harris, and had for several years enjoyed regular sittings with both, often taking a party from the home circle to share his sittings in London with the two mediums.

Little did I know at that stage of the impact that my reply to the advert was going to have on my life from then on, or just how much I would become involved in physical mediumship and its phenomena over the next 20 years or so, to the point that the subject is now the most important thing in my life (besides my family of course), with me spending most of my spare time teaching, developing, promoting, organising demonstrations and ensuring the safe practice of physical mediumship and its phenomena throughout the world, on behalf of our spirit friends. It is my joy, it is my passion, and for my sins I have been lucky enough to witness many amazing examples of physical phenomena over the years since I first 'put my toe in the water', so to speak. The vast knowledge and expertise on the subject that I have gained during this period stands me in good stead for the regular teaching and lecturing that I now undertake, both singly and on behalf of the New Spiritual Science Foundation (an important organisation which has grown out of our own home circle), in an effort to pass this vital information on to others.

But to return to the beginning. As a child, I had always enjoyed a healthy interest in ghost stories, which my parents indulged by buying me appropriate books for birthday and Christmas presents. I still have my very first of these – *Phantoms of the Night,* by Elliott O'Donnell, and *Shane Leslie's Ghost Book,* both of which I spent many a happy hour reading and re-reading. There were always the family jokes about ghosts and in my very early years these often involved my parents kidding me that certain old houses they pointed out as we passed regularly were 'haunted', causing me to hold such properties in great awe, but whilst my mother, who was naturally psychic, often took the opportunity to have a private sitting with one or other of the clairvoyant Spiritualist mediums inhabiting the Louth, Grimsby and Cleethorpes areas where I grew up, she would always take a friend with her, rather than involve me, or my father who, apart from the family jokes, tended to be rather sceptical in these matters. What a shame she never developed her own potential mediumship! With the knowledge I now have, I recognise that she could have been an accomplished clairvoyant and clairaudient medium herself. But we all have free will and it simply never happened.

Although I came from this background, with my mother's more than passing interest in the subject, she never discussed her experiences so I did not have the opportunity in my early days to learn much about Spiritualism. When I passed the local Spiritualist churches as a boy, I would wonder what was going on inside and somehow believe that everything therein from hymn books to pews and people was constantly flying about in the air! Such was the extent of my knowledge at that time and as I grew older I gave the matter little thought. Neither my father nor I ever encountered any 'ghosts', and my mother spoke little about a traumatic time in her life when she had been critically ill with a disease known as purpura, resulting in her having her spleen removed, during which period she saw spirit people around her constantly.

So I think it is fair to say that when I attended the interview at his home suggested by Elmer Browne following the advert, it was from a background of total ignorance of the Spiritualist movement and its phenomena that I approached the subject. I was, however, excited about the prospect of becoming involved but was not biased in any way towards it. If anything, I suppose it is true to say that I was slightly sceptical but able to keep an open mind as to its possibilities, due mainly to my having experienced two very vivid and evidential instances of clairaudience myself during my late teens. At the time I was a pilot in the RAF and did not know how to classify these experiences, having nobody suitable to discuss them with.

One Sunday afternoon, following lunch in the Officers Mess, and while resting in my room, I heard a woman's voice address me, apparently from mid-air. I was actually quite sober at the time. The kindly voice, which I judged to be coming from a point just a few feet in front of me, appeared to be a normal and seemingly natural human voice. I vividly remember the words spoken on that occasion, when the simple message told me: 'You can heal with your hands!'

For a few moments I was taken aback, and somewhat shocked, but then I speedily took in the message – and a feeling of euphoria and excitement came over me. Was this really true? Could I in fact, heal with my hands? Logic flew out of the window and I remember dashing out into the corridor to stick my hands on to every one of my unsuspecting colleagues who happened to come my way! The long and the short of it though was that they all thought I was mad! And in any case, they were mostly aircrew and fit young men to boot, who didn't need any healing. After much ribbing, I learned quickly to keep my own counsel. But many years later, I was to discover that I really did possess a powerful healing gift ...

On another occasion about six months later, I was on leave and staying with my parents at their home in Grimsby. Once again, while standing in my bedroom, a lady's voice, apparently speaking from space some three feet in front of me, announced that, 'You will marry Linda Mitchell.' The young lady referred to was an ex-girlfriend who was the last person on my mind at that time but sure enough, about four years later, the prediction turned out to be spot on …

I feel that at this juncture it would be advantageous to include a brief description of the different forms of mediumship and their phenomena to which I shall refer as the book progresses. In essence, there are basically two forms of mediumship: mental mediumship and physical mediumship.

Mental mediumship is by far the most common form of mediumship in the world today. It occurs when a medium sees (clairvoyance), hears (clairaudience) or senses (clairsentience) a spirit communicator. Any information thus received by the medium is passed on to the 'sitters', who are themselves unable to witness what the medium sees, hears or senses. Mental mediumship is extremely widespread and there are literally hundreds of thousands of mental mediums – good, bad and indifferent – in various stages of mediumistic development practising today throughout the world.

Those wishing to consult them in a private capacity should have no problem in finding a good sensitive (a person who is naturally mediumistic and able to give messages or readings from the spirit world), bearing in mind the fact that standards of mental mediumship do vary immensely. Anyone seeking the services of a medium should take adequate care in selecting a person who meets their own needs, ensuring that they find one who is competent, conscientious and sympathetic and who also provides a high standard of mediumship for them. (Even the best and most famous of these mediums cannot be in harmony with every one of their sitters – I have visited well-known mediums in the past who are excellent with other sitters, but for some reason, cannot get good results with me.) And it is an established fact that occasionally famous mediums, who can fill a hall or a theatre in demonstrating their wonderful mental mediumship to a capacity audience, prove to be less than adequate during a private sitting on a one-to-one basis, as their mediumship, for one reason or another, seems to work best in a situation where they are confronted by a large number of people.

It must also be stressed here that mediums are NOT fortune tellers. It is their function simply to link together those in the spirit world with friends and loved ones still here on earth and, in so doing, to provide first class evidence of survival of bodily death. Mediums cannot 'call up the dead' to order – there can be no communication unless the spirit entity chooses, and has the desire, to communicate through a medium.

It is the other type of mediumship – physical mediumship – that has concerned me more since I became involved in Elmer Browne's remarkable circle, and round which my life now revolves. Physical phenomena are very real and objective. *Everybody* present when physical mediumship is taking place can actually see and hear what is going on. Phenomena can be photographed (when permission is first given by the spirit operators) and tape-recorded for posterity. In its purest forms, physical phenomena can provide exceptional evidence of survival and proof of life after death. After all, there is little to compare with something that can be heard with one's own ears, seen with one's own eyes, and touched with one's own hands.

This category of mediumship covers many different types of phenomena – at the time of writing, we have witnessed 99 different types in our own current experimental group and there are still many forms that we have not yet witnessed. Some of the main phenomena of physical mediumship include such things as materialisation (solid, visible and animated spirit figures); transfiguration (an ectoplasmic mask over the medium's face is moulded to take on the visible features of the spirit communicator); trumpet or independent direct voice (spirit voices emanating from a levitated megaphone-like trumpet or, in the latter case, coming directly and literally from mid-air); apports (solid objects, often little presents meant for the sitters, appearing from nowhere); psychic surgery (physical spirit operations, sometimes performed by materialised spirit doctors); psychic photography (spirit 'extras' appearing on ordinary photographs); EVP – the Electronic Voice Phenomena (where extra voices occur on a tape-recording); TPP – Television Picture Phenomena (a newer phenomena where deceased persons can be viewed on a television screen as they communicate) and ITC – Instrumental TransCommunication, which is a similar form of relatively new phenomenon, but involves communication through telephones, computers and fax machines.

Physical mediumship is much, much rarer than its counterpart, mental mediumship. I have been able to trace less than 200 cases of well-documented physical mediums to date throughout the world since the start of modern Spiritualism in 1848 and, prior to my formation of the Noah's Ark Society in 1990, physical mediumship was in extreme danger of becoming totally extinct. I am pleased to say that this is no longer the case, because of the interest created in the subject by that society, by the New Spiritual Science Foundation and by the new crop of physical mediums who have come on to the scene since. It is estimated, however, that only one person in many thousands actually has the ability to develop physical mediumship to its full potential, although others may enjoy various minor types of physical phenomena which they are able to develop themselves without too much difficulty.

But to return to my narrative: I found myself, in 1973, in the company of several other potential sitters at Elmer Browne's home circle when I attended his interview. In many ways, I was quite surprised and relieved because everybody there seemed so normal. More than that I knew absolutely nothing of the subject and Bill (our subsequent nickname for Elmer Browne) took the trouble to explain patiently the ins and outs of his physical home circle. Some left but about six of us remained, fascinated by what we were being told, and it was agreed that we should join this physical circle on a trial basis.

Before we went home on that first occasion, Bill asked us if we would like to see his seance room, which was situated in a house extension built over his garage and could only be reached through the main bedroom on the first floor. Naturally we were interested to do so and consequently followed Bill upstairs in a crocodile formation. As I came level with the stairs to start climbing, I heard the sound of a baby crying – so loud that it appeared to come from the middle of our group. At least four others in front of and behind me heard it too and were startled. There were no babies in the house, which was detached with a good 50 feet between it and adjoining houses. There was a field behind, and about 100 feet of garden separated the house from the road in front. When we arrived in the seance room, I mentioned this occurrence to Bill and he ventured the opinion that perhaps it was a message for one of us.

Musing on this on the way home, I eventually let it drop from my mind until, that is, about two or three days later. My first wife and I had applied to adopt and a couple of days after this event, we had a telephone call from the adoption agency to say that there was a baby ready for us to collect. Nobody other than myself was aware of that at the interview, so what a piece of evidence it was for me, coming, as it did, out of mid-air. Today I am extremely proud of my son, whose coming was predicted in such a dramatic manner and who, having graduated from university, is now a police officer and pillar of the community. Perhaps one day he may even choose to develop his own psychic potential.

# I BECOME HOOKED ON PHYSICAL PHENOMENA

THERE IS NO doubt that the Elmer Browne physical home circle whetted my appetite to learn more about physical mediumship and its phenomena. As I recall, there were usually about 10 to 12 sitters present at each weekly seance. It was held in total darkness and the seance room was basically bare, save for the chairs placed round the edge of the room – all tight against the wall, as there was little space in the room to accommodate all of the sitters. Certainly it would have been physically impossible for anyone to move around behind the chairs, even if they had wished so to do. The room was not used for any purpose other than that of a seance room, so that its atmosphere was not disturbed between sittings, except for its being cleaned.

There was a large, old fashioned record player in a sizeable cabinet occupying the corner of the room, next to which Bill (Elmer) sat, so that he could operate it and change the records from time to time. His wife, Cath, sat on the other side of the record player, and I remember a couple by the name of Leslie and Gail who were regulars. Stan Frith joined the circle at the same time as I did, and Sue Rogers, who married while I was a member of the circle, also sat. I tended to sit next to Bill, on his right-hand side, with a very pleasant lady called Shirley on my right, and her husband John sitting opposite to me on the other side of the room. I am pleased to say that Shirley and John Berkeley have remained my firm friends to this day and Shirley taught me much of the knowledge I gained in the early days about the basic facts of Spiritualism. Another frequent sitter at the time was Alan Gauld, who was destined to become a president of the SPR (Society for Psychical Research). Even then, Alan had had much specialist experience of hauntings and psychic research and has written a number of learned books on the subject. There were a few more regular sitters and others who joined for a while and then left during the period that I sat with the circle.

Some years prior to my joining the circle, Bill had been more than impressed with a small but interesting book called *The Blue Room* by Clive Chapman. Published in 1927, it tells the story of Clive Chapman's home circle in Dunedin, New Zealand, and the development of his niece Pearl Judd as a physical medium but, more especially, as a powerful independent voice medium. In the Blue Room, where they regularly sat, they developed independent voice mediumship in the light and it was Bill's driving ambition to achieve the same results in his home circle.

Consequently, Bill took to having two separate and different periods of sitting on circle nights. The first would be held as previously described, in total darkness, with plenty of singing by the sitters, interspersed with records on the gramophone to give our voices a rest from time to time. It was quickly noted that certain songs acted as 'power songs', lifting the vibrations, increasing the ever-present coldness and generally giving better results than other songs. These we would sing several times over and it was not long after my joining the circle that we started to notice faint but audible bell-like spirit voices singing along with us, apparently superimposed separately upon our own voices. There were loud independent whistles happening regularly in the circle too, which Bill wholly accredited to a child guide of the circle – 'Joey'. Raps and taps were frequent during sittings and often these would run, in rapid sequence, the whole length of the wall behind our chairs. Since no live person present could possibly have got behind these chairs, this phenomenon was most impressive whenever it happened, and even more impressive were the few occasions when I was poked in the back by solid, materialised fingers. Alan Gauld has written of the time when, on one occasion, I commented on the bell-like voices close to my ear. Wanting to establish their reality or otherwise, he secretly lifted a microphone close to my ear, with which he was actually able to record the faint voices.

It was in this circle too that I first entered a trance condition myself: one evening, without warning, I experienced a choking sensation that seemed to go on for ages, followed by a semi-conscious state in which

I found myself speaking in a strange voice. I knew what was being said but I had no control whatsoever over my vocal organs. It only happened the once in this circle, as trance was discouraged by Bill in favour of developing the independent voice.

After the main part of the sitting, Bill would ask us to try again downstairs and, in his efforts to develop voices in the light, we would sit for a short time with just the light of the flame-effect electric fire. On several occasions there, too, we would have whistles and raps, or notice the faint voices singing along with us.

One night, out of the darkness, there were a couple of loud sentences spoken in the independent voice by a spirit communicator. How we celebrated then! A previous sitter in the circle had left a bottle of champagne cooling in the fridge to be opened specifically when, without doubt, we had achieved definite independent voice. That night, we cracked open the champagne.

Then one day, shortly after I started to sit with the circle, Bill arranged a seance for the circle with Leslie Flint. A party of about eight of us set off in two cars for London in the spring of 1974. We called on Leslie at his home in Bayswater and what an occasion that turned out to be. Leslie's house was close to Paddington Station and we had difficulty in finding a place to park the car. It was an unusual house, in the sense that its hallway was a 'tunnel' structure sticking out on to the pavement and, from the first time that I saw it, it always reminded me of an Eskimo igloo. Leslie and Bram Rogers, his secretary and friend, occupied the basement flat while letting out the rest of the property; there was a wrought-iron spiral staircase leading off the hallway down into the basement, to the living room which doubled as his seance room.

The eight of us in Bill's party sat round in the lighted room on the chairs and settees, having been welcomed and shown in by Bram. Leslie's chair was on its own in the corner, with a microphone about three feet in front of it, and somewhat higher. This was the spot from where most of the independent voices originated and it was therefore easier for Leslie to record the sitting. (Bram often made copies for clients afterwards.) About 15 minutes later, Leslie joined us, and sat down on his chair, ready for the seance. At that point, the room lights were put out, and we experienced total darkness, due to the necessary heavy blackout material around the windows and doors. The sitting was under way. The first thing I noticed was that Leslie didn't bother with music or singing but just chatted to us all quite naturally about the subject of physical phenomena and his (sometimes hilarious) personal experiences as a physical medium, relating tales of the many famous people who had sat with him over the years. In all he was an extremely interesting man to listen to and, apart from the actual sitting itself, it was worth the visit just to hear him talk.

The best was yet to come, however. About 15 to 20 minutes into the sitting, a shrill Cockney voice could be heard – loud and clear – coming from mid-air, in front of, and above the medium. This was 'Mickey', Leslie's young guide – during his earth life, a newspaper seller from Camden Town who had been knocked down and 'killed' at a very early age and now answered to the name of 'Mickey', instead of his proper name of John Whitehead. Mickey, whose voice and typical raucous laughter (sometimes loud enough to be heard outside the house) I was to come to know very well over the next 17 years, was a real 'character'. His humour was effervescent and sitters could not fail to be caught up in the almost party atmosphere which he generated by his jokes, quips, and teasing of participants, while acting as the MC for Leslie's seances. There was, however, a serious purpose behind his jollity, and that was to relax the sitters, so as to ensure that they were not tense during the proceedings, thus spoiling the harmony and sympathetic conditions necessary for the production of the voice phenomena. In addition, because of his experience of communication built up over many years during his work with Leslie, Mickey would often pass on messages from those loved ones, friends and acquaintances of the sitters in spirit who, for one reason or another, were unable themselves to speak through the independent voice, and provide evidence of survival on their behalf. Other voices were very weak and would either peter out before they had finished their communication, or break off with obvious emotion, and Mickey would finish the communication for them.

This first sitting with Leslie Flint was for me a real revelation. In all there must have been about 15 different voices which spoke to us over the period of around two-and-a-half hours during which we sat. Some were regular communicators at Leslie's seances but others were recognised by members of our party as their wives, husbands, or relatives. There were both adults and children, male and female, talking to us, some of them guides who gave excellent evidence of their involvement with us. The voices all portrayed totally different personal characteristics, and some who gave advice about Bill's home circle were sustained for as long as 15 to 20 minutes. There was a mixture of accents, from childish trebles to the cultured tones of actress Dame Ellen Terry; from an Irish brogue to the unmistakable broken English of a French communicator, and from the 'cor blimey' Cockney tones of Mickey to the distinguished speaking voice of an upper-class scientist. They were all there, and I left the sitting walking on air. This was for me. I could hardly believe what I had witnessed that day but was determined thereafter to pursue by every means available to me the elusive physical phenomena of Spiritualism. To read as much about it as possible ... to study and investigate it in depth ... and above all, to continue to develop it through the home circle. All these years later, I am still following the quest which I set for myself, though most of the objectives outlined within my enthusiastic resolution have long since been reached.

# INVADED BY THE DREADED EVP

I CONTINUED TO sit in the Elmer Browne circle for a total of about 18 months, enjoying yet another visit to London with the circle during this period to sit with Leslie Flint. I was by now making an effort to visit several Spiritualist churches, to see how various mediums worked there, comparing their mental phenomena of clairvoyance and clairaudience to physical mediumship and noting the differences between the respective methods. My job as a representative took me to all parts of England, Scotland and Wales, and I made a point of observing mediums from lots of different areas to see how their mediumship varied. Generally, at these meetings, I would be given a message myself, and often one which mentioned physical mediumship. I was learning the basic facts about psychic matters overall, reading as much as I was able to lay my hands on about the subject and becoming aware of the movement of Spiritualism itself. I was soon able to tell a good medium from a bad one, and I began, through these different mediums, to amass a plethora of 'evidence' of survival from friends and relatives in the spirit world.

While 'doing' the various churches, I remember well one instance of my receiving clairaudience myself which was so vivid that it appeared real and objective to me. I had popped into an afternoon service at a Spiritualist church in Digbeth, Birmingham, to hear a 'new' medium whose work I had not previously witnessed. The clairvoyant demonstration during the service was going well, and I was very interested in the medium on the rostrum, as she appeared to be pretty accurate, and the church, for once, was relatively full – always a testimony to a good medium. Suddenly, during her demonstration, I distinctly 'heard' a bunch of keys being rattled in the row in front of me, and this loud noise seemed to move along the row, to left and right, for a couple of minutes. I was getting cross, as I could not hear the medium very well with that noise going on but, just as I was about to remonstrate with the people in front, the noise stopped. At the time, it did not really occur to me but, thinking about it afterwards, nobody else in the church had shown any sign of having heard the keys rattle when I did, and it was so loud that surely they couldn't have missed the rude interruption. Anyway, the demonstration continued, and shortly afterwards I heard the rattling keys again, this time moving up and down two rows, and across to the other side of the hall. It began to dawn on me that no one person could have achieved that rapid movement of the keys and so, against my immediate inclination, I stayed quiet till the end of the service. Significantly, I had not received any messages myself at this particular service – the first time in many weeks that this had been the case.

At the end of the service I could restrain myself no longer, and asked the people in front of me if they had been rattling keys, or heard such a noise during the service but, of course, they had not. In fact, I think they wondered if I was a little peculiar in the head to ask such a question. However, I mentioned the matter to the medium before I left and she told me that it must have been a personal message for me – symbolising the keys to new conditions. Not long afterwards, my life was to change drastically, with a new job many miles away and a new home to boot. Plenty of new conditions there ...

Lots of things happened spontaneously to me during my early experiences. Somebody told me that I needed a crystal ball, so that I could develop clairvoyance for myself and I decided one lunchtime that I would buy one. Not knowing about these things, I left the office in Birmingham from where I was working at the time, to do a lunchtime tour of antique shops in the city, asking about a crystal ball. Today, I would consider those shops the last place to find such an object but, naïve as I was, I called on many shops and continued to ask. I had not had any luck but, on my way back to the office, I decided to try just one last antique store before giving up. There, I used the same innocent patter as before: 'I know you might think this a silly question, but, ... do you happen to have a crystal ball for sale, or know of where I might buy one?'

The lady owner of the shop looked amazed and asked me, 'Do you mean like this?' as she proceeded to fish out from under the counter a battered old cardboard box filled with straw on which was reposing a ball-shaped object, wrapped up in what appeared to be gypsy scarf. She unwrapped it, and there before me was the loveliest natural crystal ball I could possibly have imagined! I inquired about the price and was told the relevant sum, the lady adding that she could not sell it to me. The story was that the ball was about 700 years old, having originally come from a castle in mid-Europe. It had belonged for generations to a gypsy family and had been passed down from mother to daughter for hundreds of years. The elderly Romany lady, who was also a well-known Spiritualist medium in the Midlands, had died and in the traditional way it had been passed on to her daughter. Now the daughter had married, and settled down with her husband (another Romany, with the surname of Wagner) in a council house in the Birmingham area. For one reason or another, she had decided not to take up psychic work, with the consequence that she wanted to sell the ball. However, she was not prepared to sell it to anyone. She felt that it ought to go to someone who was spiritual, who would put it to good use.

The requirement, before I bought the crystal ball, was that I visit Mr and Mrs Wagner, to be interviewed and approved as a new owner. This I did, and it turned out to be a most interesting and enlightening visit. The inside of their council house was neat and clean and hung with a combination of brasses and Romany artifacts. In fact, it looked infinitely more like a caravan than a council house. They were lovely people and we sealed our bargain for the crystal ball with a handshake and nip of alcohol. Need I say that my crystal ball is now one of my proudest possessions?

Also while sitting regularly in Bill's circle there was a great interest taken by sitters, and Bill in particular, in 'Raudive Voices'. There was a lot of publicity about this new form of phenomenon, subsequently known as EVP (Electronic Voice Phenomena), which was discovered by Swedish film maker Friedrich Jurgenson in 1959, but interest in the voices was boosted when a Latvian psychologist and philosopher, Konstantin Raudive, visited Jurgenson and started his own in-depth research on the voices, culminating in the publication of his book

*Breakthrough* in 1971, which detailed his experiments. This heralded massive worldwide interest in the phenomenon which, for many years afterwards was referred to as the 'Raudive Voices', before reverting to Jurgenson's original name of the 'Electronic Voice Phenomenon', or EVP for short.

Early in 1974, Bill started to get audible 'extra voices' on his cassette tapes each week when he played back his recordings of the circle sittings. He had simply developed the ability to receive EVP, and he was extremely excited about this. So much so, that we always used to spend some time before our weekly seances listening to the EVP which had appeared on his tapes from the previous week's sitting. There were some amazing voices coming up each week – some giving their own names, or calling one of our names. Others were able to manage whole sentences and provide lucid messages for the circle. The phenomenon developed so that Bill was getting 20 or 30 examples of EVP each week on his circle tapes and, eventually, he was also able to get these messages on his own by sitting quietly with the tape. I have since learned over the years that the ability to acquire EVP can be 'caught' like a common cold by one person from another – an instance of the well-known 'knock-on effect' (which can occur with several types of physical mediumship), and it was not long before I caught this particular ability myself.

In the early days of my sitting with this circle, I could not afford to buy myself a cassette tape recorder to use during seances (they were comparatively expensive then, having not long been available), and I ventured to experiment by recording a sitting on a small hand-held dictaphone which I used for work to prepare my call reports. The tape inside was a mini-cassette which only lasted for 15 minutes, before bleeping when it reached the end of the tape. I only got the opportunity to use it on one occasion, before it was well and truly banned from the circle by Bill. Picture, if you can, ten sitters jumping out of their skins in the dark when the offending dictaphone bleeped loudly as circle members listened intently for physical phenomena.

However, when I played the first recording back, I was amazed to discover on it several instances of EVP. I could not wait to get home to try it again and once more I was treated very quickly to numerous extra voices – both words and phrases – some actually calling my name. This seemed too good to be true so, rooting through my piggy bank, I came up with just enough cash to buy a second-hand primitive cassette tape recorder. I started to experiment at home on a regular basis as well as in the circle and I was speedily getting excellent results, with better and better voices. Messages became more and more relevant to me personally, as I got to the point where I could ask actual questions, the answers to which were given logically, fairly and gratuitously on the tape through EVP. I was soon able to identify guides and relatives in the spirit world who were making the effort regularly to communicate with me in this way.

Around this time, in order to earn a few extra bob to make ends meet, I had a part-time job on two or three evenings and nights a week navigating locum doctors around Birmingham and its surrounding area, so that they could attend to emergency medical calls. One of my duties was to listen in to the radio from the control unit, to take new calls, and coordinate details of patients' symptoms and their addresses. So that I could do this, I always waited in the car when the doctor was visiting a patient. It meant that I could often be hanging around in the car for half an hour or so while the doctors completed their treatment. Throughout these long waiting periods, I took to recording the 'white noise' from the radio for periods of about 15 minutes. During these sessions, the EVP I was receiving on the tape developed to the point where I was getting 'snowed under' with messages. As many as three hundred EVP words, phrases and sentences appeared in the course of one 15-minute experiment and it could take me a whole week to play back and catalogue everything that had been received in this way.

When I mentioned to Bill the deluge of results I was getting, we decided on a little 'duel' to see who was able to get the most results in a given time. I have an amusing memory of one Sunday, when we set this experiment up so that, on a given signal, we each recorded for five minutes. We both got excellent results, although I don't think we ever actually counted the results for comparison, but the interesting aspect of this experiment was the fact that while we were both in the same room when recording and our tape recorders both started running at exactly the same time, the EVP messages on our tapes were totally different.

Towards the end of my time with the Elmer Browne circle in early 1975, I found that I was constantly getting the same EVP message, repeated day after day, and session after session. It said simply, 'Go to London.' Nothing was further from my mind at that particular moment but about a month after this EVP message was first heard, right out of the blue, I was made redundant from my main job as a UK paper mill's area sales manager. I wrote off for several jobs with paper makers throughout the country, two of them based in the London area. I believed I had a good chance of four jobs in the provinces but that I had little chance of getting the jobs in London. Guess where I ended up? Yes, in London! I was actually offered *both* of the jobs there and none of the jobs outside London.

So, in 1975, sadly I took my leave of the other sitters in my first physical circle and went to work for Bowaters Paper Mills, based at their Tooting offices. Since my home was still in Kegworth, in Leicestershire, I would stay during the week at a small commercial hotel with lots of character, situated in Streatham, and called the Thrale Hall Hotel, returning home only at weekends, but more of that later.

In the meantime, I had placed an advert in the *Psychic News,* seeking either a physical circle to join, or people of like mind to start a new one. I had just three replies – one from the Cambridge area, which was a little too far away to be of practical value. The second came from two charming ladies – sisters, one of whom was a widow living at Golders Green. They wanted to start a physical circle and hoped for my help in so doing. The final reply came from a gentleman I shall refer to by the name of 'John', who had considerable experience of physical phenomena and was living in lodgings in Romford, Essex.

I also answered another of the *Psychic News* adverts myself – from a circle looking for new sitters – which led to my joining a home circle at Clapton Common for a short period but the potential here was limited, so I gave up my place in the circle soon afterwards to concentrate more on the replies from my own advert.

# SETTLING DOWN IN LONDON

ONCE I ARRIVED in London during September 1975, apart from gravitating naturally towards physical circles and physical mediums, I continued with the process of learning as much as I could about all matters psychic, and started the beginnings of a library of psychic books – particularly, of course, those dealing with the physical phenomena of Spiritualism. I was lucky, in that several just seemed to turn up in the right place at the right time. Most were second-hand books, long out of print, but nevertheless of great value because of the information they contained. Since then, my personal psychic library has grown steadily and today boasts over 1,300 volumes – many of them quite rare.

Although I had already been sitting in a physical circle up in the Midlands, I had never, for instance, had a private sitting with a clairvoyant or clairaudient medium. I made up for this during my early days in London. After work, in the evenings, I had a lot of time on my hands before returning to the Thrale Hall Hotel in Streatham to sleep, and I used it well, visiting Spiritualist churches and pyschic centres all over the London area. Shortly after arriving in the metropolis, I paid a visit to the Spiritualist Association of Great Britain (SAGB) in Belgrave Square, where I enjoyed my first three private sittings on the same day, with Margaret Pearson, Charles Horrey and David Smith.

In the event, they all turned out to be very evidential and I obtained some brilliant proof of life after death from the communicators who returned to me. The mediums were extremely accurate, which heartened me considerably as it was also confirmed that I had pyschic work to do and that it had been vital for me to move at that time into the London area. Some 20 years further on, my tally of private sittings has reached well over 250, and I view things differently with the knowledge I now have. Poor private sittings at my first attempt (I have had plenty since) might have put me right off the subject – but it just so happened that those three mediums were all of an excellent standard.

I was very keen to get involved in another circle so it was not long before I made arrangements to meet the people who had replied to my *Psychic News* advert. Since the ladies in Golders Green had already told me in their reply that they wished to start a physical circle, I visited them first. I demonstrated the EVP to them and they were fascinated to hear the results we speedily obtained on my cassette tape recorder. I believe they were somewhat impressed, as both of their names were called by communicators on the tape, as well as their receiving a few personal messages. We enjoyed a convivial evening of conversation together and seemed to get on, so it was decided that we should sit once a week at the home of the widowed sister – a most attractive lady – although she knew very little of psychic matters.

Their hospitality was overwhelming. Both insisted on organising a meal for me each time I arrived to sit in the circle. There was usually a surfeit of food and it was obvious that they had gone to a good deal of trouble. So even on occasions when I did not feel hungry, I tended to eat what was there out of courtesy. For those of you who have met me, those meals must have contributed to my acquiring my present larger-than-life figure! It did not help my digestion just prior to the circle either, but nevertheless, results did appear to be promising after a few weeks. We quickly had loud raps and taps and, on several occasions the trumpet we placed upright on the floor each time we sat was observed to sway. The room would grow quite cold and occasionally we had psychic breezes. When, however, we tried to augment the power in the circle by introducing additional sitters, we had a couple of disastrous sessions and abandoned the idea. Despite this, all went well for a while, until one week the widowed sister asked if I minded her sitting in circle in a negligée. I must confess I thought that unusual and I became rather worried when, immediately after the circle, the other sister excused herself and discreetly disappeared home. This circle was not destined to go any farther, because at that time my attention was set firmly on psychic matters and the development of physical phenomena. My first marriage was, in any case, under a great terminal strain, partly because of my ongoing involvement with Spiritualism, so the very last thing on my mind was any sort of new romantic relationship. In all, the circle had run for just three months.

The other reply turned out to be more promising. Initially, John of Romford wrote to me to inquire about the EVP I had developed (since I had mentioned this in my *Psychic News* advert). I went to Romford to meet him and one evening we had a long chat, together with his landlady Joyce, who knew nothing at all of Spiritualism and physical circles, but was happy to keep an open mind. It turned out that John had sat with physical mediums such as Helen Duncan and William Olsen in the past and had himself been given positive indications of his own trance mediumship. Both John and Joyce were good company and, after once again demonstrating the electronic voices to them, the results of which interested John greatly, it was decided that we would conduct a little experiment to see if he could slip into an impromptu trance that very evening.

Having then had little experience of trance as such, I was quite amazed, and almost shot off my seat when the silence was broken by a loud and forcefully anguished African Zulu voice coming from the medium. This turned out to be his main guide, Khoba, who was making his presence felt in a big way and a fascinating hour was spent in the company of this powerful African, a guide that the later circle came to love dearly. On this first occasion that I heard him manifest, the guide had great difficulty in speaking and it transpired at a later date that he had initially needed to re-live his death in order to clear the way for his later conversation with us. In addition, his tongue had been cut out during his earth life by his enemies, so that it required a great effort on his part to get used to the idea of speaking again, and his first attempts were in his native language.

Comparatively inexperienced as I was, I immediately recognised in John a natural and powerful trance medium. Since he could not remember what had been said by Khoba, I played some of it back to him. Joyce, his landlady, was flabbergasted, and so was I. John was excited by this apparent breakthrough by his guide and, following further discussions, the three of us decided to start sitting on a weekly basis for the development of physical phenomena. John knew that I, too, had had indications of a light trance control in the past, and we agreed to see what happened when we got together, entering into the circle without any preconceived ideas.

Over the weeks, John's natural trance ability got better and better. Khoba came to speak to us every week, and gradually more and more guides and spirit helpers made themselves known to us through John's superb mediumship. We built up an ongoing relationship quickly with our spirit visitors, who all had their own separate and distinct personalities, to the point where they became better friends to us than many of those acquaintances we had in the earthly world.

There was a jolly Scotsman – Jock (really Angus McGregor); Doctor Dunn, a well-spoken scientist of Irish origin, leader of the team of spirit scientists who constantly worked with us. Sir Winston Churchill, speaking in an exact replica of his earth voice, was a very regular communicator at that circle. Occasionally my own Matabele medicine man guide, Zimba, would speak through me in trance, regularly joking about the bone through his nose. Sometimes, Khoba and Zimba would natter away in their own languages to each other, with John and I both in trance at the same time. Several other spirit helpers would also pop in from time to time, just to say hello.

Doctor Latimer made his presence known to us quickly, and worked from the spirit world to control the bodily functions of the sitters whilst we were in circle, ensuring that no harm came to us medically as a result of the seances. While on earth, he was a member of the medical profession who suffered from Parkinson's Disease, which eventually progressed into hyperstatic pneumonia, finally causing his demise into the spirit world.

The circle soon became established and early results were rapid. There was an occasion right at the start when my name and a brief message through the independent voice was delivered to John and me in a moment of relaxation – with full electric lighting on (I might add here that this was not actually during the circle, as we sat in total darkness).

The harmony between the three of us was extremely good. We were all sitting with open minds and enjoyed a common sense of humour, which lifted the atmosphere considerably, helping the developing phenomena along. Participation in the circle always seemed to give us a substantial appetite (something that often occurs in a physical circle, as I have later learned) and we took to frying up a batch of sausages afterwards to assuage our hunger pangs. However, as the plates were slippery, the sausages had a habit of jumping off them on to the floor and we often ended the evening splitting our sides with laughter as we chased the elusive sausages round.

It was early on in the history of the Romford circle that John came into contact with a 'Mr Cross' – a gentleman who lived in the village of Blackmore, Essex, where he ran a home circle of his own with a total of five sitters. John arranged for us to have a one-off experimental sitting with Mr Cross's circle and we duly went to Blackmore one night to see what would happen. As I recall, nothing of real note occurred at that sitting. However, a few days later, a recent prediction by Dr Dunn came true. At just our third sitting, Dr Dunn had informed us that they were trying to bring one more person into the group. Following the joint sitting with Mr Cross's circle, one of his sitters called Mike telephoned John to ask if he could sit in our circle. No approach from us had been made but Dr Dunn's prediction had been fulfilled and Mike joined the circle at the end of October 1975.

# THE SEYMER ROAD SEANCES

THE ROMFORD CIRCLE progressed very well, even though the sitters realised that it could be years before independent voice might be developed on a constant basis. Joyce's house, where John lived, was situated in Seymer Road, Romford and, looking back on that period now, I have aptly dubbed the sittings of the Romford circle 'the Seymer Road Seances'. To chronicle all that went on there over the period of two-and-a-half years during which the circle was in existence would take a whole book in itself and that is a project that I hope to tackle in the not-too-distant future. I am utterly convinced that details of the progress and results obtained in such a unique circle can make a major contribution to our understanding today of the ups, downs and ultimate triumphs involved in the development of physical mediumship.

Nevertheless, it is important here to record the bare bones of the many sessions that were held and to describe how the achievements of the Romford circle acted as a 'carrot' to my present wife Sandra and me to continue what became our joint quest in search of the ultimate physical phenomena. It certainly taught us that it *was* possible for a group of ordinary people to develop the independent voice, without which assurance we could easily have given up altogether.

Mike, the new sitter, proved to be a great asset to the circle. He was very technically minded and often turned up at the circle with one or another of his gadgets, which he hoped would augment the atmosphere and help the circle's development. I remember most vividly one occasion when he brought along his one-candlepower home-made version of an ioniser to produce negative ions, theoretically to aid the spirit helpers to produce voices. (At this time, ionisers were not readily available on the market.) Amazingly, the ioniser worked! We referred to it as the 'Happy Machine', because it really did appear to raise the vibrations and make us laugh during the sitting. However, when the lights were switched on afterwards, it actually turned out to be the 'Unhappy Machine', when Joyce spotted the soot from the candle which had deposited itself on her nice new wallpaper!

From the point when Mike joined the circle, we extended the number of sittings to two per week, in order to try to speed up the tangible results. We still received the EVP messages and voices on my tapes as I recorded the sittings and by now we enjoyed loud rappings and a build-up of intense coldness, despite the fact that we were using an electric convector heater in this usually warm room throughout the sittings. We saw lights too, which sometimes moved, but were more frequently stationary and lasted between a fraction of a second and half a minute or so. Over the months, John's trance condition gradually became deeper.

He began to feel as if he were being twisted round and round – a sort of spinning sensation – before he finally became unconscious. As this happened, the speeches of our communicators became longer and clearer, and were less influenced by John's own thoughts and feelings. Each speaker used a different voice and revealed an entirely separate character. Interestingly, however, the separate voices, once established, were absolutely identical on each occasion a particular spirit visitor spoke. Often a spirit entity would speak, totally uninterrupted, for up to 20 minutes without pausing. A feat I would defy any professional orator to achieve off the cuff. It always seemed a little odd for so many different voices to be coming from this particular medium, who usually spoke with a broad Derbyshire accent.

Our efforts, using John as the medium, were constantly dogged by his disbelief in himself and in the phenomena. Although his mediumship had by now firmly established itself as a fact, and was working on a solid foundation, John continued to be sceptical of his ability, and remained a Doubting Thomas. Despite our assurances to the contrary and owing to the difficulties and frustrations he had encountered in his early life, he just could not come to terms with the fact that his superb mediumship existed at all, which proved a great setback to the development. I am convinced that had he conquered his self-doubt, we could have achieved the independent voice within the first year, as did the medium, 'Lincoln', of whom you will read later.

It soon became obvious that the 'power' for the work which our spirit friends were doing was being taken from a combination of the medium and the sitters, as some of us felt a 'drawing' sensation at our solar plexus every week. I can only describe this as being akin to having a sink plunger attached to my solar plexus and feeling it gently pulled. Both Mike and I started to notice things happening in our homes away from the circle, and often in full light. Both of us by now were getting EVP on our tapes when we tried obtaining it at home, and I can only assume that Mike caught it from me in the same way that I had caught it from Elmer Browne.

Peculiar things were happening to our lightbulbs and electrical appliances – a sure sign that physical psychic power was around. There were also the raps. They happened at all times, and in all parts of our homes. In my case, I started to experience extremely loud raps in my room at the Thrale Hall Hotel. It seemed that the spirit people chose suitable places for such phenomena and practised in those places until the loudest noises imaginable came forth. One of their favourite places was an empty electrical junction box on the wall of my private bathroom. The knocks and bangs just got louder and louder, and more and more frequent, although I checked thoroughly that there was nothing in the box that could have caused them. Another favourite place was on the wooden headboard of my bed. That worried me more, because I had been given the best room in the hotel as a long-term resident, with the headboard of its bed against the wall behind which stood the headboard of the manager's bed. The rappings became so loud, often carrying on well into the night, that I felt convinced that it was only a matter of time till I was thrown out on to the street.

In the circle itself, the four of us felt that in order to increase the power available for the development of physical phenomena, we should be looking for extra sitters. Mike knew of a young lady who was seeking to join a physical circle, and it was agreed that we should give her a trial for a few weeks. Regrettably, the lady was as far out of harmony with the rest of the group as she could possibly be, so after two sittings, she left by mutual agreement.

We were now approaching Christmas 1975. John had built a cabinet for the circle's use, feeling that it might help the spirit operators to concentrate the power more, thereby aiding the production of any ectoplasm, thus producing results more quickly. He insisted that we took turns sitting in it, and consequently, John, Mike and I sat, one at a time on alternate weeks on the 'hot seat'. It was pretty obvious from the start, however, that the development of trance and physical mediumship was primarily through John, and not through the rest of us.

An appropriate Christmas present was our receiving two notable manifestations during the circle. The first was a series of five whistled musical notes, which were loud and independent, being heard by us all at the time. The next week – just before Christmas – we all heard the voice of a young girl communicator, saying, 'Hello'. Simple but effective.

As the new year of 1976 came in, John was continually seized with self-doubts of his mediumship and constantly announced that he was giving up sitting in the circle. I wish I had a pound for every occasion I arrived at the Thrale Hall Hotel to discover a note from John, saying that he did not want to continue, which prompted me to go rushing off on a 35-mile journey to Romford to talk him out of it. I reckon I would be a rich man by now.

We did, however, continue with the sittings despite John's misgivings and his trance mediumship continued to develop wonderfully well. Three new communicators started to speak regularly to the circle, as well as the 'old faithfuls', these being former physical mediums, Helen Duncan and William Olsen, and a very strong and forceful spirit who introduced himself as the 'Crusader', stating that he was going to try to obtain a speedy breakthrough for us with the voices. During February, I met two very pleasant people at the SAGB, shortly afterwards introducing them as new sitters into the Romford circle. These were a young lady from Woodford called Anne and her aunt, Gill. So keen was I to ensure that they attended regularly, that I took to instituting a 'milk run', so that I could pick them up and deliver them to their homes again afterwards. Not long after they joined the circle (now consisting of six members) I started, once again, to get a massive build up of EVP on the tapes during sittings, running into a hundred or so words and sentences throughout the hour that we sat. At one seance in March, by means of the independent voice, all of us again heard a series of five loud whistled notes and a lady's voice asking us, 'Are you happy?' Needless to say, we were very happy to receive such results!

I had booked a sitting for our circle with Leslie Flint for March and we were very much looking forward to the event, hoping that we might get some indication of the circle's progress while there, but it was not to be. Regrettably, there had been a mix-up with the booking and we arrived to find a group already there, waiting for a seance, whose leader's name was Roy, when the sitting was booked in my name – Foy. Somehow they had arrived on the wrong day and, although they were kind enough to leave so that we could have our correct booking, the very fact that they had been sitting around in the seance room was enough to disturb the delicate atmosphere and we had a totally blank sitting, one of very few I ever experienced with this veteran medium among the many successful seances I had with him over the years. One great point in Leslie's favour, throughout his career, was that he did not ask for his fee if a sitting was blank and would always try to book up another sitting for disappointed sitters. In our case on this one occasion, another private group sitting was fixed up for the following August.

# AN EVIDENTIAL SITTING WITH LESLIE FLINT

FOLLOWING THE ABORTIVE Flint sitting, the general morale of the circle was low but, for me, there was one bright spot during April 1976. Initially we resumed sittings without John, our medium, who wanted a complete break. For a few weeks, therefore, we reverted to using the cabinet, with me sitting in it. On the first of these occasions, I became quite deeply entranced. Through me, an entity spoke to the circle, claiming to be 'Elmer', and stating that he had been involved in psychic matters, especially with respect to the EVP, in which he specialised. The communicator continued to speak without pause for ten minutes, giving details similar to those of the Leicester Forest East circle in which I had sat. That very week in *Psychic News,* and indeed in the following week's edition, there were articles reporting the success of Elmer J Browne – my friend from Leicester – in the field of EVP. As I had not been in touch with Bill or his acquaintances for some time, I had absolutely no reason for supposing that he was not in good health, let alone dead. I knew him as a man full of vim and vigour and almost fanatical in his pursuit of the 'Raudive Voices', to the extent that he would often experiment right through the night to see what results he could obtain.

The following night, after Elmer's 'trance message' through my own mediumship, I had a telephone call from Shirley Berkeley (still a regular sitter at Bill's circle), to tell me that he had passed to spirit three days previously in London, shortly after his private sitting with Bertha Harris (his reason for visiting London, where he had collapsed in the street). So it was indeed an evidential confirmation that Elmer had been present at our sitting, just 48 hours after his physical 'death'. At a later date, I had the opportunity to play the tape to Bill's widow Cath, and she too was convinced that the communicator really was

Bill. The episode served to make me believe that perhaps, given the right conditions, my own trance mediumship might develop into a worthwhile faculty and certainly over the next few weeks it did indeed seem to progress somewhat.

After a five-week period, John returned to sit in the circle and our trance mediumships continued to develop along parallel lines for a while. The circle guides and controls, however, found it easier to continue coming mainly through John, constantly giving us a pat on the back for our achievements with words of encouragement to sustain our enthusiasm with the intended consequence that we would redouble our efforts on their behalf.

Nevertheless, in spite of our concentration and hard work, by the middle of May the circle became stale, and we were having difficulty maintaining the harmony between sitters. We started looking for further suitable interested people through adverts, entreaties and personal introductions. This yielded two further circle members who joined us on 20 May – a lady from Elstree and a gentleman called Reg, who was the Receptionist/Librarian at the College of Psychic Studies and had lots of experience in all psychic matters. Reg lived in Purley and I extended my milk run, picking up sitters on circle nights at Elstree, Old Street tube station, Tottenham and Woodford, and dropping them all off again afterwards which, after a long and exhausting sitting became a great strain for me. It was obviously not the answer.

Another new sitter, a lady from Southend-on-Sea, joined us for a trial period on 27 May but although she had a lot of physical power, by this time John and Joyce had lost patience, so following this single sitting, they suspended the circle for four weeks and nearly for good. When we resumed the seances on 24 June, the ladies from Elstree and Southend did not rejoin us and Mike, who had been with us for a long time, also left.

This reduced the number of regular sitters to six. We tried experimenting in a new direction, on behalf of a photographic researcher. He supplied us with a piece of photographic film, sealed in a lightproof and waterproof package, which he wanted us to place on the floor in the centre of the circle during a sitting. Without thinking, I carried this piece of wrapped film around with me for a week in my inside jacket pocket until the next circle meeting, at which time

I did as the photographer had asked. When the film was developed, it showed a white, fluffy mass which resembled a human embryo, showing that somewhere along the line it had been impressed with a picture of an ectoplasmic formation. Since I had carried the film around for a week, however, I was never sure from that day to this if the result was obtained through the circle, or through being in my own pocket. The photographer was nevertheless very excited at the result but the experiment was not repeated for one reason or another.

We continued to sit in token style but the circle felt wrong. The summer proved to be extremely hot, with the atmosphere in the room being constantly clammy and we were certainly not sitting in comfort. We also had difficulty in blacking the room out properly and were becoming more than a little irritated with one another. The final sitting of this phase of the Seymer Road Seances took place on 1 July 1976, after which John and Joyce suspended the circle till at least September, and although it did start again later in 1976, I was not to resume my sittings with them until April 1977. The main thing was, however, that we did part as friends after that final sitting and were therefore able to keep our appointment as a group to sit with Leslie Flint in August.

And so it was that seven of us gathered outside Leslie's house before going in to sit with him. On this occasion, nothing happened for an hour and ten minutes, and we were beginning to prepare ourselves for another blank but, finally, Mickey managed to get through and for the next hour or so we were treated to a whole barrage of independent voices, starting with Mickey, who addressed us thus:

> Hello – how are you? I'm sorry I've been a long time, but it's not my fault, just one of those things, ain't it? I see that big stout bloke's here. How are you, mate? [Addressing John.] That bloke on the couch? [John answered.] There's a lot of power round you, mate! Must be your belly! No, I'm kidding. But seriously, there is a lot of power around you, mate! Do you sit in a cabinet? [John replied that he had done.] I feel with you there's a lot of physical power round you, and though you may not think you're going to do much, you will – given the opportunity, anyway! It's strange, but you're not complete in your circle, are you? [I agree with this remark.] Is there two missing? [John replies that the circle has been

> suspended.] Yeah, but there's been some changes! They're telling me that they're not disappointed, but they're hoping you'll keep going because they don't want you to give up. You've been toying with the idea, haven't you? I think you got a bit browned off or something, or disappointed, but they say it's so silly, because after all the work that's been put in, and the power it's generated, a lot is happening, and they just want you to keep on. You mustn't pack it in, mate! You see, often when things seem to be going wrong, or when very little seems to be happening, a lot can be happening behind the scenes, and that's often when you're on the verge of achieving something. You mustn't pack it in, you must keep going!

At this point, John explained to Mickey that he couldn't help but doubt himself and his abilities, and Mickey replied:

> Look, mate, a lot of people get at themselves, and sometimes people put their own spoke in the wheel. And I think unconsciously, you've been doing just that, mate! You see, I can understand how people can say to themselves, 'Well, I don't know, it could be my own subconscious!,' but the point is, you don't want to let that worry you. Give out what you get! Let things take their course. Time will prove. Of course, sometimes a medium unconsciously interferes, but I think that you're being naughty!

Following Mickey's treble Cockney tones, a man's low voice was heard. The accent was markedly Scottish, and the voice familiar to us all as he gave us the following message:

> Can you hear me? [We answer yes.] Aye, it's Jock here. I've been standing here waiting for the opportunity to get a few words through to ye! Actually, it's a bit difficult for me. We're all doing our best. Just want ye to know we're all here! Aye, don't give up the meetings. Keep the circle going. Don't give it up! Ye must start the meetings in a few weeks. I want ye to start up again as soon as ye possibly can. Ye must not doubt yourselves. Ye must remember and realise we're doing everything in our power. We'd be very upset if ye gave up now. Because we're on the verge of getting quite a few things through, and I'm sure if ye continue, eventually we'll succeed. But it would be fatal now to give up. I think youre wrong! Ye're going to start in September? [John answers yes.] Well, we'll be there!

It is interesting to make here a comparison between Jock's voice through John in trance, Jock's voice heard independently at Leslie Flint's, and his voice later heard independently in the Romford circle. All three were taped and retained by the group, and all three are *almost identical.*

Jock's voice was followed by a lilting lady's voice with a mellifluous French accent:

> I do not know if you can hear me? [We answer yes.] I am so anxious to come and talk with you. Maria is my name. I am very anxious – you know – for you to know of my presence. You are lucky here. Many come to you. Some of them you know, many you don't know. But all come in love, and we want you to continue with the circle, not to give it up! Maria Theresa. Sister Maria. God bless you!

We had never previously been aware of this lady but her message was as clear as all the others. Carry on! Shortly after this, another communicator's voice came out of mid-air to talk to us:

> White Feather come with blessing to children! White Feather here, I White Feather. White Feather come, say, continue circle. Please, White Feather want you to continue circle. Please, no give up circle! White Feather send blessing to children.

This clear, Native American sounding voice and personality was also at this time unknown to us. But like the voice of Jock, an identical voice, introducing himself as White Feather, was later heard independently in the Romford circle during October 1977.

There followed a period when a departed relative came to speak to two of the sitters, these being his sister and his aunt. The nature of the communication was very personal and not connected with the circle in any way. It was, however, very evidential for the sitters and they were in no doubt as to the identity of the communicator. The proof that they received was further substantiated by bits of information Mickey kept volunteering to them.

Next came a man's voice with a heavy Italian accent, who announced himself as 'Roberto'. Again, a personality of whom we had no previous knowledge but he was subsequently heard to give his name independently during the Seymer Road Seances:

> Roberto. I come and talk to you. I have been to your meetings and I am very interested, you know. Many people love to come. One day we will come and speak at your circle. But I want to come and help you. I am most interresant in everything you do. In the main, I come with other people. We want you continue the circle. Many people send their blessings, you know. All come together to help you.

Mickey chipped in here to tell us:

> He's somebody who seems to have attached himself to your group. I think he's probably Italian, and actually he's quite a character. Are there seven of you in the circle? [We answer no, six.] Oh, that's what they're on about, then! One dropped out, cause they're talking about seven. But you're not going to pack it in, are you? I can see that you've gone through a very funny phase if you know what I mean; and you've been toying with the idea of packing it in. [We answer yes.] Thinking you ain't made much progress. Well, you are, you know! You are making progress, and as for him over there [referring to John], he doubts himself. He's a bleeding Doubting Thomas, he is! [John here stated that there is one person in the spirit world who comes to the group who he doubts very much and at this stage we agree with him.] What person? You mean over here? [We say yes.] You doubt him? Really? I appreciate he's on our side of life, but why should you doubt him? [We were referring to Sir Winston Churchill but did not volunteer this information to Mickey.] Well, if he was important on your side, he might be just the reverse over here. Sometimes a person who was famous on your side has to go in through the back door to get in over here. They don't get the front door and the red carpet, you know! He may have to come down a peg or two on this side! Anyway, if he's present, he may speak to you. I don't know. But it seems odd that you should doubt him.

We were, of course, fishing to see if Winston would speak to us but did not disclose this. However, within a few minutes of Mickey's comments, a stentorian voice, well known to millions, was addressing us:

> Winnie! Winnie! I say, what's the matter with you all? Well, this is far different to what I expected. Can you hear me? [We chorused

> yes.] What's the matter with you all? Winston, Winston here! Winnie to you! What the deuce is the matter with you? What are you doubting for? I, I know that you come here with a particular desire to have confirmation. Of course, I don't know how I'm going to give you sufficient 'evidence' if that's presumably what you want but if you don't darned well believe now, you never will. I do hope you'll continue the meetings. I mean, don't doubt. I'm having a bit of a job to speak to you through this box – no doubt, when one gets used to it, one achieves a much better end product or result from your point of view. I don't want you to go on doubting, otherwise you'll get nowhere. Now, I hope you'll be satisfied.

Further evidence was to follow, as Winnie continued: 'As a matter of fact, what about the photograph? Yes, a special photograph! You know what I'm referring to. This photograph of me.' One sitter asked where? To which Winnie replied, 'Where you've been going of late.' (It was a fact that a recent photograph taken by John and Mike had a spirit 'extra' on it.) Mike asked, 'That was you, was it?' and Winston replied, 'Yes. I desperately tried to impress myself in every possible, conceivable way, and all the damn time, you're doubting! Anyway, I'll come and talk to you again and if you should come back here – if it's possible – I'll make every attempt. But don't give up! Goodbye.'

Needless to say, each and every one of us was extremely impressed by Sir Winston's independent voice. We had found the confirmation we were seeking. Even Leslie Flint was impressed by what had taken place and he expressed a great interest in our circle. The final evidence was provided by Mickey, who now spoke again:

> Do you have your little do on a Wednesday? [We answer no.] Well – wait a moment. I can't understand this because it's that stout bloke, and they're laughing, and they say they were very amused about Wednesday. But why Wednesday? Have you ever been to where that gentleman's buried? [John answered no, but told Mickey that he had considered visiting Sir Winston's grave.] Well, evidently he's got a bee in his bonnet. You've been discussing or thinking about some sort of, not pilgrimage, but going to this place where he is resting, and he says, why bother, because there's nothing there. I suppose it's natural that you doubt sometimes but he's a very forceful character, you know – very concerned about the state

> of the world and especially concerned about what's happening in England. But you've got some tape recordings of him, haven't you? [We all agreed.] Because he's talking about the tapes. You've been experimenting in some way with the tapes, ain't you? [In the light of our EVP experiences, everybody agreed.] And also, you've had some other people trying, as well as him, haven't you? [Again, we could but agree.]

At this point, the power began to fade, and the voices started to get fainter. Mickey hurriedly said goodbye and went. I felt that the evidence was overwhelming, as did the other circle members. I regret to say, however, that as we emerged into the afternoon sunlight I was torn asunder. One part of me wanted to continue with the circle regardless and yet I could not forget the disharmony which had been rife before the circle was suspended. If I had felt that the circle would not resume without my being there then without a doubt I would have continued as a sitter. As it was, I was satisfied in myself that John, Joyce and Mike (who had indicated that he wanted to return to the circle) would continue to sit. My emotions were in a real turmoil. I was not sure that I would continue to be an asset to the group in my then frame of mind and felt that they might do better without me. My own doubts of the situation were many and while I had never lost the fire in my heart for my quest in search of physical mediumship, I was now impressed to strike out for pastures new and consequently followed my instincts.

## TEMPORARY LEAVE OF ABSENCE

HAVING DECIDED TO move on from the Romford circle and because I was fired with enthusiasm once more from the sitting we had enjoyed with Leslie Flint, I was soon off in search of the Holy Grail again – that elusive physical phenomenon of the independent voice. Reg and I kept in touch as Purley was not too far away from my Streatham hotel and, through his work at the College of Psychic Studies, Reg came into contact with many first class mediums.

One of these, who was doing more work for the college, was the medium Charles Horrey. I knew him first of all from my initial three private sittings at the SAGB and I had since had two more excellently evidential sittings with this clairaudient medium over the last eighteen months. Since Charles had started to work at the college, Reg – in passing – had mentioned to him that I wanted to sit for the independent voice. Charles was very interested in this too and was therefore kind enough to offer his flat at Stockwell as a venue for a new circle.

So it was with this in mind that I met Charles for the first time on a social basis, rather than professionally. I had a great regard for his abilities as a medium and was pleased that he wanted to help. After a preliminary meeting, it was agreed that Reg and I should form a physical circle with Charles in September 1976 to sit for the independent direct voice. Additionally, Charles was at that time developing his own trance mediumship at the College of Psychic Studies by sitting with Reg there. With September fast approaching, it was clear that Charles, Reg and I needed at least one other sitter to complete the circle. Right out of the blue, a casual acquaintance – a lady by the name of Eve – telephoned me to ask how the Romford circle was progressing. I explained the situation to her, as she was not aware of the current position, and the upshot was that she asked if she could sit with us at Charles's flat on a regular basis.

When we started the Stockwell circle, Charles said that he was prepared to let us sit there for six months to see how far forward we could go in that time and we began on that understanding. He was quite sure in himself that if we were intending to develop the 'voice', then we would at least have had plenty of pointers by then and he felt that we should concentrate on the development of my own physical mediumship.

During the initial period in the Stockwell circle we seemed to progress well. Back came all the familiar minor phenomena such as raps, whispering sounds and lip-smacking noises from mid-air, etc. On the very first occasion that we sat, the room door opened noisily half-way through the sitting and the two trumpets, which we placed in the middle of the circle, had both moved about a quarter of an inch. Trance communication, through both Charles and myself, formed the nucleus of the circle, the aims of which were identical to those of the Romford group. Progress was, however, very slow, although I continued to get EVP messages on the tape and we heard the occasional word of independent voice, albeit not very loudly or clearly.

Regrettably, the harmony never did feel just right, and it seemed that we were duplicating the non-harmonious conditions that had existed in the Romford circle prior to its break. It was true that everybody at Stockwell was a conscientious sitter but somehow we didn't quite gel together as a group. Charles was not a well man, due to a blood condition, and he tired easily. His work was exacting and draining and he felt we were not getting anywhere with our development, which was basically true because, optimistic as we were, the phenomena did not build beyond the usual psychic coldness, the whispers and the raps. After five months of sitting, Charles's work took him off to Switzerland for a month and, although we did continue sitting while he was away, the circle broke up naturally on his return. The timing could not have been better, as it proved to me my lifelong belief, as you will see, that 'when a door closes in life, a window opens'.

At the time the Stockwell circle started in September 1976, the Romford circle re-formed without me. Because of the evidential sitting at Leslie Flint's in the August, John's confidence had returned, and John, Joyce and Mike started sitting again but, after only six weeks, Mike left. Like the classic story of the ten little Indians ... then there were two! John and Joyce did not feel that it would be worthwhile just the two of them sitting by themselves so, once again, the circle broke up for a few weeks. John placed adverts in the *Psychic News,* to search for suitable sitters, because his renewed enthusiasm and motivation, generated at the Flint sitting, was still strong and he did not wish to abandon the task. On this occasion, several replies were received and appropriate interviews were arranged to assess the suitability of the applicants.

Despite my starting, and sitting in, a new circle, I had stayed on friendly terms with John and Joyce and popped in to visit them from time to time, albeit infrequently. It just so happened that I called in there on one occasion when two lady applicants came for their interviews. One of these, Sandra Hutson, later joined the circle and in the fullness of time was to become my second wife, with whom I have since lived happily ever after, and without whom (we now work together as a team in our psychic work) I could never have hoped to achieve the amazing psychic successes that have been chalked up over recent years. Three others, a journalist called Harry, and a couple named Mick and Susan also joined, along with Mike, who decided he would give it another try now there were some new sitters.

So, while I was steering a parallel course in Stockwell, the revitalised circle really got down to some serious work during November 1976. The sitters now seemed to get on well together and there was a general air of optimism within the circle. The atmosphere during the sittings was lively and the communicators, speaking through John's trance, were as encouraging as ever, constantly urging the circle on and assuring everybody that development really was taking place. On one occasion, an independent voice was heard by the sitters giving the name 'Roberto', thus fulfilling the promise of that spirit entity at Leslie Flint's that he would visit the Romford circle and make himself known.

Towards the end of January 1977, Mick's wife Susan was obliged to leave the circle in order to have a baby. Looking after the new arrival prevented her from returning to the circle afterwards and, at about the same time, a new and refreshing communicator started to manifest in the circle. This was Neville, a boy who had been run over and 'killed' at the age of ten. He endeared himself to all the sitters by his innocent witticisms and prevailing sense of humour. Over the next few months, he was to develop into one of the main communicators and helpers within the group.

During their initial sittings prior to the beginning of March in 1977, the circle changed little. The new sitters got to know one another better and became more confident. John still had the millstone of unemployment around his neck and consequently spent much of his time in a depressed state. To overcome his anxious state of mind during the series of sittings, he was therefore drawn deeper and deeper into trance until he was totally unconscious.

Then one day in early March, when two of the sitters were unable to attend, the four people present experienced levitation of the trumpet. On that occasion, it raised itself into the air by several feet, before falling back to the floor with a noisy clatter. A small coffee table in the circle, upon which the trumpet had originally been placed, made scuffling noises on the carpet with its legs as it circumnavigated the room under its own steam.

These were the first properly controlled physical phenomena which had been received by the group. John did not really approve, because he wanted to carry on and get the voice and he felt that movements of this type would waste the available power. But one has to bear in mind that apart from John himself, none of the other sitters had previously witnessed levitation and movements of objects around a seance room. For them, it was superb evidence that the spirit helpers were constantly working around them.

This spate of phenomena prompted one of the sitters to produce a luminous plaque for use in future seances and thereafter this was placed on the mantlepiece. Maybe this, too, could be levitated, or used to show materialised faces. Nobody knew what was likely to come next, but certainly a great deal of excitement was generated by this bout of telekinesis. The trend of these first physical phenomena continued for some weeks and further movements of the trumpet and table were noted, building up in intensity until, on 30 March and 6 April, they were at their strongest. Both sittings also produced a barrage of raps and taps which persisted throughout the whole seance, along with intense coldness and a series of psychic breezes. The luminous plaque floated down to the floor, a loud whistle emanated from mid-air in front of the medium, this being followed by the crash of a small table falling over onto its side. Before the sitting, this table had on it an ashtray, connected to the table by a detachable pedestal. When the lights went on afterwards, it was discovered that the ashtray, which contained several used cigarette ends, had carefully and gently been removed to a safe place on the floor prior to the table falling over, to prevent the messy ash from spilling out.

Khoba, Jock and Dr Dunn (the scientist) spoke at length through John during the sitting of 6 April, indicating that the phenomena they had been able to produce that night was just a start, and that they would now progress rapidly towards independent voice. The guides asked that I be invited back into the circle to augment the power and Joyce undertook to contact me accordingly.

# BACK IN HARNESS

I WAS SOMEWHAT surprised to receive a telephone call from Joyce on behalf of the Romford circle during the second week of April, but nevertheless delighted to hear of the positive results which were now being obtained there. Whilst I *had* kept in touch with John and Joyce, it was some months since I had heard from them and now I listened, enthralled, as Joyce explained everything that had been happening in my absence. I was asked to return as a one off, just to see how things might progress with me there and, needless to say, I jumped at the chance.

My first sitting with the new Romford group was on 27 April 1977. The circle now numbered seven in all of whom two, Harry and Mick, I had not met before. The atmosphere was, however, distinctly happy and relaxed. Shortly after the sitting started, the room became extremely cold. The odd factor (typical of a seance for physical phenomena) was that the coldness was localised near the floor, and whilst our legs and feet felt frozen, the temperature appeared to be much warmer around our upper bodies, arms and shoulders.

The Scottish guide Jock spoke through John, explaining that they were trying to extend a psychic rod. (Psychic rods are often fashioned by the spirit helpers in this type of circle to help them achieve phenomena. They are formed out of ectoplasm, can be anything up to several feet long, with a diameter of a couple of inches or so, and can change instantaneously from being soft and floppy in texture, as though constructed of fabric, to being as rigid and strong as an iron bar, quite capable of lifting or moving heavy weights around a seance room.) We were warned not to move under any circumstances, or to touch anything whatever transpired, as the phenomenon was at a critical stage, and ectoplasmic substance was coming down John's nose. Jock further asked us to relax as much as possible and not to become too tense, thereby keeping the atmosphere jolly. Something was heard to slither across the floor and we presumed this to be the psychic rod. I began to experience the now familiar feeling of my solar plexus being gently pulled. Harry's chair was pushed from behind and I commented on being able to see misty clouds of ectoplasm floating around the room.

The spirit scientist Dr Dunn told us – again through John – that an ectoplasmic voicebox had been formed on the end of the psychic rod they had produced and that persons unknown were constantly trying to talk to us through it. Cold breezes were then felt around the room by some of the sitters. Shortly afterwards, Dr Dunn explained that their efforts were being frustrated by the fact that the medium had not drunk enough water prior to the sitting and was fast becoming dehydrated. In future he needed to drink plenty of fluid before sitting. These comments were immediately followed by a loud rap, almost by way of a confirmation, and we then heard a couple of unintelligible words spoken in the air by a squeaky-sounding voice, followed by a loud independent whistle. A faint voice managed to say, 'Hello'. Things were happening all at once, as we caught the sound of several whispering voices, which preceded a scraping noise from the small table in the centre of the circle. John was coughing and spluttering – a natural reaction to the extrusion of ectoplasm – and I felt a blanket of wet substance moving over my knees before wrapping itself around my legs like a second pair of trousers. A few moments later, the sitter to my right felt it moving over him, too.

There was a peculiar odour in the room, a sort of earthy smell – a little akin to the smell of wet fern in the woods. The sitters on the other side of the circle now felt the same thing happening, as the substance crept over Joyce's hand and Harry's lap. Further lip movements and whispering sounds followed, and again we heard a faint 'Hello' spoken near Harry. I saw a bright light, about the size of a cricket ball, quickly flash on and off near Joyce. We then had another whistle and, almost as a finale, one of the luminous plaques toppled off the mantlepiece, falling like a leaf on to the floor.

A short silence ensued and then came the voice of Khoba, John's 'doorkeeper', speaking through him. He explained that the circle would have to close as the medium was extremely dehydrated, and it would have been dangerous for him to go on. Khoba felt that our sitting had been a good one and that our spirit friends were quite close to bringing us the full and controlled independent voice. All the members of the circle had been excited but at this point I left quietly to go home, while the others stayed on to discuss the night's events.

To me, returning to the circle on this first occasion, it seemed that all the sitters were now acting more professionally, and as the spirit world wanted. An excellent blackout had been achieved, and I noted that there was now considerable harmony within the group, plus a genuine interest in the phenomenon itself. I had felt quite comfortable in the company of all the members of the circle, and hoped that I might now be given another opportunity to witness more of the proceedings at Romford. What I did not know until later was that the group had decided democratically to ask me to become one of its permanent members again and Mick had been selected to telephone me the following Sunday. The prospect appealed to me and I was delighted to accept.

From May onwards, therefore, I once again became a full member of the Romford circle, sitting each week in the Seymer Road Seances. The incidence of trance speech increased to the level we had enjoyed before the circle broke up the previous year and there were constantly excellent indications that the independent voices were imminent. The communicators started and maintained a flow of their philosophy, which was most enlightening. During the sitting on 18 May, Sir Winston came to speak to us through John, telling us that he felt our first independent communicators would be those who we knew and loved on this earth before they 'died'. An hour into the sitting, the luminous plaque (which on this occasion had been placed on the central table along with the trumpet) leapt off the table to fall on the floor by Mick's foot. Shortly afterwards, the trumpet began to rock violently on the table, until it fell off on to the floor, near Harry. We were asked not to move about, because an ectoplasmic rod was linking the trumpet to John. Harry's foot was nevertheless in contact with the trumpet as it lay on the floor and every time John coughed (some ten feet away from it), Harry could feel vibrations in the instrument. Lip movements and faint unintelligible voices were then heard to come from the wide end of the trumpet.

Several communicators spoke to us at length on that occasion (through John in trance), as they also did the following week on 25 May. This was to be an even better sitting from the point of view of physical phenomena. Shortly after the circle commenced, the trumpet began to shake and rattle as it stood upright on the table. Cold breezes were felt around the room as the trumpet rocked, eventually falling off the table on to the floor, with its wide end pointing towards the medium. A moment later, it soared off the floor in a looping movement, in the course of which it must have covered 20 feet or so. This time, it 'floated' back to the floor. The whole manoeuvre had taken no more than a couple of seconds, and all this only 15 minutes after the circle had begun. Less than five minutes afterwards, the table was heard dragging its legs along the carpet, obviously moving around the room. A couple of indistinguishable objective words were heard independently in the air and, as we discovered afterwards, had been recorded on the tape.

Dr Dunn, through John, urged us to be patient and converse more, as we were tending to become tense. They would also prefer us to dispense with the trumpet in future, as we tended to concentrate on it too much. A further independent voice was heard by all calling John's name, before the table moved again – first shuffling round the room, before we heard it pick up speed and rush at Joyce. Had it hit her at that speed, she would have been hurt but, as it happened, immediately it reached Joyce it toppled over, pinning her legs gently into the confines of her chair.

A few moments later, the trumpet started to moved round the floor – not rolling along it, but skimming the surface, before it came to rest with the wide end pointing towards Sandra. Two of us heard a faint scratching noise coming from inside the trumpet and all the sitters noticed the intense coldness in the room.

Dr Dunn, speaking through the medium's trance state, explained that the system of independent voice using an ectoplasmic voicebox was not, by any means, the only method which they were employing. One idea which they had in mind was to harness natural and spiritual energy, amplifying a spirit communicator's thought energy into audible speech which they could transmit to us. There would be several advantages to using this non-ectoplasmic means – less danger to the medium, for instance, as well as being able to use the system in artificial light. At the time this idea seemed somewhat revolutionary to us but now, 18 years later in 1995, this is *exactly* the method which is currently being employed and pioneered in the Scole Experimental Group to produce the wonderful phenomena we now enjoy.

A third sitting on my return to the circle also produced excellent results by way of physical phenomena. As requested by the spirit operators, we left the trumpet out, although we did have a small coffee table in the centre of the circle. At one stage of the seance, we began to sing the classic song 'The Keel Row'. Immediately the table started to dance about, stamping its legs on the floor in exact timing to the music. In fact, the movement of the table was so strong, that one of the leg supports broke at its top end. There followed a lay-off of two weeks, while two of the circle had their annual holidays.

I am sad to say that when the circle reconvened two weeks later the gremlins had struck again and there was once again disharmony in the group. One of the sitters was desperate to bring all sorts of research projects into the circle, despite the fact that we all knew the development was not yet complete by a long chalk. The 'ordinary' format of the circle was too boring and mundane for this particular sitter, despite the encouraging phenomena he had experienced, and he wanted infra-red cameras with light sensitive trips, special microphones and a host of different gadgets. Not unreasonably at this stage, he was refused permission to use them, but it did not end there. Totally out of the blue, he started to talk of the physical phenomena we had experienced to date as having been 'rigged'. It seems he had chosen to forget the original purpose of the group, this being to develop the ultimate phenomena we sought properly and before all else in the circle, leaving any thought of research or visitors until later, when such projects could be approved by the spirit team that worked with us. With that attitude he was holding the circle back as well as creating disharmony and it is not surprising that the sittings of 22 and 29 June (his last with the group) produced few results of note.

On 29 June, Dr Dunn told us via trance of his own pending temporary departure from the team:

> I have to tell you that I shall be leaving you in a short time! I have completed the groundwork, as it were, and my function will be taken over by someone else. And I wish to say to you that the relationship between yourselves and this man will be like a sergeant major to the troops in the army. So I am just warning you! He's not quite so easy going as I have been. I will, however, eventually be back myself.

John was so upset during this session on 29 June by the disinterested attitude of our 'rebel' sitter, that he was persuaded to write him a very strong letter, suggesting that if the sitter did not feel happy with everything as it was, he should leave the circle. Back came the reply, with the circle member tendering his resignation forthwith, and stating how for some time he had suspected John of faking the phenomena. So much so, he admitted that he had taken to smuggling a camera into the sittings each week with the express intention of catching John out when phenomena occurred. I was horrified. If the camera *had* been used when there was ectoplasm about, the health of all the sitters could have been permanently impaired. At worst, John could have sustained an internal haemorrhage, which *might* have actually led directly or indirectly to his death. The prospect did not bear thinking about – especially as the sitter concerned should have been fully aware of the drastic consequences such actions could have produced.

Since the circle had always been run on democratic lines, John showed us all a copy of his letter to this sitter, and the subsequent reply. We were greatly surprised when another member of the circle disagreed violently with what John had written and stood up declaring that if the 'rebel' sitter left, he would leave too! Whereupon he walked out, never to be seen at the circle again.

We later discovered that both had been in contact with one another outside the circle for some time, believing in unison that some phenomena had not been genuine. The rest of us, however, could account for the majority of what we had witnessed and that was good enough for us. Subsequent experience has taught me that during the development of a physical medium, various sorts of odd things in unusual circumstances *can* occur, and it is the responsibility of the home circle members to provide a loving, harmonious, confident and sympathetic environment, so that the medium's gifts can unfold – after all, the medium at this stage is not expected to sit under 'test' conditions; and since thoughts are living things, added to the fact that the developing physical mediumship is of a complex and fragile nature, the very fact that one or more sitters are thinking negatively during a seance with a fixed belief that 'this or that particular thing is fraudulent' can actually cause fraud to happen.

# THINGS ARE LOOKING GOOD

IN VIEW OF the circle losing two sitters under such upsetting circumstances, the seance of 6 July produced little other than trance, but trance communications through John were still very good. The first to speak was the new entity on 'attachment', whom Dr Dunn had warned us to expect. Winnie had christened him 'Reggie', because of his army rank (he had been a Regimental sergeant-major during his lifetime), and he lived up to his rank in every way. His manner was curt and precise. 'Bristling', is the expression that comes to mind, as he spoke to us:

> I'm just having a little look round here, as I've got a job to do. This question of independent voice! Well, what I usually do when I'm asked to assist at these kinds of proceedings is to ask you why you think you deserve independent voice? [We gave a few mumbled responses, regarding honourable intentions, etc.] Yes, well, my function is physical mediumship, and my interest is in the independent voice. That's what I have been brought here to try and do. And I am willing to give you three months of my time if you cooperate fully with me when I take over. I've already sorted things out. You have talked of gardening in this circle. Well, I was interested in gardening when I was on earth, but I think mainly I spent my time weeding out. And this is one of my functions here. But I'm just making a preliminary reconnaissance to see what I need to do, and what I need to collect from you all. And as I say, I'll give you three months of my time. In return, I expect you to give me three months of your time, excluding holidays, of course, and sickness. And if you can maintain the dedication, patience – whatever, then I don't like to fail!

He didn't mince his words, this Reggie – and it was obvious that as a spirit operator he knew his job. Things were obviously starting to happen fast now and for once we could not help but feel that the circle was going in the right direction, as our confidence returned. It seemed that everything from now on would all be worthwhile, with the door to progression opening wide for us.

Jock also returned to speak to us that evening for the first time in several weeks. He had, he said, been away on a journey to one of the other planes of existence. He tried very hard to describe this to us, but to no avail, because he could not find the words in our language to put over the concept of such a wondrous place. His personality had undergone a notable change – the normal joviality had disappeared but, although he now seemed to be a bit of a 'sobersides', he was still there to help us in what we were trying to do. An interesting factor of his message, however, was that he had seen, on this brighter plane, a completed copy of the book Sir Winston Churchill wanted us to write on his behalf, covering his life in the spirit world. (Winnie had often spoken of this book, which he was intending to dictate, piece by piece, through the independent voice, when the facility was available to him.)

Winston himself had something to say on this occasion, too:

> I am anxious to get on with it and I hope you have now sorted yourselves out. This should now be akin to a Cabinet of War! Please keep out for the time being all who wish to intrude upon the manifestations that might occur here. I am pleased that I have got, by pulling a few strings, this person – this man who was the backbone of the British Army, the sergeant major - and I'm sure that if he and you can coincide at some point at least, the job will be done. It will be hard perhaps, for you, but I think – in fact I'm sure – that the two who are now absent were not very amenable to discipline of any kind.

On his concern for England, Sir Winston had this to say:

> What's happening to this country? Each time I come here, I find the fog growing thicker and thicker! What's happened to that Clean Air Act? I don't see any sign of clean air! Bloody moral pollution, I call it! I hope you ladies will forgive me. I haven't changed a great deal. My friends, I wanted to come back because I, too, am aware of what has been happening. In fact I have been partly responsible and I accept that responsibility. And I want to endorse what has been said already. Time passeth, and we must get

back some of the spirit that was evident in the old days! There's nothing old fashioned about guts and courage, is there? Then what the hell's the matter with everyone? Anyhow, I feel that I must do my best to give some assistance to a country that I led. And if the only way I can do this is by communicating with you in this manner, then I have to ask you, even implore you, to give your all to what we both want. Our ideas and ideals are coincidental, but the result will not be common, my friends. My revelations to you will be far from common. And it has been arranged, or is being arranged, already that my book will be published. So please remember that you sit here with a sacred duty and a very heavy responsibility. I don't come for any idle purpose, I assure you of that. Not that any do. All the funny people. All these coloured chappies – they have got a purpose too. It's all part of the divine plan. And one day you will all have to go to their world, so may I suggest to you that if you were going abroad to a country for the first time, would you not try and find out some of the habits, the customs, and the language of the natives? [We agreed at this point.] Then there's your answer! You must endeavour to find out about the habits and customs of the land to which you must all go, eventually!

Stern stuff, this, coming from so eminent a personality as Winnie! It did, however, have the desired effect and, as the rallying speech it was intended to be, rekindled much of our enthusiasm. We felt that it really had been intended that the circle would continue on to success with only five sitters, who were now prepared to carry on to infinity, if necessary, to achieve results.

From now on the struggle towards achievement, however, was to be a downhill one. On 13 July, Dr Dunn addressed us at length, through John – his speech, without breaks, lasting almost 25 minutes. He spoke of various matters, ranging from the helpers of the individual sitters in the circle to the subject of trance control itself. On that subject, he had this to say:

The fact that you recognise the problems of trance control will help towards harmony, simply because you recognise the problems of each and every one of you. In this control, as you see now, I sometimes have problems. I have sometimes to fight the medium on occasions, trying all kinds of methods to force my ideas through, and by your own controls, you will recognise the problems that each of us have. It's terribly important that none of you should be in any way cynical or sceptical of controls, and I would hope that you would never use the word 'alleged'.

Because subconsciously these things are true, we become part of a medium's consciousness, and we don't take away personality, by any means, so I hope that point will be taken. Please do not concentrate too hard at the moment on listening for taps or odd sounds, and do not comment at length unless you hear an obvious voice, because this could cause some difficulty now we are close to our goal.

At this same sitting, on 13 July 1977, Winston returned yet again to further urge us on, and to comment in his unmistakable way on the state of affairs in the country:

I think I told you that I should, or could if I wished, move on to pastures new. But I find, more and more, as I come closer to you, that my presence in my own modest way – as you've heard of me – is needed. I am dismayed, disgusted and horrified at the manner in which this country's affairs are being conducted. I recall, quite vividly, that my father, Lord Randolph Churchill, himself resigned from the government when he was Chancellor of the Exchequer, over defence cuts. During the time of my own office, we knew the enemy, and we knew where the enemy was. But now, where is the enemy? In our midst! In our midst! But who, and where, and how, can we fight and find this common unity, over the forces that are creeping, like a slow stain, over this land? This land that I loved so much, and stubbornly defended.

You will have coming to you during these sittings, hopefully when it is the time, free speech. By that I mean independent speech, available to us here, and you will be told of the beauty, of the harmony, of the wonder of the heavens, and of the spirit world beyond.

I don't come to you with such messages. I come to you as I did, closer to the heart of the people. Not trying to give you soft soap! Not trying to lead you astray ... Not trying to bring insincerity to you. But I want you, for me, and for those who think like me, to recognise that there is a fight! And that in this room, we must have a council of war. We must keep out and exclude those who would tend to injure, who would corrupt us, and swerve us away from our purpose.

And I feel I may contribute something of the greatness that once was; because I may communicate to you something of pride; and we must recognise that the lot of men is to fight. Not always with the sword, but with the pen, with the mind and with the heart. With the very soul and spirit! To fight for the freedom and the unity of individuals.

What kind of freedom have you now? What happened to the victories? Weren't they Pyrrhic victories? Have we not lost more than we gained? What I want to say to you is this. That whatever may come to you; whatever may be said to you about the release and the benevolence of the spirit world; I have seen little of this. What I have seen are the weepings, and the wailings, of those who wish to communicate themselves to those on Earth. The young men who gave their lives for you are amazed and dismayed.

And I trust that you will help me, and a thousand others, to throw a bridgehead across this river between us. Between the Spirit World and the Earthly World. That we may be able to cross this bridge, and bring forth our battalions; that we may sweep before us, and sweep away the corruption. All that is destroying us, slowly and stealthily.

To give you an analogy, inside your own bodies, at the moment, your corpuscles are constantly on guard against the bacterial agents, the enemy within, and those agents that seek to penetrate from without. Can you see what I'm trying to say to you?

Life on earth is no picnic! I was lucky. I was fortunate, because I was active. In the Army! In politics! I lived life to the full, but there are those who didn't have my opportunity, and I want you to dedicate yourselves to allow these people to come. The boys – 16 years old, 17 years old – whose lives were ended. Not that it matters that life was ended; but that life was ended for a purpose; and if that purpose has not been cast aside, then you have failed them. Not you in particular, but everybody has failed them.

As the weeks rolled by, the messages of encouragement and the instructions from the spirit helpers to help us improve the conditions they needed for the independent voice began to build up into some kind of a logical picture. As we understood it at the time, the communicator who was doing the majority of the spadework behind the scenes was our sergeant-major friend, Reggie, whose attitude to his work with us was amply summed up as follows, when he spoke to us through John on 20 July:

> Blood, toil, tears and sweat is about all there is, you know, and there's nothing wrong with that. I've got a job to do, on a certain level. I have to examine the potential here, and this will be judged once I present my report on you. There is definitely potential here. Recognise that you do only spend one hour per week in the circle. I want you to trust each other, and give each other any help you can. I want you to generally do as I tell you. Well, I've got work to do, so I'll be off. Just carry on! Don't worry about little sounds that don't mean a great deal. Don't start listening hard and concentrating. Give yourselves up to what you feel, and we are doing all we can here. If we make a success of it – well, that's good for everybody.

We continued throughout this period to get all the previously enjoyed signs of physical phenomena. Perhaps we were so used to them by now that we became almost blasé in their consideration. Every week there was the intense coldness, the breezes, the raps – we tended to see the odd light here and there, and several sitters noticed the pulling sensation at the solar plexus, as power was extracted for use by the spirit operators. There was a cotton-wool feeling round our foreheads, or out of one or both of the ears. Whisperings were heard almost constantly in the background and I continued to 'clock up' several EVP voices each week. Often these would be duplicated on somebody else's tape recorder, suggesting that such voices were in fact, objective.

Harry was by now being 'controlled' from time to time in a light trance condition and other communicators in addition to John's main guides and helpers would speak, either through Harry, or through me. Sandra, too, was beginning to show some signs of incipient trance control. Joyce heard whistles around the house at all times of the day and night, apart from those heard within the circle, and we all noticed that progress was going ahead in leaps and bounds.

On 3 August, after the table had danced about the previous week, Reggie had some straight talking for us yet again:

> There's a rumour going around that I'm a bit of a hard case. Well, I'm a very reasonable man – I shall treat you all just as badly. I want to give you a motto, for you to imprint on your minds, and this is

it: 'Be reasonable ... Do it my way! Right? That's how reasonable you've got to be.' Now, about this table-moving business. Perhaps you've heard the phrase 'ideoplastic'? It seems that ideas can have an effect on matter. And there's no doubt that it's a very uncertain, incomplete medium that I'm using at the moment. In addition, the rest of you have still got thoughts on your mind that are affecting the phenomena adversely, in the sense that you still want something to happen. This is what we call 'ideoplastic'. Very important to realise that you all affect the phenomena.

And I remember what was said. Each of you said that you weren't thinking of table movement. Well, the circle is not run on intellect. It is run on imagination – on emotions; and when each one of you said, 'I wasn't thinking of table movement, or levitations, or things like that', you forgot that you've all got a subconscious mind, which is like an iceberg – seven-eighths of which is below the surface. But what about the bits that you didn't know you were thinking?

Remember, this vehicle is one of imagination and emotion. You create an emotional atmosphere and you use your imagination. I can't keep coming here and digging at you all the time. I can't waste my time, or Sir Winston's either. He's very anxious to get on with this thing! And it's up to you as a group, to get together and think about these things.

I want to get all these things cleared up, because it is so important we get together as a team. Get together, and become dedicated! You must realise that *everything* you do is important. Every thought that goes on here is as important as any other. Don't forget, I want to make a favourable report on you, and to get independent voice for Winston's sake. That's why I'm here, for *his* sake. He's happy to come, otherwise I wouldn't have touched it with a barge pole. Right?

You must have realised by now what my function is. I have to correct what I think is wrong in the circle, and put you on the right road. So let's hope we will get somewhere now!

Over the next few weeks, things were looking more promising at each sitting. The medium settled into a new job during this period, and the guides and helpers came regularly to add their own individual encouragement and excitement to the whole. Sir Winston referred to the eagerly anticipated day of our ultimate victory as IV Day – Independent Voice Day!

# INDEPENDENT VOICES AT LAST

ON 14 SEPTEMBER 1977, just four days after my birthday, Harry had not yet returned from his holiday. Four of us – John, Joyce, Sandra and I sat in the usual manner, with no reason to expect that this sitting would differ in any way from the other recent sittings.

Winnie and Dr Dunn spoke through our entranced medium, once again giving out the usual mixture of hope and encouragement for the phenomena we were ultimately seeking – *the independent voice.*

They were followed by Neville, who came through John. On this occasion, he was very excited:

> I've got some good news for you – I've been picked for the first team! They told me tonight that I'm going to be the compére – like Mickey for Leslie Flint. I was waiting for a bit of promotion you know, and now I've got it! I'll be boss, won't I? And I'll have to go and find people for you. Like Mickey. I can be all fancy, and say, 'It's your turn now – you're on stage now – come on, five minutes, please!' I'll tell 'em, you know! I'm ever so pleased about it. I was wondering if I was going to be picked. And if you don't do as I tell you, I can shout at you, can't I? I was hoping that I would be the first to speak proper to you, but I'm not sure about that now. OK. Well, I've got to go because they want to try something.

Things started to happen then. Something heavy moved round the room, tapping all over. Immediately afterwards there was a piercingly loud whistle which made us all jump. This happened three times, with short intervals in between the whistles.

John was making 'puthering' sounds and coughing violently as he had done before when ectoplasm was being produced from him. I heard what I judged to be a psychic rod fall on to the carpet and move across it, just a few inches in front of me.

We had now been sitting for around three-quarters of an hour and things were looking lively. Joyce spotted a dark shadow move across the circle. Suddenly, without warning and quite simultaneously, something landed on the laps of Joyce, Sandra and myself. This turned out in each case to be a bundle of tissues but, bearing in mind that this had happened in total darkness, and quite simultaneously, it was a wonderful exercise in precision.

Jock spoke through John to ask:

> Have ye not heard anyone at all yet? [We answered negatively at this point.] We're doing our best. Dinna worry aboot the things flying aboot. We have to use the energy. If it's not used up properly, it can damage the medium. I thought ye could hear. I whistled, ye know! [We said we had heard this.] Aye – that was independent. I was trying out the box. Ye're doing quite well now. But ye have to sit a little longer to give us the chance to build. Ye have to realise, it's a long way to here, but not very far, really.

Shortly after this, there was a noise representing something between the rushing of the wind and the crackling of tinfoil. It was followed by a voice. An *independent voice, no less* – obviously quite controlled now. Our very first independent voice! And loud too. Clearly audible to all of us:

'KHOBA – KEBO – KHOBA – KHOBA – KHOBA.'

The name was repeated ten times. The independent voice of Khoba was very different from the voice he used when speaking through the entranced John. Although initially it gave the impression of someone talking through a foot thick barrier of soap bubbles, it was definitely there, and came from a point some feet away from the medium. It took several moments for the full implications to sink in. We were all ecstatic in our congratulations. This was indeed IV Day! We had finally made it, and here we were, with independent voice at last! (Let me remind the reader here that the term 'independent voice' refers to a voice which sounds identical to a normal human voice but comes from a point in mid-air, not from the mouth of a physical medium. It is produced by the spirit operators creating a voice box resembling a human larynx out of ectoplasm, then moving it around the room on the end of a psychic rod to the point from where the voice will be heard, as a particular spirit communicator 'activates' the artificial voice box.)

We had been sitting for approximately 70 minutes. If we could get this with only four of us, we wondered just how good it would be when we were back to full strength. The important thing, however, was that the breakthrough had been made. Immediately he had finished speaking independently, Khoba reverted to his trance control of John, and continued to address us. He was obviously very happy himself:

> This is me, yes, it's me – I come first! I got through good, because I waited many, many years for making noises. And me, I was all those years with no tongue, no speaking, but I can use the box now, and you will be able to listen to me. I am thanking you very much for what you have done. And don't worry about what's happened in the past because it's been learning for you.
>
> There's been many pathways, many blind alleys you all go up and down – and efforts evaporating like bubbles in the air. And now you beginning to see a little light, to make your way forward. It is a long way to go yet, but the light is there now. We can get through, and you'll hear me sing a song from the ceiling one day. But at the moment, we still near medium. You wait a little, and voices come from much further away. But it's been a good night tonight. Weather right for us too! Many times before – we got through – but accidental then, my friends. This time we got a controlled one!

As I closed this historic sitting with a short prayer, the small table shuffled round the room a little, presumably to disperse the excess power. We were all light of heart that night, and our enthusiasm over the voices knew no bounds. Everything seemed just perfect!

The following week was an occasion for much joy and a little sadness. Joy, because on this occasion, we had four separate independent voices, but exuberance was tinged with sadness when Reggie, the one personality we felt had enabled us to achieve our goal, came through John to say goodbye:

> I can say farewell to you now. I've been around, and as you know I've done my part. It's all in order, and now it's up to you. You must keep together. I've done all I can do, and I think you're on your

> way – it's just a matter of building it up. So I'll say 'cheerio' to you all, and thank you for your efforts.
>
> We have decided that it's best to keep it lighthearted for the time being, so we can raise the atmosphere as much as possible. All we want now is to try and bind the ties, if you can understand that. And that's all I've got to say to you. I'm very happy that we've been successful, and I'm leaving it entirely in the hands of all of you now.

On this second week of our obtaining independent voices, we were back to full strength by way of the number of sitters, and feeling in fine fettle. All we wanted now was to help our spirit friends to build on what had already been achieved. The foundation stone was laid but the rest needed working on.

The first voice during this seance was fairly weak. A child came through as follows, her voice emanating apparently from mid-air:

'Maggie, Maggie. Can you hear me? I know all about you – come along. Mum, my mum, Mummy!'

A short message, which did not mean much to any of us at the time. During it, Sandra started to cry uncontrollably – she felt she was the mother of the child, and was controlled as such, an entity declaring through her:

'The baby, my baby! I want my baby!'

John was beginning to make vomiting sounds and something was heard to spill on to the floor as this happened. One of his controls asked for water to be passed to him, as he was becoming very dehydrated. Khoba also came, and asked that in future we ensured the medium always had enough fluid available to him, otherwise our helpers would have problems.

The second independent voice that week was Jock's. He came through, and called his name out three times. This was followed by the voice of Neville, coming from the middle of the room:

'Can you hear me? Neville, Neville, Neville.'

This was accompanied by several incoherent words, part of what Neville was trying to say to us. The quality of the voices at this stage was not very good. They tended to sound like someone speaking and gargling at the same time. Occasionally, one could smell that peculiar odour – a sort of earthy smell, reminiscent of damp ferns.

Just one more voice made itself heard during this sitting of 21 September:

'WINSTON, WINSTON, WINSTON. IT'S JUST THE JOB! I'M DOING THE JOB!'

Over the next few weeks, the voices grew in number, strength and clarity. Some that came were there for personal reasons. All those of us sitting in the circle had somebody through the independent voice in turn who we had known when they were on earth.

Those who proved to be most proficient in the early use of the voicebox were Neville, Jock, Winston, Khoba and Helen Duncan, but each time any of the communicating entities spoke to us in this manner, they showed some improvement over the previous occasion.

Around this time, we also began to hear from a new communicator. His voice had a musical almost hypnotic quality and he informed us that during his earth life he had been a bishop. He appeared to have been drafted in to help us with our more spiritual development – a facet which in the past, although not ignored, had been pushed very much into the background, as our drive to get the independent voice breakthrough gained momentum.

He urged us to have quiet periods for meditation purposes during the sittings and these added tremendously to the peace and harmony we felt within the Romford circle. Our emotions became much keener while the phenomenon was developing in the group, and most of us noticed that we could suddenly jump from emotional highs to lows, almost crying on occasions at sad sections of TV films, etc. All our senses in fact became much augmented during the course of the Seymer Road Seances.

The bishop's voice really was a pleasure to listen to; he would encourage us as we drifted off into our meditational periods, urging us to accept that God lies within, and it was from this direction that our comfort and solace should come. Of the circle, he had this to say:

> I thank you on behalf of those who are desirous of communicating, for your willingness to make yourselves available and to endure with courage and patience the frustrations and the vicissitudes of this communication in these times of stress. You'll never know how much you have helped these people here. Even those who cannot

communicate with you – they thank you for the things you have given them – for the sacrifices you have made. And don't forget that the sacrifice has only just begun. It is sad, perhaps, that there are so few places to which these souls can come and be welcomed, and be given something of yourselves. If I could only describe to you the joy on the faces of those who manage to once again come back to the earth as they once were! And they are forever hopeful that you will bring, in time to come, their own loved ones to this place. That they may assume again from each of you the cloak, the earthly cloak around their spirit forms so that they may feel and touch – that love – that rapport which existed for them many years ago.

Early in October, Dr Dunn urged through the medium's trance that the circle members did not become too insular:

It is felt that in some ways you are becoming a little too insular. By that I mean that you have excluded further possibilities, and I suggest that you, in your own good time, try and enlarge the circle by the addition of one or two members. Although experiments in this direction have, in the past, in the light of your experiences not been too successful, it would be a great help if you were able to find one or two people.

This is a very delicate and tenuous stage, this consolidation part, but I'd like you to accept that the blueprint is laid down, and whatever happens now cannot destroy the nucleus – the egg – as it were. So if you can, or should come across anyone who you think is reliable, or with whom you could achieve rapport, then give it a trial. Bear in mind that at the moment, the power is not great. By this, we mean that we have no reserves, and that constitutes a problem. It can mean that there is a certain loss, or a draining of power, as perhaps some of you have noticed. More sitters would prevent this.

During this same sitting on 5 October, Winston reverted to trance communication to speak to us, and he had this to say:

What was it he said? Insular? My friends, in some ways I think you are getting a trifle arrogant! I hope you realise, whatever has happened, that I have been the force, the dynamism behind the selection of people. I have urged you. I have exhorted you. I have tried to reach you in every way I can, and I don't want you to fail

> this time! I have searched for a place where I can be heard. Where my words and thoughts can be recorded. And here I've found somewhere where I can be heard. Perhaps even understood!
>
> I hope you realise the terrible and difficult problems we have to face in our attempts to bring you a facsimile – that's all it will ever be – merely a facsimile of what we used to be. But if I can convey to you just one thousandth part of the awesome and terrible infinity in which you live and move, and have your existence – if I can bring to you one speck of knowledge – if I can turn over for you one pebble on the beach of wisdom, then I think I can say I have achieved my purpose.

The independent voices during that week were also impressive. Sixteen of them in all. Among the communicators were Field-Marshall Lord Montgomery of Alamein and, evidential for me, Elmer Browne, who spoke from a point in the air no more than six inches in front of my face! The scent of jasmine in the air was perceived by all of us, and commented on by Jock, speaking independently. Jasmine happened to be the name of one of Sandra's guides, who was apparently making her presence felt. Neville also had plenty to say as his independent voice gained momentum.

Following this sitting, the general feeling in the circle was that we should do as requested and look around for a couple of sincere sitters to make up our numbers. We had been lucky enough to have secured another sitting with Leslie Flint at the end of November and he was not aware that, in the meantime, we had achieved the independent voice. We were looking forward tremendously to the sitting and to receiving from it possible confirmation of where we were heading. While we therefore agreed with what Dr Dunn had to say about extra sitters, we felt that it would not be right to bring anyone else into the circle until after our appointment with Leslie.

The week afterwards, on 12 October our helpers explained that for psychological reasons, John, the medium, was a little upset to be unconscious when the phenomenon was going on, thus missing the voices himself. The intention, therefore, was that the mediumship would be transferred on to a group basis, rather than one person doing the whole thing, so that John could be conscious and able to hear the voices himself. We were very pleased about this decision, as it effectively put us all on an equal basis, with identical privileges in hearing phenomena.

From that week onwards, as promised, John was at least partially conscious, and was able to hear the voices himself. It was noticed too that there was an immediate improvement in the clarity of those communicators' voices which spoke independently to us.

As the weeks passed by, the voices continued to come. We learned more and more about the process from Dr Dunn and the other regular communicators. It may be interesting for readers to note Dr Dunn's comments on the need for potential communicators to practise:

> They have to rehearse you know, even to say 'Hello', and Neville is practising as hard as he possibly can. It takes a long time for these people to become orientated. By that I mean several weeks, even months, before they can use the apparatus effectively – and even at your sittings, it takes a long time to become accustomed again. I want you to recognise the enormous changes that they have to undergo, and also that they're not really aware of your own voices initially. They cannot necessarily hear what you are saying. In some cases, they don't even know that they have been heard. So please do not prompt them.

On the question of who was in charge of running the circle, Dr Dunn had this to say:

> I'll tell you something now that I haven't told you before and that is that I have my superiors too. They are known as the 'Brotherhood', and they are very interested in what we are doing here. I am now in constant contact with this Brotherhood, and I want you to realise that there is a great interest taken in these matters by those evolved beings.

The voices were by now coming from points in all parts of the room. From the ceiling, from the floor, from the walls, and all places in between. The instant shifting of a voice from one place to another was most impressive, and added to the confidence we had in the phenomenon by this time.

We were told that it was being planned for the group to get full materialisation eventually and that the medium for this would be different from the current medium. Who could doubt what they were saying when we had already had so much proof?

Although a decision had been taken to not accept any new sitters into the circle on a regular basis until after our appointment with Leslie Flint, John had already tried an advert in the *Psychic News* to test the response. After sifting through the replies we received, it was decided that two or three of the applicants would be invited to attend on 2 November 1977 for a trial sitting. In the event, two of these applicants joined us on that occasion. To say that we were all apprehensive about the sitting was an understatement. We could not help but wonder if the presence of two strangers in the circle, so soon after we had obtained the voices, would inhibit the phenomena, or even prevent the voices from occurring altogether.

We were, however, proved absolutely wrong in our doubts and fears. A total of twelve independent voices came to speak to us that evening, in spite of the misgivings we had. Amongst the independent communicators was an ex-schoolfriend of mine from Grimsby, who had entered the RAF a year or so after me, and had attended Cranwell, the elite RAF College. He had proved to be an ace pilot and had become a member of the famous Red Arrows aerobatic forma-tion team, before being 'killed' in an air crash when operating as an instructor.

William Olsen, a physical medium in his own lifetime, also spoke to us independently on that occasion, and the following week the voices were even better, as we were informed about the presence of several souls who had been connected with the acting profession. Amongst others, Ellen Terry spoke to us independently.

We were now approaching the sitting at Leslie Flint's. On 9 November, Winston reminded us of Remembrance Day, of those who gave their lives for their country, promising before he left that he would be present at Leslie's.

The next week was one that I will remember vividly for the rest of my life, as my own sister came to speak to me independently. It was an extremely emotional moment for me as a great joy, hard to comprehend by those who have not experienced it, came over me.

I realised that if such feelings as this could be generated among the members of the group who were already used to this sort of communication, then the help and joy brought to casual sitters at some future date, caused by the impact of being reunited with their loved ones, must be immeasurable. I recall that I was then tremendously proud to be a member of this privileged group, which obviously had so much good work to do in the near future.

# FINAL CONFIRMATION AT LESLIE FLINT'S

HAVING ACHIEVED THE independent voice, our group felt extremely uplifted. However, the human element in us demands the ultimate proof at all times and it was with this in mind that I approached our sitting with Leslie Flint. The weather was not ideal on 24 November that year but all the group members arrived on time and the atmosphere when we saw Leslie again was cordial and optimistic.

We could not yet know it but this sitting was to prove to be one of the most evidential that any of us had ever experienced, both from a personal point of view and from the general aspect of the circle interests. Leslie seemed to be reasonably healthy, but looked rather drained; it was obvious that the past year since he had retired from public life had aged him considerably. Nevertheless, this time we did not have long to wait in the darkness. The voice of Leslie's main guide, Mickey, was heard after only about 25 minutes. Although the words were difficult to hear at first, the voice gradually grew in volume.

Mickey's greeting, in the independent voice, was almost that of an old friend. One of our main intentions at this sitting had been to confirm whether we ought to increase the number of regular sitters at the Seymer Road Seances from five to seven or so, in order to augment the power. Our question remained unasked, as Mickey answered it evidentially without prompting almost as soon as he first came through, in the following manner:

> Hello. I remember you. I've been to your place, when I came and let you know I was there. [A correct statement!] And I wanted you to know that, because I take an interest in your little group and I think that you've got great possibilities.

Mickey then addressed me personally and correctly referred to two of my healing guides, one of them German. He spoke of the healing work I had been doing recently, before continuing:

> There's a little group of spirit people who work very very close to your circle, and they are most pleased with the way things are going. I think you're much better as you are, and I don't think you should make any alterations. You've been concerned, and uncertain in your minds about something. I believe you've been talking about the possibility of increasing the numbers, but with all due respect, I think you'd better stay as you are. It's better to be small in numbers and strong in power, love and harmony than you get a couple leave, who might upset the whole apple cart.
>
> I'm told that you'd be better to stay as you are, and not make any changes. You could open the door, and although newcomers might be all right, they might not really fit in. If they then, perhaps, packed it in, you'd be right back where you started, wouldn't you? But I know you've had some very good indications of things lately. There's a tremendous amount of energy and power you know.

Here Mickey broke off, promising to return before long. Another personality came to speak to us – one who had been visiting our circle for some time, namely Sir William Crookes. During his lifetime he was an eminent scientist, psychic researcher and champion of Spiritualistic beliefs, following his in-depth researches of the mediumships of D D Home and Florence Cook (through whom he witnessed, and 44 times photographed, the much-publicised full-form materialisation of Katie King). His advice to us and encouragement for what we were doing was long and remarkable during this sitting:

> As a matter of fact, I'm very pleased that you've come here today, because one has felt that you might have made a great mistake by allowing others to intrude into the group, which I am quite sure would not have worked out. I think you would be well advised to stay as you are. We are quite happy about it, and we do not feel that any addition to the circle would be of any real benefit.
>
> It seems that you are now well established. The power is excellent. The conditions are right, and there's great love and harmony between you. We have every reason to believe that in due course we should achieve what we set out to do. You have already begun to see some

> of the signals and signs and have you noticed that the conditions have changed a little?
>
> There has been a slight change, and the atmosphere begins, I should imagine, from your point of view to become colder. This unfortunately cannot be helped. I'm sorry if it inconveniences you. Have you, by the way, heard the whistling sounds? We have endeavoured to do certain things to encourage you, naturally, and the whistling sound is more than likely, from our point of view, a signal.

As it happens, this information was very evidential for us. We had indeed been feeling the extra coldness in our circle for some time. Whistling noises, too, had been a regular feature in this group almost from the beginning. Sir William went on to explain in greater depth:

> This vibrational thing is very difficult to explain. We have to lower our rate of vibration. This may sound odd to you, but to enter into the atmosphere and conditions of earth, our vibrational rate becomes less than is normal for us. You to some extent heighten your vibrational conditions whilst we lower ours. Once we are as it were tuned in, which we definitely are, there will be certain signs and signals.
>
> You may get cold breezes, and you may have other things which from time to time will happen. Do you hear any unusual noises? [We answered in the affirmative.] Don't be surprised if you hear some noises which are not what you would call natural or normal noises in the room, and there will possibly be other things happening, such as the moving of objects or the perfume of flowers.
>
> I'm not suggesting that you are an impatient crowd. Far from it, in fact you're very sensible in your approach and attitude, and patient, but we also feel that sometimes we must do something that will give you a little encouragement. Our task is to eventually bring into being the phenomenon that we're sitting for, but the point is, it may take and will take quite a while, as we can't promise it quickly.
>
> From time to time we think 'well, we must try tonight to do something a little special' to give you an extra boost. The power with you is quite, quite extraordinary. I have no doubt in my mind, and I know that others here have no doubts in their minds, that we shall achieve what we set out to do – so it is not necessary to make any alterations in the sessions.

> The singing is a help to us at the beginning, as the vibrations are helped by sound. It doesn't necessarily mean to say that you have to continue that all the time, however, once the vibrations are at an acceptable level.

Sir William Crookes went on to say that should there be any questions which we felt disposed to ask, or should we require of him any advice or help, he would be only too happy to do what he could for us. John thanked him here, as he had already answered our main query, and the matter was discussed in more detail by this same communicator with further confirmations of what had previously been said.

Circle member Harry inquired as to whether prayer helped in the circle, and on that subject, Sir William had this to say:

> Well of course, prayer always helps, but the point is this – that prayer is something which obviously must come from the innermost self. It is an asset and a help, and generates goodwill, thus creating a harmonious atmosphere. It is only natural and right that one should approach the subject from a prayerful aspect, and one could go into depth regarding prayer.
>
> However, from my point of view, prayer is what you are yourself, deep down inside you. How you conduct yourself in your earthly existence, and how you behave to others. In short, prayer must be a living thing, even if it's not verbal. You can, for instance, sit and enter into prayer in a mental way, without necessarily vibrating the atmosphere to create sound so that people can hear your prayer.
>
> I'm not saying that you shouldn't pray out loud – yes, by all means pray if you feel so disposed. You must realise, however, that the prayer is what it is, a verbal thing. Real prayer is your innermost soul, your innermost self. Your action and reaction with regard to life, to human beings generally, and to all those who enter into your environment and conditions; into your way of life.

Sir William was asked about his previous visits to our circle.

> I have been on many occasions. Not every time, as that is not possible or practical. I do – as it happens – know most of the souls that come to you and have great regard and respect for them. I know too, that their intentions are the highest.
>
> You see, I was very caught up with this subject myself, many years ago, when I was on your side of life. I sat with various mediums,

> taking a great interest in the subject. I advocated it and I am sure that some of you must have read books in which I stated my views.
>
> I visit your circle basically because I am interested in the manifestations of the Spirit, with regard to the mechanics of communication, either in this, or that way – such as the direct voice, or materialisation – that sort of thing, which provides something tangible that one can deal with.
>
> Everything that is done in the circle is for a purpose, you can be sure of that. And I can honestly say to you that those here who are very close to you have your welfare at heart. Some maybe will speak to you here today; others will not. But from our point of view, everything to do with your group is as we wish it to be. No reflection on other friends who may wish to join you but we would rather you stay as you are.

There were a few more remarks and observations from Sir William Crookes before he concluded his long talk, which had lasted for over ten minutes. As Sir William's voice faded out, there came the next communicator, and a lady's dulcet tones announced with a French accent that she was Sister Maria. We recognised the voice immediately:

> Maria – I have come too, you know, just to let you know of my presence. Everything is there with you, and so we are content to be patient. I know that we shall eventually succeed. I come to you often, and sometimes I am able to give you a little hint – yes. And one day I hope you will see me, and also other friends here, and hear our voices. The power, it is there between you!

Sister Maria then invited questions, and Harry, who was fascinated by her accent, commented on her voice, to which she gave the following explanation:

> Well you know, I have learned many things in this world, and it is very difficult to explain certain things to you. When I come back to the earth, I suppose it is because I have the old idea of things, and I suddenly, almost automatically, find myself thinking and speaking, I suppose, as I did.
>
> Because, you know, I had many years in convent, and languages was one of the things that were very dear to me. This is very helpful, and very essential, in the work that we now do. Over here, you know, we don't have to speak. We can communicate entirely by thought. But when we come down to you, we have to concentrate

> our thoughts very hard, so that we can come through to you independently, like this.
>
> Today the conditions are wonderful, but there again, this is because of yourselves, you know. Generally the conditions in your world are terrible. So much malice, hatred and intolerance. There's an atmosphere of unrest in your world. Sometimes it is as if we are piercing a fog.
>
> But when I come to you, that is another thing altogether, and all of us are conscious of this. The air around you when you sit is light. Almost like a light in the darkness for us. We are so grateful to you. Just be patient now.

Mickey came in swiftly here to tell us of some of the spirit children who are in the habit of visiting our circle – most of whom had been described to us in the past, and so Mickey's descriptions were very evidential for us. He also mentioned that there was a Scotsman who came to us. He was obviously referring to Jock, and then Jock himself broke in with his broad accent:

> He's talking about me! Just thought you'd like to know I was here – there wouldn't be any show without Punch! We've got great hopes for the circle. I don't think you should alter it.

Jock continued by giving me some excellent personal evidence, the nature of which precludes my detailing it here; and it wasn't until much later that I discovered his information to be one hundred percent accurate in its content. The medium (Leslie Flint) could have had absolutely no way of knowing beforehand the information which Jock gave me, as it concerned something which was happening at the *actual* time of the Flint sitting – but over one hundred miles away! It also helped in making a correct personal decision on a matter which was important to me then.

Mickey had more to say to John. Again, personal evidence for him, and this was followed by a now familiar voice; that of White Feather, who had spoken to us at Flint's a year previously, and had since then spoken independently in the Romford circle:

> White Feather; White Feather come; bring blessings to children. I am very pleased, like all friends here with circle. You make no difference, no change! You carry on as always.

White Feather was followed by a man with a 'corblimey' Cockney accent who addressed Harry, identifying himself as Jimmy Hawkins. He spoke of his wife's visiting these 'spooky meetings' when she was on earth, although he considered it a load of Tommy rot. Now he had no option but to change his ideas. He offered his help at the circle meetings.

Mickey followed up this communication by announcing that John's brother was there, and wanting to speak to him. It was obvious from the conversation that followed that John had recognised his brother at once and he was very happy and somewhat excited to have had the contact. During the many years that John had spent following his interests in psychic matters, he had never before had anybody return to him from the 'other side' whom he had known personally and now here was his own brother, speaking to him, apparently out of thin air.

As soon as this well-recognised relative went, Mickey returned to speak to us all about our plans to hold a special Christmas sitting this year for the spirit children, complete with Christmas tree and presents. This was an excellently evidential reference, as we had only just recently decided to do exactly that.

Mickey continued, speaking to John at length, and giving him accurate personal details about his past life and problems – about the life and death of his brother – and about a lady who also wished to be remembered to him from the spirit side of life. Every bit of this information being given by Mickey was subsequently verified by John after the sitting.

Although we were sitting in total darkness, Mickey proved that he could see because Sandra was told off for having her legs crossed – she had forgotten in the excitement of the sitting that this is not allowed in a physical circle as it prevents the flow of energy and power necessary for the continuation of the phenomenon.

Mickey followed up his comments to Sandra with some evidence for her, before telling me that Elmer Browne sent his regards and was anxious to let me know that he had not forgotten me. Through Mickey, he confirmed that he came regularly to the circle and, again, this was evidential as Bill had communicated independently at Romford. Circle member Joyce was also given some excellent personal evidence at this juncture, and a few other communicators who were present were acknowledged by Mickey, and described to us.

An interesting aspect of all of Leslie Flint's seances, including this one, was the fact that when Mickey spoke, he would sometimes turn aside, to address another spirit entity who happened to be present. When this happened, Mickey's side of the conversation was frequently audible to sitters as a whispered aside. That proved on many occasions to be a most amusing interlude; it was rather like listening to somebody speaking on the telephone, without hearing the other end of the conversation.

Often, Mickey would be speaking at the same time as Leslie, or when Leslie was coughing. This happened more than once during this particular sitting. At one point Leslie yawned, and simultaneously Mickey chided him, 'Oh stop yer blooming yawning!'

The Flint sitting was not quite finished. Our best known communicator had yet to come and Mickey went on to introduce him thus:

> There's a man here, Winnie, Winnie Churchill. He's here. He comes through at your sessions sometimes, and he seems deeply interested in what's going on.
>
> You've got a photograph of him that you've hung up, haven't you? [This was accurate.] Because he's talking about his picture that you've got. Winnie Churchill. He's laughing, or beaming as you call it, and he says, 'They often say it's a pity he ain't here with us now – we could do with him.'
>
> He's quite a character, ain't he? He liked a drop of drink though, although it's not necessary over here. He comes and he controls occasionally, but he seems to be interested in your group. I think he's hoping that one day he'll be able to speak in a sustained independent voice. But he's grateful for the opportunity, and he says he'd been to one or two other places, but ... [here, Mickey is heard to speak aside to Winston, 'Hey, why don't you do it yourself, Mister!']

And without any further ado, the voice of Sir Winston in its familiar tones, was heard:

> Hello. Well, well, well! It's me here! [Harry interjected here, 'Pray continue, Sir Winston.'] You can drop the Sir. I'm quite happy to be just referred to as 'Winnie', although some people would prefer

'Winston'. Can you hear me? [We confirmed that we could.] It's a bit difficult for me to know whether you can hear me.

I'm very pleased to be able to talk to you for a moment or two to let you know I'm here, as promised. I must say, I don't find it too easy. No doubt, with experience and opportunity, I shall be better at it.

But I'm happy with the group, and I come every time, without fail. So don't worry. Carry on! It does mean a great deal of patience on your part. Anyway, we'll get better at it, eventually. Just carry on the good work. Bless you. Goodbye.

The power was getting very weak now and Mickey's voice was faint as he came for the last time to bid us farewell. Our sitting at an end, the lights were once again turned on. The results of the day, and the accompanying evidence, had been fantastic. We were overjoyed with the confirmation we had received about the circle. As always, we had taken the precaution of giving Leslie no background information whatsoever about ourselves or the circle beforehand.

Needless to say, each and every one of us from the Romford circle was in exuberant mood after the afternoon's events. And the euphoria was not just confined to ourselves. Leslie Flint himself had been amazed by the sitting and by the extent of the communications. So impressed was he, that he asked us if *he* could sit with *us* at a future date. We would have been happy to oblige if the Romford circle had continued to run for long enough but, regrettably, that was not to be. For now, however, our feeling was jubilant, and we all celebrated afterwards with a meal in one of the local Bayswater restaurants before setting off home.

# END OF AN ERA

THE 'HEADY EUPHORIA' of that November 1977 Flint sitting faded after a few weeks and circle members were faced with the question 'Where do we go from here?' According to the advice given at Leslie's, we should not alter the constitution of the circle for the time being by bringing in new sitters. Our medium, John, once again began to question his own psychic ability and his mediumship as there had actually been a request from our own helpers to increase the number of circle members. With this dilemma before us, none of us could explain fully why such an apparent contradiction had taken place, although today, in the light of much more experience, such an explanation would be comparatively simple; in that even with the purest of physical phenomena, the mind of the medium *can and often does* affect the messages, to a greater or lesser degree, *whether delivered through trance or through direct and independent voice.*

Even Leslie himself, with his 60 years' practical experience of physical mediumship, was always happy to admit that this sometimes happened in his own case and, of course, the depth of the medium's trance greatly affects the validity of the communication. In any event, the intervening years have taught me that while long-term development is taking place with physical mediums, messages should not always be taken at face value. Cross confirmation from another source is helpful; whilst proof and evidence will come in its own good time through the physical medium who is undergoing the development of their mediumship. Certainly sitters should be sympathetic throughout the development period of any physical medium, thereby providing at all times the correct and harmonious conditions for him/her to develop their gifts without making an issue of information and messages which are regarded as suspect.

Although we were still getting the independent voices following this Flint sitting, they did tend for a limited period to be short and concise – just the odd word or name. We obviously needed the further breakthrough and incentive of achieving sustained independent voice contact of the type we had witnessed at Leslie's home in Bayswater.

Early in December 1977, through John's trance, Dr Dunn had more to say on the subject of the Brotherhood;

> You may recall that I mentioned the Brotherhood. Well, at the time when I did so, I had the distinct impression that you were thinking of some esoteric figures, dressed in raiment rather like the Ku Klux Klan of America, or some phantom figures in flowing white robes.
>
> I can assure you that this Brotherhood is nothing like that. In fact, the Brotherhood of which I speak is composed of people – scientists mostly – who were involved in this Spiritualism before their passing over to the spirit world, and they are currently working on a revival of 'real' Spiritualism if you like.
>
> Sir William Crookes is a member, Sir Oliver Lodge, Sir Arthur Conan Doyle, too. There's W T Stead, there's Miles and Gurney. Lots of people like that, and this is the Brotherhood. They are trying to bring back physical phenomena again, and they are also in contact with Konstantin Raudive.
>
> In fact, these are the two things which they are currently working on. They are interested in Raudive – we call it 'Raudive', in regard of this being an accepted term for it on this side, and they are very concerned that you recognise how important it is for this group to progress, now that you have drawn these people to you.
>
> This brotherhood is not, as I have said, some esoteric clan, but these are very determined and anxious people – anxious in the sense that they are so incensed with the mediocrity that in many cases passes for mediumship these days – and they wish to bring something of repute back to the movement in which they were involved, because as you know, their names have been somewhat tarnished in the past, and indeed, presently too.

I was urged by Dr Dunn to continue my experiments with the EVP in addition to my circle work, and was told that I would be assisted by my spirit friend Elmer Browne and indeed, Konstantin Raudive himself, in this work.

On 14 December 1977, shortly after the 'death' of Lady Churchill, Winston spoke to us through John:

> Yes, Clemmie and I are together now. Now that I can walk again, side by side with the one who supports me, then together we can – *I* can devote more of my time to you.
>
> The question has been asked: Where do we go from here? I'll tell you where! Imagine yourselves standing in the middle of the Antarctic. Where would you go from there? Which direction would you take? [None of us could come up with a useful answer to that question.] Well, there's only one way you can go; forward and onward.
>
> And now that you've learned what you have, the intention is that we're going forwards and onwards to materialisation. This is the aim.

Sir Oliver Lodge than came to speak to us, offering constant encouragement, and referring to several experiments they were attempting currently in the circle as the progress continued. I had for some time been contemplating writing a book on the Seymer Road Seances and Sir Oliver told me:

'With regard to your book – Sir Arthur will help you with it! Sir Arthur Conan Doyle! This one won't be fiction, though.'

Some way into the sitting, after we had heard several communicators speak independently, there was a touching incident. A lady's voice, also speaking independently, was heard by all to say:

> Hello, it's Clemmie here, Clemmie! I've come to see you. Winnie made me do it but I don't mind at all. I'll be here with him all the time. I didn't realise that it would be like this. He told me I was so beautiful. It's like old times. So lovely!

Several of the guides now came to tell us that it was their intention to speed up the circle's development so that our first goals would be realised quickly, and that this process could leave us a little drained of energy following sittings. We were asked to forgive them if this proved to be the case.

For some weeks, we had been getting odd words and phrases spoken independently in German (incidentally, a language totally unknown to the medium). From the content of these communications, it was obvious that the speaker had been a member of the Nazi party when he was on earth. The obvious connection made us think of the erstwhile Führer, Adolf Hitler, and to satisfy our curiosity, we sounded Winston out on the current condition of the former leader.

Winnie had promised to investigate whether such a personality might be brought along to our circle at some future date to provide an interesting and historic meeting of minds. However, when Winston spoke to us on 21 December he had this message for us about Hitler:

> Yes. I've investigated the possibility of the great self-seeking Führer and what opportunity he may have to join us, but I am afraid my investigations have proved to be fruitless. Apparently the man has no redeeming features whatsoever which would be of any possible use to us. Maybe of interest to historians, but I think ... better to leave that to the psychologists.
>
> It's a shameful waste indeed, but one lesson we have learned from such a man is that orthodox religion, orthodox practices, socialism, conservatism and liberalism in all its forms have not given to the people what they desire.
>
> So it could well happen again, I'm afraid. There is this vacuum to be filled and one day, some other maniac will stride into it. And with his inherent volubility, with his stridency and his charisma, will lead the human race into a premature, early chaos.

This was an all-sobering thought for a Christmas sitting but, nevertheless, we were in a happy mood and sang several carols. Shortly afterwards, the independent voices started in earnest.

Leslie Flint's guide Mickey said a few words of greeting, and then the loud and clear voice of Sir William Crookes was heard coming from the area of the ceiling. The voice was virtually identical to the one we heard at Leslie's, and completely independent:

> As a matter of fact, I've been able to come to you this evening and I wish to endorse what has already been said regarding the intentions of the Brotherhood. We are terribly anxious to return to what we were. To things as they were in those great days, when the movement was at its height.
>
> However, we cannot afford to destroy the bridges in the process. And we must go slowly and carefully over the ground, to bring you your own version of what we think should be available to all who can be accessible to you. I can't stay long with you, and you've already heard me speak before.

> Here, we have rejoined together in this great Brotherhood, and we see that the time will come when the only thing left will be to have to bring to you – to usher in the new millennium – the reality which will not be based on some abstract theological theory, but will be grounded on the solid fact that 'life after death' really is true, and can be substantiated.

There was no doubt that the independent voices were now able to sustain themselves and we at last *had* the breakthrough which we had long sought. It seemed that from now on, we were going to enjoy some very interesting and evidential sittings.

Elmer Browne greeted me independently and made a joke. His voice on this occasion was pretty much identical to his earth voice as I remembered it when sitting in his circle. Then came Sister Maria, who spoke for a few minutes, and expressed the hope, as she had done at Flint's, that she might be able to fully materialise for us.

Not to be outdone, Neville also came along and chatted to us for a sustained period in his usual jocular manner, causing us to laugh loud and long. All the communicators were now speaking fluently in the independent voice, and we were hearing them clearly. Khoba came too, in order to tell us that they had at last perfected the 'apparatus'.

Lastly, at this particular sitting, the overall prospects for the group were summed up by Dr Dunn, as he referred to the children that had been present at our Christmas sitting:

> There are lots and lots of children present, and they find pleasure in being here. You will find that they will come in the future, too. And please, please let us not say to the children 'Once a year we'll have Christmas'. Let's make it Christmas every week.
>
> Anyway, I want to say that although we have what you might call rather advanced, and perhaps impossible, plans for the future, we are, in fact, taken along with these things. We have tonight achieved, I think you will agree, rather a great breakthrough, and I don't wish, on Khoba's advice or indeed on his insistence, to tire the medium any further – or any of you, for that matter.
>
> Just as you, Robin, record these sittings, so too do we record everything in minute detail. Nothing is missed by us – no word, no gesture – nothing at all is missed. And all this is referred back, for the sake of future sittings.

> Where you were all wondering a few weeks ago as to whether we would bypass the independent voice to achieve materialisation, I can assure you that this will not be the case. Nothing will be bypassed here. If you come together in love and harmony, we shall achieve materialisation of solid forms, and you will hear the voices coming from the mouths of the people you see.

The indications were, therefore, that as a circle we would continue to move onwards and forwards to achieve even greater things in the future. After such a superb sitting as this 'Christmas special' had been, we were once again fired up with enthusiasm, and looking forward very much to our sittings in the New Year 1978.

Over the next four months, we had some really fantastic sittings. The communications made through the independent voice were far too numerous and too full of detail to include in this book. They were encouraging in the extreme, and the quality of the voices, including such communicators as King George VI, were amazing.

We continued the seances with the five regular sitters for a few weeks into 1978, until Harry decided to leave the circle because his work schedule no longer coincided with the times of the sittings. Funnily enough, the loss of one of the sitters did not adversely affect the quality of the sittings – in fact the phenomenon continued to improve after he left, with just the four of us – John, Joyce, Sandra and me.

Regrettably though, John's health continued to be poor. He suffered terrible mood swings and during the early part of 1978 this problem became more acute. Joyce felt that his mediumship was causing him additional psychological problems and he was encouraged to give it up altogether. Neither John nor Joyce could see a valid reason to continue the mediumistic development, despite the superb results that had been achieved so far.

However, in fairness to both parties, neither had ever professed the overwhelming desire and dedication to serve mankind and the spirit world which is vital in every sitter in a truly successful physical circle such as our current Scole Experimental Group, although we *had* hoped that some spiritual motivation would come naturally, along with the success of the circle.

Instead, looking back on the situation in the cold light of day, the drive to develop the independent voices had seemed to be more a matter of curiosity for them which, once satisfied, left them, as they saw it, in something of a cul-de-sac with nowhere to go.

By March 1978, the voices had developed to such a degree that John could easily have made his living in the same way as Leslie Flint, as an independent voice medium but I do not believe that such an idea appealed to him, perhaps because he lacked the desire to serve others. His psychological problems would perchance have caused him to be unsuitable for such a role, since he was prone at a whim, in all the time that we knew him, to turn round at the last moment when everybody was present prior to a seance, and announce that he was not going to sit that week. Such behaviour could be frustrating in the extreme and particularly so when sitters had travelled some distance just to be there.

In addition, I had personal problems of my own at that time. My first marriage broke down completely and I moved into a bedsit in Chelmsford Road, South Woodford, during March. Thereafter, the Romford circle headed quickly towards oblivion.

The very special sitting with Leslie Flint during November 1977 was, as I recall, the very pinnacle of the Seymer Road Seances. But far from the dizzy heights we sitters had hoped to reach, with ongoing independent voices, and maybe eventually materialisation, so that we might be in a position to give solace and help to those who needed it and provide for all and sundry the wonderful proof of 'life after death', the circle was destined to go the way of numerous circles before and after it, and break up entirely.

John and Joyce suspended the circle for a month during the last week of March and we were destined to sit only twice in April (with the final sitting on 26 April 1978) before they decided that they did not want to continue with it any more. Subsequently they announced that they were going to give up psychic matters altogether, for reasons best known to themselves. I suspect, however, that the true reason was John's inability to come to terms with the psychological aspect of the development of his mediumship, a process that he found to be traumatic in the extreme, as a consequence of his mood swings.

There was nothing that Sandra and I could do to persuade them otherwise. We were both devastated to lose the wonderful phenomena which we had experienced during the life of the Seymer Road Seances. In a way, we felt guilty, too, that we were letting our spirit friends down and denying them their rightful opportunity for carrying the circle forward to its correct conclusion, so that we could give help to those in this world who needed it.

The feeling of loss was dreadful. We felt so close to the guides and helpers that they were almost 'family' to us and we experienced a period of grief somewhat akin to losing most of one's family in a single tragic disaster.

But as life gradually got back to normal again and things settled down, we realised that whatever the outcome had been, we had been truly privileged to be a part of that remarkable circle. It was indeed a 'carrot' for us to aim for again in the future. We *knew* now that a dedicated group, sitting under the right conditions, could develop the independent voice, and more besides.

The shared experience drew Sandra and I closer together as 1978 progressed and gave us the determination to succeed in our quest for physical phenomena, come hell or high water. It was not until years later that we realised it had all been part of a much greater plan.

# BACK TO THE DRAWING BOARD

As the Seymer Road Seances receded into the mists of time, in the words of the song, I 'picked myself up, dusted myself down, and started all over again'. Spirit had not finished with me yet as, during the first days of May, I discovered in the *Psychic News* a number for the South Woodford Spiritualist Church (closed down at that time) and duly contacted George Gray, whose number it was. It turned out that the previous South Woodford Spiritualist Church had been compulsorarily purchased and subsequently demolished to make way for a new bypass (now part of the London North Circular). Adequate compensation and a piece of land had been supplied by the local authority when this happened and George Gray, supported by a small church committee, had taken on the task of having the new church architect-designed and built. Surprise, surprise, the new site, reached by a footbridge, was no more than a few hundred yards away from the bedsit in which I was living.

I met George and his wife, Isobel, and volunteered my services to help on the committee in any way I could with the building and administration of the new church. Since the committee was small, my offer was taken up and I was duly seconded on to the committee of the South Woodford SNU Church.

While chatting one day to George and Isobel Gray, I happened to mention in passing the Seymer Road circle, outlining to them the circumstances under which it broke up, adding that Sandra and I would dearly like to get back into a physical circle. As we had no suitable venue, we were unable to start one of our own.

Immediately both of them, being the generous people that they were, offered their home in Hainault and it was agreed that we would have our first sitting of the new physical circle on Tuesday 9 May

1978. Five of us sat on that first occasion, with the sitting taking place in their lounge. Despite our efforts, it proved impossible to achieve a good blackout and the sitting consequently was totally unsatisfactory. The following week, however, we sat upstairs in their spare bedroom, where the blackout was so much better with only one small window to cover, as opposed to three large ones in the lounge.

The Hainault circle continued weekly throughout 1978, running until the end of February 1979. It was a pleasant enough circle, but singularly unspectacular. New sitters came in from time to time, and others left, but apart from a smattering of trance, raps, taps and coldness, there was little to get excited about by way of phenomena.

I lived in the South Woodford bedsit for the whole of the year, and stayed there until the end of the following February. Sandra and I continued to have a number of private sittings with various mediums from time to time, constantly seeking some form of guidance as to how we could achieve physical phenomena again.

Most of these sittings were encouraging, pointing to the changes that were going on in our lives. I was in the midst of a divorce and, during September, I changed my job to work for a Finnish paper firm, where I was employed until recently, when half of my department and I succumbed to the every-hungry monster, redundancy.

Occasional committee meetings for the South Woodford church took place but there was little to be discussed, since the church was not active, in fact the new building was not to be constructed until 1980. We were basically a caretaker committee, with George Gray at our helm, personally undertaking most of the essential meetings with local authorities, the SNU building fund, and the architect, etc., in fact, generally overseeing the building project.

Sandra and I also met and befriended a lady who was also a friend of Leslie Flint's. This was Gladys Hayter, who ran a physical circle (with promising results) in nearby Ilford. She often told us of how she had sometimes visited restaurants with Leslie Flint and Bram Rogers, where phenomena had occurred during their meal in fully lighted conditions – the touching by apparently materialised hands and the movement of glasses and crockery across the table. In addition to the phenomena in her circle, for a number of years Gladys had been able to get superb spirit photographs, which we found very exciting (she had several albums full of examples) because we were not aware of many other people then who were showing any progress with spirit photography.

Gladys also took over the Green & Woods library of Leslie Flint audio tapes, and spent much of her time distributing them to those people she felt they would help, with their detailed information on the spirit world by hundreds of souls who had returned to Green & Woods over the years through the mediumship of Leslie Flint, to describe their experiences of 'dying' and providing an audio panorama of their current lives in the spirit world.

We met Gladys following our purchase of the classic book on Helen Duncan's mediumship by Alan Crossley. At the beginning of the book, we noticed that there was a tribute to her generosity in sponsoring its publication, with mention of the fact that she lived in Ilford. She was very experienced in the matter of physical mediumship and its phenomena and had been lucky enough, while enjoying a holiday on the South Coast and visiting a trance healer, to have been invited by his guide to a sitting of their home circle, where materialisation took place. On this first occasion, a dear friend had materialised and embraced Gladys and she had since had many opportunities to visit the circle again, to her great delight.

At the end of July 1978, following the sale of my previous home, Sandra and I made a snap decision to go on holiday. We took her two daughters with us and drove through France and Germany without bookings, but staying in hotels as and when the fancy took us. It was a most pleasant holiday and, after staying in Paris, Nancy and then Titisee in the Black Forest region of Germany, we headed towards Austria, arriving at Munich. We were a little off the beaten track when we spotted a sign for Dachau Concentration Camp. Since we were there, we felt that just once in our lives we ought to make an effort to see the place, and so we followed the sign for a mile or so until the camp came into sight.

Unfortunately, the time was about 4.45 p.m. and the former camp was about to close for the night, so we set about finding a hotel close by, from where we could resume our visit first thing in the morning.

As it happened, there was a small private hotel in the village of Dachau itself, which turned out to be run by a Jewish couple whose relatives had died at the Dachau Camp.

The whole experience was traumatic in the extreme. It was just as if we had walked on to the set of a Hammer horror film. As we entered the village, and then the hotel, the local heads all spun round to look at us in classic style. The hotel was unable to offer us an evening meal and there was a curfew imposed by the management of 10.00 p.m., after which time the hotel would be locked up. We booked our rooms, and then set about finding a local restaurant for a meal.

The atmosphere in the village was awful – the whole neighbourhood felt heavy and unpleasant. There was an air of unease and unrest about the place, one could even describe the feeling, in layman's terms, as spooky.

After we had eaten in Munich and returned to the hotel, we went to bed, but none of us could sleep as the unpleasant atmosphere persisted. I got up to go to the toilet and once in the corridor outside the room activated the timed light switch there. I carefully paced out the distance from the toilet back to the bedroom door, in case the light had gone out before I finished in the bathroom, and sure enough, as expected, the corridor was in total darkness following my ablutions.

No problem, I thought to myself as I remembered the number of paces I needed to take and counted away merrily as I walked back along the corridor. At what I believed to be the right spot, I turned to my left, expecting to find our bedroom door. There was indeed a door there, and I turned the handle, intending to enter the room.

The door was surprisingly locked, and I thought to myself that Sandra must have locked it by mistake, so I knocked on the door and waited ... and waited ... so I knocked again. This time, a very large lady opened the door, shouting in German that I was trying to accost her! That was most certainly the very last thing which I had on my mind, but with my limited German, I dare not try to explain to her in her own language, so took the line of least resistance by feigning ignorance of what she was saying, shrugging my shoulders, and returning to my own room two feet farther along the corridor.

The next morning, at breakfast, I noticed the large lady sitting there with her husband, who looked very insignificant and somewhat henpecked. She was speaking excitedly to him in her own language but I did not let on that I understood what was being said as she pointed me out to him, and repeated that I had tried to molest her in the night, whilst he – her miserable husband – had hidden under the bed!

I was not unhappy to leave that hotel behind us as we went on to visit the Dachau Concentration Camp, an experience which I will never forget. Although our visit, and this whole episode, is strictly not a psychic matter, it is valid in that both Sandra and I had been aware for some time of the presence around us of a number of spirit people who had been imprisoned in similar camps during their lifetimes. We had been told on various occasions by mediums we had visited privately that we do draw many of the souls to us who were unfortunate enough to have passed into spirit in these dreadful places. Over the years we have had contacts from a variety of such souls.

I can only describe the area of the camp as 'sterile'. There was no feeling of an 'atmosphere', or of 'bad' vibrations as such. Amazing to note was the fact that no birds flew over the area, or were seen to settle nearby on any of the trees in the whole time that we spent there. Although the place had been closed for 33 years, and was now a museum of its former activities, the memories were there, and the real smell of death was ingrained into the timbers. We found it hard to believe that such cruelty could have been perpetrated by any human beings upon their fellow men, women and children. It made us more determined than ever to help in whatever way we could, through physical mediumship and its phenomena, to bring the message of spirituality and the truth of survival to the world in general, so that atrocities like the Holocaust, with its roots here at Dachau, might never happen again in this world.

On a more pleasant note – on the same holiday we enjoyed a curious but unusual and thought-provoking experience when we drove into Switzerland for the day in order to visit Lucerne. The place is very picturesque and, having found somewhere to park the car, we walked into the town. I recall it was somewhat busy, so it is possible it may have been a market day. As we walked farther into the town and away from Lake Lucerne, we passed through a town square which was packed, with people milling around everywhere. Suddenly, through the crowd and striding towards us, came a monk in a brown habit. We noticed him particularly because he was walking with his head down towards the ground, apparently paying no attention to the people around him. Quite spontaneously, and without warning, when he drew level with us, he raised his eyes, looked me straight in the face, and smiled, as if he knew me. It was a personal thing, as he did not appear to notice Sandra or the girls who were with us. I smiled back, thinking what a pleasant surprise it was, and wondering in vain if I had ever seen him before.

About half an hour or so later, we were returning to the car, and once again passed through the same square, which was still very busy. This time, however, as we were halfway across the square, we spotted a nun, who was walking in the same manner as the monk – eyes cast downwards. Guess what! As the nun came close, she suddenly looked up at Sandra and, without acknowledging me or the children, beamed at Sandra before once again returning her gaze to the ground. Could *two* similar incidents be pure coincidence? Somehow, I doubt it. But it kept us smiling for the rest of the day.

It was in the September of 1978 that we decided to pay a visit to Borley, in Suffolk. Many years previously, Borley Rectory had been dubbed 'The Most Haunted House In Britain' by psychic researcher Harry Price, who wrote a book of the same name on his experiences and researches there. The rectory itself had been almost destroyed by fire on the night of 27/28 February 1939, as chronicled by Harry Price in his sequel, *The End of Borley Rectory,* and the remains had long since been demolished, making way for a modern building which now stood on the site.

Ever since Harry Price had immortalised the village in his best selling books, Borley had been a mecca for ghost hunters, sensation-seekers and psychic researchers because, although the rectory itself had disappeared, rumour had it that much of the psychic activity had transferred itself to the church, just across the road from the rectory site. Over many years, psychic researchers of all ages, sizes, shapes and nationalities had visited the church with varying results. Some had even held all-night vigils in the church, occasionally witnessing ghostly happenings in the middle of the night and/or recording ghostly noises, footsteps, creaking doors (when one of the church doors had opened) and similar occurrences on their tape recorders. It has always been my secret ambition to take part in one of these all-night vigils at Borley but regrettably, the current vicar and villagers do not encourage such activities, keeping the church locked most of the time.

Nevertheless, when Sandra and I visited the church with Sandra's daughters in 1978, this was not the case. The church was open and there was nobody else there apart from us. I had my tape recorder with me, so we decided to record for a while as we walked around the small village church. It was a fine and warm day, with the sun shining brightly outside, but there was a definite coldness about the interior of the church, which did not feel entirely natural. We wandered around inside the church for about 15 minutes, after which time we left and played back the recording we had made. The tape was full of some of the loudest and clearest examples of EVP voices I had ever received to date. Among the words and messages were several examples of all four of our names being called individually, plus the names of many of our family, both still on earth and in the spirit world. After Sandra's daughter Tina had taken an abortive photograph in the church – she forgot to wind her film on in the camera, causing the shot to be doubly exposed – a voice on the tape, speaking in a foreign accent, announced, 'Huh, that's another one waisted!' At one point, an EVP voice said loudly, 'They are evil here!'

In the churchyard before we left, I took a few photographs of the church and its environs. When these were developed, one of them appeared to have a misty figure on it, standing by a bush, and I am still unsure to this day whether or not I actually captured a 'phantom' on film.

It was towards the end of 1978 that Sandra and I met 'Dutch Harry' as we came to know him, in unusual circumstances. The Hainault circle had shown very little sign of progress, and members felt that perhaps the addition of a couple more sitters might help matters. We were still searching everywhere for ways and means of improving our knowledge of physical phenomena and their *modus operandi* and had arranged to attend a lecture at the SAGB in Belgrave Square, London, by 'Battling' Bertha Harris, on physical mediumship. A few days before we went, Sandra had a very realistic and vivid 'dream' one night, in which a man came forward to speak to her. He was tall and thin, with a slight stoop and 'grizzled' face, having a gaunt look about it. By his appearance, Sandra thought that he might be Czech or Polish, but certainly felt that he came from Europe somewhere. In her dream, the man mentioned Leslie Flint's name. On asking if he knew Leslie, the man answered that he did, and had come to sit with him. Sandra remembered asking him who he was, and the man replied, 'I am your new sitter.'

A strange 'dream' – perhaps, if that is what it was. We duly attended Bertha's lecture, which was most informative. When she took questions at the end, one man raised several points about the independent voice in a slightly foreign accent. He also mentioned Leslie Flint. With a shock, Sandra suddenly realised that this was the man she had seen in her 'dream'. Arie Mechelsen was the man's name, and he was a native of Holland, so he consequently became 'Dutch Harry'. Since we were obviously intended to meet him, we suggested to 'Harry' that we all went for a coffee following the lecture, where we were able to exchange information on our joint interests. He was a most unusual man, who had spent his last working years before retirement running his own shop in Holland. Their state retirement scheme, however, had generously allowed him to retire early, so that he could follow his research into physical mediumship, in particular the elusive independent voice phenomenon.

During his lifetime, Harry had done many jobs, working on occasions for celebrities, such as Douglas Fairbanks Jnr. He had enjoyed opportunities from time to time to sit with Leslie Flint and had been very impressed by Leslie's mediumship. There was no physical mediumship that our new friend was aware of in Holland at that time, although there was a healthy interest in the subject. Since the 'mountain couldn't come to Muhammad', Harry had now come to England to study physical mediumship and to try to arrange sittings with Leslie to enhance his studies.

We spoke of the EVP, in which he was greatly interested, but he had been unable to get the phenomenon himself. I arranged to go to his bedsit in Clapham (where he was living frugally to eke out his Dutch state pension) so that I could demonstrate EVP to him and Harry was duly impressed with our results. Gradually, after a number of similar visits, the knock-on effect seemed to work, and he 'caught' it from me – thereafter going on to get some outstanding examples of EVP himself. It was when doing joint experiments in Clapham that we discovered the principle that EVP results could be enhanced by running a tap quietly in the background as recording took place, and thereafter I have always found this to be a useful tip for EVP experimenters.

Sandra and I realised that with his particular interests, and seeming dedication to physical phenomena, Harry would indeed be an excellent sitter and consequently, after agreeing matters with the other members of the Hainault circle, he began to sit there with us once a week, travelling by tube to Hainault, where Sandra and I would pick him up at the tube station, depositing him back there afterwards.

Dutch Harry stayed with us in the Hainault circle until the group broke up at the end of February 1979 and he became one of our earliest sitters when we started our own circle the next year.

Early on in 1979, Sandra and I had become quite close, and we decided to get married in April. The hunt was therefore on for a suitable house for us to live in, as although Sandra had her own house in Romford, it was a very small one with no room suitable for holding our own physical circle – needless to say that was one of the main considerations in choosing a home.

We looked at all types of properties, including an old rectory in an outer Essex village. Both of us felt that an old rectory might have the right sort of spiritual atmosphere for our circle but it was soon apparent that this type of house was right out of our price range. The one exception we did look at was a beautiful house – old and large, as well as having been a former rectory, but it came with a massive crack (leaving it open to the elements) running down a main outside wall from rafters to ground. It was a hopeless 'chicken and egg' situation: we would not have been able to get a mortgage until the structural work was done, and we could not afford to do the structural work until we got a mortgage. So we had to shelve the idea of a country rectory for a few years.

Finally we settled on a property in Harold Hill which we thought would be suitable, only to find that we had been 'gazumped' by some other buyers when we tried to complete the purchase. Eventually, however, we did find a suitable house nearby in Queens Park Road, Harold Wood. This was a largish semi-detached four-bedroomed home, with a loft extension. The layout of the property allowed us to have the bedroom on the front of the first floor for ourselves, with what had originally been the back bedroom next to ours on the same floor acting as a circle room which could be kept permanently blacked out and where I could also do some healing work when necessary. We had the usual bathroom and toilet on that floor more or less to ourselves.

Sandra's two daughters had a bedroom each on the top floor, which was almost like a self-contained flat, with its own toilet and shower – so the overall plan of the house was pretty much ideal for holding our own physical circles.

Everything was therefore ready, and it was just a question of tying the knot, dotting the i's and crossing the t's. At the end of February 1979, I gave up my Woodford bedsit and moved into Sandra's home at Romford, where we were to stay until we could take possession of the Harold Wood house in late April.

The Hainault circle simply faded away at the end of February, and it was decided that we would not sit again until we were in the new house. Although the circle there had not been particularly spectacular, it had been friendly and useful. We were extremely grateful to George and Isobel Gray for allowing us to sit in their home for over nine months. I was still a member of the committee of the South Woodford SNU church, and we continued to see George and Isobel regularly thereafter.

The psychic activity around us in our everyday lives was remarkable. From the moment that I went to live with Sandra in Romford, there was a tremendous build-up of physical phenomena in her small home. We regularly heard independent voices in fully lighted conditions in the house. This was *not* clairaudience, as we were mainly together when this happened, and each of us heard the same things. Often, this would centre around the voice of a little girl, who was heard by both of us to shout 'Mummy' from time to time or 'Get down, Benny!' referring to Sandra's dog. This phenomenon could also be exceptionally useful. On one occasion, when I was away, the little girl woke Sandra up in the middle of the night to tell her, 'Wake up, Benny's been poorly', and when Sandra went to have a look, sure enough, Benny had! Another time when Sandra was woken up by the same little girl's voice, she was told, 'Go, see Benny! Go, see Benny!' When Sandra complied, she was greeted by a kitchen full of smoke, since she had forgotten that she had previously been cooking melts for the dog's dinner next day, and had not turned the pan off. The pan had boiled dry, and was about to burn through, so the situation could also have resulted in a house fire, had she not been woken up by the independent voice.

Shortly after we were married, Sandra went to bed early one night when I was very late home from work. Her back was giving her problems, and was painful. She heard a gentle lady's voice tell her to turn over on to her front, and open her psychic centres, because spirits were going to bring her healing. Trustingly, she followed these instructions to the letter, and shortly afterwards felt two massive materialised hands placed on her back. Somehow she was sure that the hands only existed up to the elbows, and she was very scared. So she sent out the thought to spirit that she appreciated their efforts to help her, but as she was scared, would they please take the hands away. Instantly, the phenomenon ceased, but to this day, her back has remained much better than it ever was previously.

One morning, after my early start for work, Sandra heard a male voice in the bedroom call out the name 'Bill', in a voice reminiscent of Elmer Browne's. She was not too happy, as she was still in her nightclothes! But there were many such incidents happening on a regular basis, almost as though the physical power was gathering ready for the new circle which was planned for Harold Wood.

# LAUNCH OF THE HAROLD WOOD CIRCLE

THE DAY ARRIVED at last when we moved into our home in Harold Wood. By now it was the end of April 1979 and we immediately set about getting the circle room ready, our number one priority. As we decorated the room, we screwed the windows permanently shut, shuttering them with a large sheet of marine plywood, which was also screwed into place and painted, before finally being covered with wallpaper, to match the rest of the room. The edges of the door and its surrounding frame were given a fixed fringe of black felt to seal the cracks and complete the blackout, while a special shelf was fitted to the wall close to my seat to take the ioniser and microphones, etc. which would be used during our seances.

Our advert for potential sitters was duly placed in the *Psychic News*. We interviewed those applicants who replied, and chose the ones we felt would be suitable for our new physical circle. The stage was set, and we started our sittings on Friday 18 May with a total of eight participants including ourselves. Five were new to us, but Dutch Harry also sat, travelling to Harold Wood from Clapham each time he came.

The first night seemed promising, considering that at this stage we did not know each other too well. A substantial coldness built up in the room (always a good sign with physical circles). There were a few flashes of psychic lights observed by some sitters. Our trumpet did not move, but we reckoned that these were early days, and were content to bide our time. One of our new sitters showed some promise with her trance control, and it was also obvious that my own development in this direction was to be ongoing, as one of our known helpers spoke through me. The ioniser we used seemed to be having a beneficial effect, keeping the atmosphere 'light', and so it was decided to make this a permanent feature of the circles.

Week two resulted in a little more progress, as we introduced another sitter, now making nine in all. This time, in addition to the coldness, several sitters were feeling a slight 'pulling', sensation at the solar plexus, as power was being extracted from them. Some also felt a 'cobwebby' feeling over their faces (often associated with physical circles and ectoplasm).

We sang rather a lot to keep the atmosphere rousing and played taped music during the lulls. Sitters commented that they could hear whispering during the singing and, on several occasions, independent whistles were clearly audible during the music. At one point we heard three words spoken independently, which were picked up on our recording of the circle but they were not clear enough for us to decipher exactly what was said.

Two communicators spoke words of encouragement through my own trance utterings, one of these, Elizabeth Garrett Anderson (the first lady doctor in the UK), commenting on their success from the spirit world in their attempts to influence the authorities to keep her hospital open (The Elizabeth Garrett Anderson Women's Hospital on London's Marylebone Road). News of this reprieve was made public the following week.

On playing the sitting back afterwards, it was discovered that the tape also contained several EVP messages. Clicking of fingers was heard in the seance by more than one sitter, and several saw lights in the room briefly. Three other sitters, besides myself, had been close to trance during the evening. The signs were good.

This became a regular pattern. Development continued, and several different communicators spoke; some briefly – others at length, controlling me and two or three more of the sitters from time to time. Of the communicators themselves, some purported to be guides; others just helpers, or indeed casual visitors to the circle. The first indications of physical phenomena were constantly there, too. On 1 June a Czech communicator spoke through Maureen, one of our sitters (while another sitter was weeping uncontrollably with emotion), about the time he spent in the Treblinka Concentration Camp.

On 8 June there was to be a breakthrough. Early in the sitting, a female communicator, using me in trance, told the circle that they were trying to create a voicebox for the production of the independent direct voices. Much later on, a gruff male communicator was speaking through Maureen, saying, 'I help you! I help you! I help you!' At this point, we could *all* hear *two* distinct voices speaking together, saying exactly the same words at the same time. One of these was deep and gruff (obviously coming through Maureen, who was entranced). The other voice was pure and seemed to come from high up – about three feet above the medium. It suddenly dawned on us that this was independent voice in its early stages.

Shortly afterwards, a female communicator with a very high voice spoke in the same way but this time left us in no doubt that we had independent voice.

Over the next few weeks, the progress was slow, and not dramatic. There were several attempts by our spirit friends to speak in the independent voice but, unlike the rapid development of the voice that had occurred in the Seymer Road circle, attempts were made less frequently, and proved not to be as successful as the results we had obtained there.

There were, however, constant signs that trance communication, through me and through Maureen, was developing well. A myriad of different communicators succeeded in speaking to the circle, the majority of them offering encouragement for the advancement of the circle's phenomena.

We were always looking for confirmation that our efforts with the circle were worthwhile and so Friday, 6 July 1979 saw us again visiting Leslie Flint. All the members of the group were present – nine of us in total – and we were greeted warmly by Leslie as we arrived.

Mickey must have been on a coffee break though, as it was almost an hour before he came to speak to us in the independent voice. After the usual introductions, and banter about people being 'windy' in the dark (several of the group had not experienced independent voice as clearly as this before), the phenomenon really got under way with the young Cockney guide telling us:

'Mixed bag, your circle, ain't it? There's a lot of power though, ain't there? I reckon as how you've got a good circle if you can keep it together.'

Following a few questions from the assembled company, Mickey spoke a little about people in our world relating to those in the spirit world:

> You have to laugh, don't yer? Takes all kinds, don't it? After all, the people that constitute, as you call it, our world, once was on your side. So, some people have changed for the better, and some people are – well! Still clearing their way. You don't suddenly become an angel when you kick the bucket, you know. If we're not talking to you like this, we don't go running round playing harps and singing all the time. I mean, over here there's loads of ordinary people. Not everybody, of course – some people come over here dead religious, ha ha! But actually, I think sometimes the very religious people are the ones who find it more difficult – 'cos they've got to *unlearn!* You get some of these bishops who – you know – the 'Bless you, friends' types, and they have to come down to sort of normal. Hah! It takes all kinds, don't it? It makes me laugh; some people don't know what to make of me – but I do me best! I can't please everybody.
>
> Rather like those two women – you know – who came here some time ago. Posh, they was! They'd got fur coats on – minks and all that – they was real posh ladies. When they went on their way, I followed 'em down the road, and one woman said to the other, she said, 'Well,' she said, putting it on a bit, 'what did you think about it?' and the other one says, 'Well, it was all right, you know, but that boy – ain't he common!' She didn't know I was right behind her!
>
> But at the end of the day, I like to make people laugh. I like people to be happy. I don't want people to think that kicking the bucket's a miserable business. I want people to be happy, and know that life goes on. You're still much the same after you kick the bucket, and the process of change is gradual. You learn, and you get a much better understanding – and you love people – and make allowances for them. After all, no-one's perfect.

With that, Mickey got on with his work of marshalling all the communicators, and Sister Maria came to talk to us in her French accent:

> I do not know if you can hear me? [We assured her that we could.] I want to talk to you. We have been very close to you, you know,

> trying to help you in your circle. Maria – Maria Theresa – I have so looked forward to your coming here today. We have great hope for this circle. There is great promise, you know, and you must stay together. You must not lose heart. These things take time, and you cannot expect too much, too soon! But we are very happy for you. We know that we can make very good progress. Each one of you here has the power to speak – each one of you here can be used in some way or another. But you must be patient. You must not lose heart. It is a long time, huh, since I was able to come and talk with you. But I just wanted you to know I was here today. And to give you all my love and blessings. Au revoir!

As the mellifluous voice of the nun Sister Maria faded away, a very familiar voice, that of the Scottish guide, Jock, who had helped us from the spirit side of life during the Seymer Road Seances, began to speak:

> Aye, I just thought I'd pop in for a minute to let ye know I was around. Aye, you've got the right circle now, and I hope you'll all stay together and work together fer a common good. We've got great hopes for this circle in more ways than one, and there's a lot of physical power there, ye know that. And we've got great hopes in that direction, but of course these things take time. But we don't want ye to make any changes. Ye don't want to make any alteration – no – I think you'd be wise to stay as ye are, and to not have changes of any kind. And don't take any new people, 'cos I think you'd make a mistake, and I think that it might be bad in the long run. Stay as ye are now.

Jock went on to discuss my healing work which by now I had got well under way and spoke for a short while on the whys and wherefores relating to the reasons for every patient not responding positively to spiritual healing:

> I think, of course ye know – I think ye do realise that – I don't want to give a bad impression, or distress in any way, but ye cannot expect to heal everyone. Ye know that! We've gotta have some people come here sooner or later. Aye, but there's a funny side too. When the work begin to run out, perhaps ye can do a few running repairs, and relieve some pain or what have you at times, but ye can't always cure; that's impossible. Just remember, ye can't put a new engine in an old body!

Jock was followed by a new communicator, a lady who addressed us briefly:

> Evelyn – Evelyn! My name is Evelyn. Can you hear me? [We responded.] I don't know if I can say very much. I'm rather new to this. My name is Evelyn. I was for many years with the Salvation Army. I come to your circle sometimes, and I hope I may be of some service. Like so many other people, one has to change to some extent one's views, and of course, I'm afraid I had very strong views. But now I see things very differently, although we're all part of God's creation. We are all His children, and we must come closer together in love and in harmony. I do so enjoy coming to your meetings.

At this stage, another of Leslie Flint's main guides – Dr Charles Marshall – came through to talk to me at length and in depth about one of the patients I was treating with spiritual healing. The discussion was long and it was obvious that Dr Marshall knew exactly what he was talking about from a medical point of view. I was given evidential advice about the patient's condition and medical advice on how to proceed with the healing. It is perhaps interesting that my patient benefited tremendously from the healing following Dr Marshall's advice.

Mickey kept slipping back in to talk to us generally, between the other visitors and he gave several of the sitters some evidential personal messages from loved ones in the spirit world. Mickey mentioned the presence of an Irish priest who wanted to speak to us and shortly afterwards we heard a soothing voice with a definite Irish accent:

> This is Father Michael here! I'm not quite sure that you can hear what I say, but I wanted to let you know that I was here today. Can you hear what I am saying? [There was a positive response.] I've just come to give you my blessings and to say that you ought to know we're doing everything in our power to help you in the meetings. And we've got great hope of the meetings, and you've to stay together, now, and leave the rest to us. We're not far away. We're always round and about. You're in good hands, and the power of the Lord is with you. Can you not hear what I'm saying? It's very difficult at times – we're not always aware of whether we're

> being heard or not, you know. It's very difficult when you are trying to speak clearly through this box business. It's very odd, you know, to be natural – while trying to speak clearly – and one can't be sure as to whether one's getting through or not. And how are you all today? You've got a fine group of souls here; a fine circle. You must keep it going now, and leave the rest to us. We will not fail you! You're in good hands.

Now we heard a voice speaking faintly to begin with:

'Arthur – Arthur speaking.'

Leslie Flint tried to help out here by encouraging the communicator and asking him his surname, only to be told by Mickey, speaking separately, 'Oh, shaddup!' Leslie asked Mickey to help the communicator, once again to be interrupted by Mickey. I include this little interchange to illustrate how two or more voices might be speaking at the same time at a Flint seance and, as here, the medium (Leslie Flint) could also be speaking. But back to Arthur:

> Arthur Tracey. My name's Arthur Tracey. I've been to your meetings on several occasions. Very interesting. I came over here very suddenly, but I've no regrets. I'm very well, and very happy here. I must say it's a great joy to be able to come and speak, maybe only for a minute or two, but I must say, your little meetings do help, not only from your point of view, but sometimes from ours. You'd be surprised the number of people who come along from our side. I'm very fascinated and interested in all this business, 'cause you know, many years ago, I used to be on the stage.

Arthur Tracey faded out, and we were treated to a real laugh as Rose, who was one of Leslie's regular communicators, came to talk to us, and tell us of the flower stall she used to have at Charing Cross Station in London, next door to Joe Lyons Corner House. She spoke of how she had progressed in the spirit world since she first started coming through many years ago and told us that she had been to our own circle, where we had some great potential. Then she said:

> Course, you know, I go to the 'spook' meetings now. I used to laugh about that, you know, when I was on your side. I had a friend of mine – Emmie her name was – she was always going to the Spiritualist meetings, and I used to pull her leg. I used to say,

> 'How are the spooks, Em?' You know, and she'd say, 'Oh, I went to the service last night – very nice!' and she'd say, 'Why don't you come?' And I'd said, 'Well, I don't know, dear, don't think it's up my street.'
>
> I mean, I wasn't supplying flowers for funerals! All that business. I mean, it's bad enough when you have to go, isn't it? Without going to them places and talking to the dead. I used to say 'Gives me the bloody creeps,' I'd say. She used to get real annoyed with me, you know.
>
> Course, now I'm dead, myself, it's a different cup of tea, ain't it?

Rose was a real 'character' and her witticisms had us rolling about with mirth as we listened to her Cockney humour.

Our final communicator during this Flint sitting was the Frenchman – Maurice. He was familiar to us all as we had heard him on previous visits to Leslie's and he too had words of encouragement for us, speaking in his striking French accent:

> Maurice! I just thought I'd pop in to tell you all we are very thrilled, you know, very happy with your circle. It is making excellent progress, and many wonderful people are helping you. Each one of you is being assisted and helped in various ways. But you know, we still have great hopes of doing something – eventually – very striking. We are very concerned with many things; but I personally would like for you to have the voice, you know, the box. That is what we are most anxious for; but of course there are many other things too. You have good friends – many souls; we have great hopes of the circle you know, and this is why we come today to cheer for you up. But it is important for you to keep up, and not to get depressed, and to know that everything that is possible is being done, you know. It is wonderful to be able to come and talk with you. I look for this ver much forward you know! I have been many a time to your group, but not always to speak, huh! Today everyone here send their love embracing to you – gives them great joy in their heart to come to you – for you all.

Maurice bade us all goodbye, as did Mickey, when he told us in a very faint voice that the power was going. The sitting finished shortly afterwards. I feel it is relevant here to remind readers that all the communications and evidence given at this and other Leslie

Flint seances were volunteered by the souls who spoke to us in the independent voice. Nothing was solicited from the voices when they spoke, and I had pre-warned sitters to be careful not to give any information about ourselves or our circle away to the medium prior to the sitting. Leslie simply knew us as a 'home circle', and although I had counted him a friend for many years, he knew very little of my background, or of the background of any of the sitters in our various physical circles. Yet the 'evidence' was abundant.

For some reason which I never understood, the harmony of the circle suffered after this sitting at Leslie Flint's. The very next week, one of our lady sitters left without a word, and we never heard from her again. Our friend, Dutch Harry also deserted us, he returned to his native Holland to continue his retirement. Nevertheless, the circle maintained its weekly sessions throughout the rest of July at about the same level as we had enjoyed prior to our sitting with Flint, and we then broke up for a three-week holiday before resuming on 17 August.

We discovered when we returned that there had been some discord between several sitters while we were away on holiday and this was very definitely evident during that sitting of 17 August. The harmony had gone altogether, and the atmosphere between sitters was dreadful as, immediately after we had opened the circle in prayer, three sitters launched into a heated argument about the necessity or otherwise of darkness in the circle while the phenomenon was developing. It was pointless continuing with the sitting and so we closed early.

Immediately after this fateful session, it was painfully clear that there was some sorting out to be done, and so the very next day, following several phone calls in both directions, the number of sitters reduced even further from the nine we had started out with to just six.

You could have knocked us down with a feather when, totally out of the blue on Sunday the 19th, John and Joyce – our former colleagues in the Seymer Road Seances – rang us from their home. They asked us if they could come over for a chat the next day, and this was duly arranged. Their visit went well and the possibility was discussed of their returning to the circle, which they were now in favour of.

The following Tuesday, Mick and Doreen (two of our regular sitters) came over for a social evening and it was suggested that Sandra and I should have a short sitting just with them. We went ahead with this suggestion and the impromptu session proved to be jolly and harmonious. It also led to a striking experience. Afterwards, while we were sitting down enjoying a cup of tea and a bun, the telephone rang. As I picked it up, a faraway voice announced, 'It's me!' With a great shock, I recognised it as the voice of an elderly neighbour of mine from 30 years previously, when I was a child of six years old – a Mrs Grantham, who would surely by now had passed to spirit!

The voice continued, 'I want you to carry on with the circle!' before the line went dead. As you might imagine, there was much excitement after this incident, and I remember clearly that my enthusiasm for the circle, which at this point had waned somewhat due to the disharmony, was instantly restored. I had heard of phone calls from the 'dead', but had never imagined that I might personally experience one.

At the next Friday sitting, with just six sitters, the atmosphere felt 'right' again, and we experienced trance, independent whistling, and some remarkable examples of transfiguration through sitter Maureen in red light at the end of the sitting. The rest of the circle members were happy to invite John and Joyce to sit with us again, and they consequently joined us the following week.

I think that we had somehow imagined that with John and Joyce sitting, we would just be able to pick up where we left off at Seymer Road and in that we were sadly disappointed. With much more experience under our belts now, we should have realised that to build up the phenomena again would take time.

However, there *was* a lot of trance through John – and from time to time, a little through me. It was most pleasant to renew acquaintances with the guides we had come to know well at Seymer Road, and amongst others, Khoba, Neville, Jock and Dr Dunn had plenty to say to us about the long term possibilities of the circle.

Fairly early on in the sitting the trumpet, which had been standing upright in the middle of the circle, fell over noisily with a bang, making us all jump – and we were told to take it out of the circle as it was not needed. Throughout the seance we were all singing away merrily, as singing had always been an integral part of our sittings for physical phenomena. Today, of course, we realise that singing is not absolutely necessary for the development of physical mediumship. Much more important is the harmony between sitters and soft, taped classical music playing in the background is often sufficient for the power to build up in the circle.

Once again, following the sitting, we were treated to three or four distinct transfigurations through Maureen in the red light – and everyone was able to see clearly an Arab, complete with beard, and an Oriental gentleman with drooping moustache.

# REGROUPING AT HAROLD WOOD

IT WAS AROUND this time, during the autumn of 1979, that we first started to notice things happening around the house which we were later able to attribute to a very playful spirit helper – a young African girl who was always playing tricks on us at Harold Wood.

'Beth', as she came to be known to us, had a fascination for gadgets and knobs. However, from the beginning, she was particularly taken with the radiators in the bathroom and on the first-floor landing. She had a penchant for turning them off or on – always the exact opposite of the setting we had selected, and at first it did not really occur to us that the 'fiddling with the knobs' had anything to do with our spirit friends.

It simply seemed to us that we were gradually losing our memories. Nevertheless, the activity became stronger and stronger, and more frequent. As soon as we discovered that they had been turned off or whatever, we would turn them back on. But the phenomenon became so prolific that as soon as our backs were turned after we had restored the 'on' setting – they would once again be turned off.

Through many of the private sittings with clairvoyant and clairaudient mediums which we were still enjoying, the activity with the radiators and other phenomena around the house was frequently confirmed to us, along with the name of the 'culprit'.

There were instances when Sandra went to put on the kettle for a cup of tea or coffee, only to find that the electric point had already been switched on, and the kettle was almost ready to boil when Sandra reached it.

Her daughters would frequently hear spirit children playing marbles on the wooden staircase between the first and second floors, and this could occur at all times of the day and night.

On one occasion, we were awoken in the middle of the night by the girls screaming that the shower on their floor – the second floor – had suddenly come on, and that they could not turn it off. Needless to say, Sandra and I rushed to the scene, only to discover that we couldn't turn the shower tap off because it was *already* off. What had apparently happened was that the centre of the tap had been dematerialised so that there was a constant flow of water through the shower. I remember sleepily pleading with our spirit friends to restore the situation to normal – and shortly afterwards watching as the flow of water ceased abruptly without us touching anything.

Beth just could not keep her spirit fingers in check and we were once considerably embarrassed when we visited an old smugglers' inn on the seafront at Scarborough, Yorkshire. The Three Mariners had been turned into an attraction resembling a museum, and was open to visitors. The inn had been a haunt of smugglers in past centuries, and many of its secret passages and priest holes were left open to general view. In addition, by reputation the inn was haunted! Sandra and I toured the various rooms, which at the time were filled with Victoriana and bric-a-brac.

It was a quiet day in the resort and we were in the building by ourselves. We moved through the first floor, and joked about the 'ghosts', noticing at the time that in one room, there were two very large biscuit tins filled with hundreds of buttons, sitting in a cupboard. We walked into another room and looked around but then Sandra had a sudden urge to go back into the first room.

However, as soon as we entered that room again, we saw that the floor was completely covered with buttons! It was apparent that the two biscuit tins were still sitting in the same position within the cupboard but they were now totally empty. Without waiting for any reaction from the staff, we propelled ourselves as quickly as possible out of the Three Mariners in case the caretaker thought that we had scattered the buttons ourselves, and labelled us vandals.

While we were staying there at Scarborough, we also visited the local Spiritualist Church. I found its location most amusing, as it was sited next door to a motorbike shop which many years ago had been a high class grocery store by the name of Hopwoods. For me, that revived some wonderful memories, as my grandfather, having returned from active service in the First World War, was its manager for most of his working life. To this day, I can still recall the delightful range of smells I encountered within that old-fashioned grocers; not least the aroma of the coffee-bean roaster. As a young boy, I had stood spellbound, watching the whirr and passage of the message containers as they sped round the store on a pulley system, returning with the customers' change. However, had my grandfather still been alive, I can well imagine just what his comments might have been at the thought of a Spiritualist Church right next door to his beloved place of work.

Nevertheless, as we attended the service, the medium of the day as I recall, a gentleman by the name of Alan Weetman from the Doncaster area, gave us a very accurate and evidential description of our little spirit friend, along with a message from Beth, admitting to the naughtiness with the buttons.

At home, there were also constant raps and taps around the house which we both heard, and for which there was no logical explanation other than psychic activity.

But I digress. The circle sat throughout the rest of 1979, and staggered into January 1980 with the necessary enthusiasm from the sitters waning once more. The trance through John, Maureen and me continued to develop slowly, and we had a few good communications over this period, but the physical phenomena we were really sitting for actually seemed to recede without moving forwards at all. Looking back now, I believe that the essential commitment from sitters wavered somewhat and this held the circle back.

Consequently it was decided to give the circle a rest for a while, and to advertise for more and varied sitters at the beginning of May 1980, to revitalise the format.

In the meantime, the committee of the Woodford National Spiritualist Church became more active, as the actual building of the church had now begun. It was suggested that I took on the job of medium secretary, and with enthusiasm I busied myself getting lists of working mediums and speakers up to date, knowing that most working mediums book their appointments a year in advance. It would soon be necessary for me to start booking better known mediums for the church. In these early days of the building work, we anticipated that the church would possibly be ready for commissioning in the September or October of 1980, so I set about speaking to various mediums and sounding them out, bearing in mind that as the old Woodford church had been closed for some years, the list which I possessed was somewhat out of date. In addition, I spoke to most of the medium secretaries from the local London Spiritualist churches, to pick their brains as to the standard of some of the mediums whose names I had and to glean from them their recommendations of mediums then working the circuit who were not known to me.

I felt that for such a beautiful major Spiritualist church as the new Woodford Church was going to be, it was my duty to try to ensure that we only booked the pick of the mediums, to provide potential churchgoers with the best possible evidence of survival through the regular clairvoyance, clairaudience and clairsentience demonstrated in the new church. The plans for the church building were very exciting, having been fully architect designed. When George Gray had asked the architect for 'circle rooms' in his original brief, the instruction had been understood quite literally by the architect so that they had been designed as rooms that were actually circular in shape.

I wrote to mediums all over the country to inquire after bookings and I still have in my possession today letters from well known mediums such as Ursula Roberts, Margaret Pearson and Queenie Nixon (the transfiguration medium from Clay Cross, Derbyshire), offering their services to the church in response to my own inquiries. The actual opening was to be performed by the then President of the SNU, Gordon Higginson, with clairvoyance by Doris Collins, who had long-standing links with the old Woodford church. In the event, however, the building took longer than anticipated to put together and the actual opening did not take place until February 1981.

It was through this process of sounding out unknown mediums that I happened to meet Geoffrey Jacobs from Chelmsford, Essex, who was highly recommended as a clairaudient medium. A friend of ours, Joan Dragon, who was involved with the Westcliffe-on-Sea Spiritualist Church, knew him well, and she explained to us that in addition Geoffrey was an excellent trance and physical medium, able to produce ectoplasm and trumpet voices. In fact, Joan's husband Bill had sat with Geoffrey for many years, and was usually present when Geoffrey did his occasional physical seances.

Naturally, as soon as physical mediumship was mentioned, my ears pricked up, and I hoped that Sandra and I might get the opportunity to sit with Geoffrey if that was at all possible. As it happened, the first time we met Geoffrey there was an instant rapport and we became firm friends. Not long afterwards, we booked a private trance sitting with him, and I recall being most impressed by his trance mediumship, when several spirit people spoke through him.

Our trance sitting with Geoffrey was such that we spent several hours after the event just chatting with him and his wife Brigid about our interests and experiences with home circles and with physical mediumship and its phenomena. For some time, I had felt that it would be an excellent idea to try to re-form the private Link of Home Circles which had been started by Noah Zerdin in 1936 so that, as then, home circles consisting of people of like mind could meet up socially to exchange ideas and experiences, thereby generally helping one another in the development of their mediumship and psychic phenomena. As we chatted with Geoffrey, it soon became apparent that for a number of years he too had thought along the same lines, and we enthused together about the possibility of actually bringing such a link to fruition.

Our talks on this subject turned out to be somewhat prophetic as, during 1980, I came into contact with Eileen Roberts, president of the Union of Spiritualist Mediums. Eileen lived close by to us, in Ardleigh Green near Hornchurch. The USM had a very active branch in the Gidea Park, Romford area, which met once a month and, after getting to know the USM president, Sandra and I started to attend the branch on a regular basis. It was not long before we were invited to join the committee of this Romford branch and, following our recent talks with Geoffrey Jacobs about a link of home circles, I mentioned this to Eileen Roberts as being a good idea.

Surprise, surprise! It turned out that Eileen had herself been actively pursuing the possibility of re-starting the Home Circle Link through the USM but had simply been waiting for someone to come along who was willing to undertake the work involved in starting and running such a link. Sandra and I indicated that we would be happy to take on the bulk of the work and it was arranged that I should be seconded on to the national executive committee of the USM in order to look after this aspect of their work. This was done as speedily as possible and it was planned that the USM Home Circle Link would come into being during 1981.

A further contact through Joan Dragon was made with Mrs Maud Gunning, of Westcliffe-on-Sea. One evening, Sandra and I went to the Westcliffe church to see Bill and Joan Dragon work, and we were introduced to a very elderly lady, with a forceful character, at the back of the church. This was Maud Gunning, and it was not long before we discovered that she had been a superb physical medium in her day, when she had run a regular circle for materialisation, amongst other notable physical phenomena.

Having similar interests, it was not long before we befriended Mrs Gunning, seeing her on several occasions, including one very memorable day when she came to tea with us at Harold Wood. Her stories of physical mediumship generally were legion, and I remember listening, enthralled, as she recounted to us some of her personal experiences over the years. Many of these were confirmed to us years later by one of her regular sitters. What a character that lady was! She would not, even at her advanced age, stand for any nonsense, and was one of the 'old school' of physical mediums.

Through her mediumship, Abdul Baha, founder and leader of the Bahai faith, materialised to one of his followers. There were well-attested instances of water being turned into wine, and often apports of masses of fruit and flowers (sometimes of an exotic variety) appeared, which almost filled the room and would afterwards be distributed to local hospitals for the patients. Occasionally the apports would be of expensive watches and valuable gemstones, etc. Once, all the ivy from the side of Mrs Gunning's house was apported into the circle room. The guides asked for the white light to be put on, and it was noticed that the ivy was so deep, it reached from the floor to a point above the knees of all the sitters. Instructions were then given to turn the light off momentarily again. This was followed shortly afterwards by a further request to reinstate the light. While the ivy had disappeared once again (having presumably been restored to its rightful place on the wall of the house) the sight that greeted them was amazing. In front of their very eyes, the floor was now covered with insects, which had come in with the ivy but had been left behind when it vanished.

During another sitting, an 18-stone man was levitated to the high ceiling, and rolled over it, gathering distemper on his clothes to prove he had really been up there. Mrs Gunning was not always in deep trance during her sittings and, on one occasion, a full-sized lady's human head (nothing more, just the head!) materialised in the circle. Initially it sat on the lap of one of the sitters, looking up with moving eyes and lips, saying that the communicator was looking for her daughter. As each of the sitters in turn said that they were not the correct recipient, the head simply jumped from lap to lap until it was recognised by one of the sitters as being the head of her mother, and a long conversation ensued between them.

My intention was to write a book on Mrs Gunning's mediumship as I was so impressed by the stories of phenomena that happened during her seances and, with this in mind, I conducted just one of the necessary interviews with her in order to get the story of her life right, before once again, I got diverted on to another path. When I was ready to continue, I discovered that unfortunately Mrs Gunning had by then passed to spirit and I had missed the vital information that I needed. One of my main regrets in psychic matters today is that I never managed to complete that book on Mrs Gunning.

But back to the Harold Wood circle. In May of 1980 we advertised for more and varied sitters and had a number of interesting answers. John, our medium friend from Romford, had once again given up sitting for phenomena, and not everybody who sat in the previous phase of the circle was right for us. We therefore set about putting together a whole new circle, with just two of the original sitters, apart from Sandra and myself.

* * *

We started to sit again on a weekly basis from about July and it took a few weeks of settling in before we started to get some encouraging results. However, it was not long before we entered into what turned out to be the best overall period in the history of the Harold Wood circle for phenomena in the whole of the time that the circle ran.

On 6 August, to see if we could get a little help and advice, we once again visited independent voice medium Leslie Flint, where we had an excellent sitting, as you will see from the details in the next chapter. For a few members of the circle, this was to be the first visit of its kind but all were extremely impressed by the voices they witnessed, and this sitting was followed by some excellent ones in the Harold Wood circle itself.

For instance, on 12 September, loud, sustained whistling was heard by us all, in tune to the song we were singing. When we commented on this, a loud whistle was heard in confirmation. The following week, during the sitting, five flowers were removed psychically from a vase in the centre of the circle, these being thrown to four of the sitters. They were all on target, and fell on the laps of the intended recipients in total darkness. Twice during the sitting, there was a pronounced beating of birds' wings against the wall, which we all heard.

On Friday 26 September, the table in the centre levitated and fell over. The vase on it fell in the corner, and was undamaged, as were the flowers within, which landed some distance away from the vase. Twice during this sitting, water was sprinkled on the faces of the sitters from a point just above face level.

The next week, the chairs of two of the sitters vibrated violently for a sustained period, and again, sitters had water sprinkled on to their faces. Suddenly, all sitters felt something akin to birdseed falling on their hands and in their hair. We discovered after the sitting that this was several handfuls of uncooked, hard rice, which had been apported into the circle room. The only other rice in the house was in a large, sealed tupperware bowl in the kitchen, and this was found to be undisturbed. Interestingly, some of the rice was stuck to the skirting boards, which was consistent with its having been moved in contact with a sticky substance, and we concluded that this must have been ectoplasm.

One of our sitters was a policeman, who was shortly to be married. None of the rest of us knew this at the time, but it seems the spirit people did! Hence the rice.

On 17 October, all the sitters' chairs were vibrated and the atmosphere became extremely cold. Some sitters were prodded by unseen fingers and had their hair gently pulled. While we were singing a rousing song, the tambourine we kept in the centre of the circle was tapped in time to the music. A week later, water was poured in abundance over all the sitters. None escaped! Constant whispering was heard around the room throughout the sitting. A loud thump seemed to signify that the table had gone over, but afterwards it was discovered that the table was in its normal position. A vase of flowers was lying sideways near the foot of one of the sitters. However, the flowers were still in it, along with some water. A cross, which normally sat on the wall, had been carefully removed and deposited on the floor, along with the trumpet which had been placed there before.

During the sitting, the trumpet had been lying in contact with a sitter's foot, and he was able to say that he had felt its vibrations clearly through his foot as it pulsated like a living thing.

Reviewing these results in the cold light of day, and over 15 years later, what Sandra and I failed to realise at the time was that the phenomena only occurred in the presence of one of the newer sitters – Lisa, and that when she was unable to attend, the atmosphere was flat, with no spectacular phenomena. I have since analysed sittings of the circle in depth and it is clear that our friend Lisa was in fact a powerful developing physical medium. Lisa, who had much previous experience of physical mediumship herself, had in the past sat with a number of famous physical mediums, including William Olsen and Estelle Roberts, and in so doing had witnessed materialisation, direct voice and levitation.

Had we recognised at the time the important role that she was playing in the circle (I don't believe that to this day, Lisa herself has ever realised that she was the one who was fast becoming the medium of the circle), then we would undoubtedly have changed the format of the circle to concentrate more on Lisa's potential.

However, there was little change in the phenomena for a while, although the circle kept going with enthusiasm. On Friday, 30 January 1981, it was a very foggy night when we sat, and there were just four of us including Lisa present at the sitting. Despite the fact that phenomena were supposed to be adversely affected by fog, the trumpet suddenly shot up in the middle of the sitting, with its wide end suspended over the water bowl, before it dropped again just as suddenly. When we put the lights on afterwards, there was a single white rose on a four-inch stem sitting in the water bowl. Clearly an apport. And this at a time of year when there were no fresh roses around in anybody's gardens.

All of the psychic activity around us seemed to be quickening somewhat and accelerating in its intensity. We were just weeks away now from the opening of the Woodford National Spiritualist Church, which was planned for Saturday, 21 February 1981 and preparations for this important event were at their height. The church was – and is – a beautiful and unique building. It had been designed with separate three-bedroomed living accommodation at its rear. The committee had decided to let this accommodation on a furnished basis to bring in extra funds, and the task of finding suitable tenants fell to me.

Knowing that it would be better to go for tenants who held down regular jobs, I had the idea of approaching the main branches of the High Street banks in the City of London. In the event, it was not long before Barclays came up with three of their young lady employees who would be happy to share the accommodation we were offering, and when we had furnished the building, they moved in and a regular income for the church was assured.

During the first week of February, we were contacted by our friends John and Joyce, of Seymer Road fame, who had once again dropped out of the Harold Wood circle some months previously. They asked if they could visit us and perhaps participate in a one-off sitting for old times' sake. The thing was that although it seemed practically impossible for them to fully commit themselves psychologically to a circle on a regular basis, whenever Sandra and I sat with them just as a foursome, whatever our moods happened to be at the time, there was always a distinct and unique chemistry between us which made it possible for phenomena to occur.

So it was that they came to see us on Saturday 7 February, and the four of us sat as agreed. One of the two trumpets rocked violently and fell over, while the other moved several feet. The tambourine also moved and rattled. Water was sprinkled on to all of us as the central table moved around the room, and the water bowl which had been standing on it fell heavily to the ground but without spilling a drop of water. There was a strong, earthy smell of ectoplasm, and I was pulled quite painfully at the solar plexus, as power was drawn from me to help towards the phenomena. In addition, there were two independent voices which addressed us from mid-air, one of these being the voice of our old friend and guide Jock, and the other being that of a new communicator.

Naturally, these exciting results fired us up once more with enthusiasm, and it was suggested that we might repeat the experiment in the near future, maybe even leading to a second circle at Harold Wood, to be held on a different night. The suggestion was approved by all and we agreed to have another sitting later in the month.

# A TALE OF TWO SITTINGS

NOT LONG AFTER the new format Harold Wood circle had started to sit, we were once again privileged to attend a sitting with Leslie Flint on 6 August 1980 and what a sitting it turned out to be!

It involved one of the longest conversations we ever had with Mickey, Flint's young Cockney guide, and this proved to be Mickey at his very best. He had lots of comments on various subjects and interesting information to give us, as well as exhibiting an impish sense of humour, which those of us who visited Leslie on a regular basis soon came to recognise as his trademark.

I am sure that you will recognise the common thread which runs through my book of Leslie's wonderful mediumship, which was instrumental in my initial enthusiastic involvement with physical mediumship and continued to represent the light at the end of a long tunnel. It was something to aim for and provided a guiding hand when our various circles seemed to be faltering. There was never a lack of encouragement during these sittings.

The content also of the Flint sittings was always interesting. You just never knew who would be coming to talk to you next but, in my experience, there was always an input from our own individual circle guides and helpers.

My father became a real Flint fan later in his life, though a little sceptical of the whole subject earlier on, and he would wait eagerly for Sandra and me to play him the latest sitting when we visited Grimsby. He knew that we only ever told him the absolute truth as to how the voices could speak – loudly and clearly – from mid-air. Amazingly, although he never had the chance to meet Leslie on this side of life, he has confirmed that they have since met in the spirit world.

But to return to the story … on 6 August it took about 50 minutes of chatting with the medium in the darkness before any voices were heard and Mickey was very faint when he first came through. Typically though, it did not take him very long to get his steam up once he started and he was soon addressing us in his usual breezy manner:

'How are you, Robin? Have you got your gang with you?'

One of the sitters commented that she loved all the spirit people, to which Mickey replied:

> Well, we love you too, mate! We love all of you, but course, mind you, it's hard going, ain't it, to try to love everybody! That's what we're supposed to do, ain't it? You know all that but by gawd! Cor, stone the crows. There's one or two odd bods here and there. You think well at times – but there you are. I mean, how can you love Hitler? [Another sitter commented that somebody did.] Yeah, it must 'ave been 'is mum before 'e grewed up …
>
> How are you getting on in your circle? I've been several times, you know! There's a lot of power with you lot. You know, I reckon you ought to get something more physical. It takes time, though, don't it? Course, you've 'ad one or two ups and downs, ain't yer? And a few changes, ain't yer? [This was evidently correct information.]

Mickey continued for some time to chatter away generally until the voice of Maria Theresa – Sister Maria the nun – broke into the conversation in her strong French accent:

> I do not know if you can hear? Maria! I am ver' 'appy that I am able to come and talk with you. It means so much to us over here when you come together, you know. And you know that there are times when, perhaps, you get a little down. But we are with you and we are doing everything we can! We just want you to continue. Stay together, and know we are never far from you. I now how marvellous it would be if we could speak like this but we have hope of it, you know! But we are managing in others ways, huh? You have sometimes communication of a different kind, no? But we are 'appy in everything we try to do. If there is anything, you know, that I can do, or any of us can do – anything you want to ask – you know, we will be ver' 'appy to try to answer you and help you. You know, it is for you to ask.

Mickey broke in at this point:

'Ask and thou shalt receive – get cracking!'

One of the sitters had been showing signs of trance but he told Mickey he still doubted himself as a medium as he was not in deep trance. Did Mickey think he was imagining it all? The answer was interesting and may help those currently developing, or contemplating developing trance mediumship:

> Well, I believe you may just be receiving genuine communication but, at this early stage, it is obviously of a mental nature. I mean if I want to try and transmit something to you through, say, your circle, I have to send out my thoughts, hoping that you will pick up the thought vibration that I'm giving you. Of course, you may put some of it in your own way of interpreting it, and sometimes perhaps you may unconsciously misquote. I suppose it's a matter of patience and time – and experience; but you do receive a lot of mental impressions and thoughts and ideas, and you give out; for instance, you may not go in a deep trance – you may go in a semi-trance. You may be conscious as to what you're saying, but have no command over it. Don't let it worry you. Don't sit there analysing yourself with it. Just give out what comes; let it flow, and you'll find that the easier it becomes, the better it will get, because you're not sort of getting in the way. You see, a lot of people, unconsciously in the early stages I think, interfere. They don't mean to, but they're not even aware of it sometimes. Just let what comes, come! Leave it till later to analyse it, or let other people pass their opinion or idea about it, and you will find that a lot of things will come which are obviously nothing to do with you; and sometimes things which are not common to your knowledge. Maybe in a personal way, or maybe about other things. But I just think that the best thing anyone can do is to stop concerning themselves or worrying themselves as to whether what they're getting – or what is coming – is correct or incorrect. Just let it come – and if you allow yourself to relax and let yourself be used, you'll find in most instances it will improve in value, and it will improve in what is coming. And don't worry yourself as to whether it is personal or evidential or whatever. Be serious, but not to the extent of being analytical. [At this point, the sitter broke in to say that it just becomes difficult

for him to distinguish.] I know that – but the point is this, mate! That there is no such thing, or very rarely – even when I come and talk here – I mean, old Flint keeps out of it to a certain extent; I mean, he can't help it; but the point is that all communication is necessarily on a mental level. If I can't talk physically then I have to transmit my thoughts. This voicebox, or whatever you like to call it, which is artificially produced – reproduces what I'm trying to convey. But it may not necessarily always reproduce exactly. It may reproduce exactly to demonstrate what I *wish* to say but it may not always reproduce my temperament or my personality. There are some times when I'm able to speak loud and clear and all the rest of it; other times when I find it difficult and occasions when I can't get through at all. In other words, be grateful, cock! Forget about how it comes and when it comes. You can record it and when the sitting's all over, you can listen back to it and you'll find lots of interest and help in the recording. And if you do find a few bits and pieces that puzzle you, well, that's still all interesting and helpful. If you're going to be too analytical whilst the thing is working, you might as well pack up and be done with it, mate.

'Ere, you're a real case, cock! You're a real case, you are! But you've gotta laugh, 'aven't yer? There's no point in being too serious. You know, some people think that because we're over 'ere, we're all flying round playing bleeding harps! What a dreary world! I wouldn't want to be in a world like that. Who'd want to go on eternally singing hymns? Bad enough in church, singing a couple! Ha, ha! I'll make you laugh, Robin! No harm in a giggle, is there, mate? Who wants to – when they kick the bucket – who wants to go to a world full of misery? I mean, if there's not brightness, and cheerfulness and happiness – who'd want to survive? Can you imagine anything worse than what some of these religious people think it's going to be like? All the world running round like mad things, singing at the top of their voices – 'osannas! And they all want to kick the bucket and dive in.

One of the sitters broke in here to say that she would want to do a little bit of exploring when she first passed over and Mickey responded:

I thought you were doing a bit of that now! [He laughs.] You mean you want to find out more and more about life over 'ere? Well, that'll come gradually. You don't suddenly become aware of

> everything. Otherwise, what's the point? Everything is an adventure. When one door shuts, another opens. You go a little further along up the ladder – you know – of experience. Oh, you'll learn, mate!

Following his interesting observations, Mickey started to tease one of the sitters lightheartedly about her short blonde hair and that led to him reminiscing about the old days, when he was a child in London's Camden Town:

> Cor, stone me – the old days, you know, when my old mum used to put 'er 'air up at the back, then put a comb in it and put a maid's cap on, with 'er apron on too; then she used to go across the road to the pub. Cor, women 'ave changed since then! Now when you go to the pub you go all dolled up in the 'ope of meeting somebody who'll buy you a drink! [He laughs.] You gotta laugh, ain't yer? The times I've stood outside the old pub! Cor, my mum and dad – when they'd 'ad a row! My mum would go in one bar and me father'd go in the other. Yeah, but it worked out all right for me – I got *two* bottles of lemonade, and *two* snacks. I used to go to one door and shout 'Dad!' and out 'e'd come and say, 'What the 'ell do you want? I suppose you want a drink?' and off 'e'd go till 'e come out with a lemonade or something and a big arrowroot biscuit like dog biscuits. Then I'd go down to the other entrance, and shout 'Mum!' and she'd say, 'What do you want?' Yeah, I'd usually do well when they'd 'ad a row. It paid me, that way. And then, of course, there was my mum's sister, who took to religion. Cor, she was round the bend with religion, she was, but she was always good for a tanner! Cor, I could tell you some stories about them days.

There were a lot of personal evidential and accurate messages from Mickey at this stage and he managed to keep us all in fits of laughter with some of the things he came out with. Nonetheless, there was a serious purpose to it all as several went away afterwards with superb proof of the survival of their loved ones. Then Jock, our Scottish circle helper, came through:

> It's all right – it's only just myself! Aye. I thought I'd put in a few words – let ye know I was around. Aye, I didn't know what ye feel about it, but we're quite happy about the circle. We think it's getting on quite well. Course, as ye know, these things take their time, but the poower is at times very strong, and I think that before

long you'll begin to see some effect from all our efforts! But ye must not get down in the dumps! [I comment that it is a problem at times.] Aye. Well that's human nature – at times, ye think we're not making any progress, but I can see that a lot's going on behind the scenes. A lot's happening of which ye don't realise at times, and I think that individually most of you are making some individual development all right. Some, perhaps, might not feel they're doing very much, but everyone's making a contribution! Everyone's important to the whole. No one should feel that they're perhaps not pulling their weight. We're quite happy the way things are. Sometimes things are seen to be thriving and other times there's little or nothing happening. But just when it seems that there's little or nothing happening, there's often a lot going on in the background. I ask only that you'll be patient and leave the rest to us. Well goodbye, God bless, and keep going – you'll get there in the end!

Another of our own home circle helpers – Elizabeth Garrett Anderson came quickly on Jock's heels to give us a message of encouragement for the circle and Mickey cut her communication short with some more evidential messages of a personal nature. Following that, the faint voice of a little girl, who called herself Marie tried to talk to us, but she faded away in the attempt. As her voice faded away, the commanding tones of Sir William Crookes addressed us:

As a matter of fact, I do think it's very complex at times but one does attract an enormous number of people. Not necessarily always people that you'd expect, either. Course, one's guides, and people that you know will, from time to time, appear and come through; but quite often you know, a lot of souls are drawn and attracted, sometimes in need of your help. You know your circle's gone through different phases, obviously, but the point is: the main purpose of it is really that the physical mediumship which we still have faith in *will* develop you know but, however, that doesn't alter the fact that over the last year or so there have been these changes, which do have some effect of course.

Nevertheless, there are other forms of mediumship which each one of you have to some extent functioning in you in one direction or other. I think the obvious thing is not to be unduly perturbed about it. Indeed, people do sometimes get very concerned – like our friend here was saying [meaning the sitter who had told Mickey he doubted himself], wondering if some of the things that were coming through were from his subconscious. But actually, I wouldn't allow that to worry one unduly although, of course, in the initial early stages of development, there will be some aspect of the instrument [medium] there. Indeed I think it would be true to say that it's practically impossible to completely cut out the instrument. This can only come with perhaps a number of years of development; being able to submerge oneself deeply and allowing, as it were, those souls to come and speak freely in their own way and their own jargon if you like, using their own method. You see, these things do not necessarily come as quickly and as easily as one would wish. There *are* exceptional cases; instances perhaps, when you least expect it, that maybe someone takes over and they really *do* take full control; and then they do get over tremendously – aspects of themselves – their personality; and subject matter which they talk about and discuss is something which is perhaps even foreign to the individual – the medium – but as far as I'm able to gather, and I've been many times to look at the group and know many of the souls who come regularly to it, we are very convinced that you have indeed a wonderful circle in embryo.

There's a great deal happening there; a great deal developing; and in due course, I know that you'll see many benefits. The thing is just to stick it out and work together in love and harmony as indeed you are. You are a very happy little crowd and this is half the battle too. There is great understanding and sympathy and each one of you feels that you have some part to play. Each part is important to the whole you know, although perhaps, from your point of view, it sometimes seems something rather like a jigsaw puzzle and you don't seem to be able to get the bits in the right places. However, you leave that to us. We can see the full picture that you can't see and each one of you is a part of that picture. So carry on as you are. Don't get distressed. Don't get unduly concerned or worried, just leave everything to us – and we will do everything that we can. Anyway, bless you – it's been wonderful talking to you again. Goodbye! [Sir William confirmed his name before he left.]

Finally, after a short blessing by White Feather, one of our circle's well-known helpers, Mickey weighed in with a short burst about how he sometimes watched television:

> Do you watch that series *Coronation Street*? [A chorus of yesses greeted him.] Well, I thought I'd better tell you that the woman in it that died in a car accident [in the soap] – she ain't 'ere, you know! No, but it wouldn't surprise me if she came through at a circle, ha ha! You know what I mean? You get some people, bless their 'earts and all that but they believe that some of the characters on the television are real, you know. It takes all kinds to make the world, don't it? But old Flint watches it you see and he goes and sits down to watch *Coronation Street* and I sometimes watch it with 'im. [One of the sitters asks if he watches a lot of telly.] Well, in a sort of way, but it's very funny that! You'll never perhaps grasp exactly what I'm trying to say but we can watch things through people's memory – their thoughts. You know, if old Les gets caught up in something on the television and I'm in tune with 'im, or at least with his auric emanation, as you term it – if I'm close to 'im, like, then I can sort of take on 'is thoughts and all that. Because it's a very funny sort of thing with mediums, 'cause being a medium is being sensitive and you take on the thoughts and emotions and feelings and experiences of all manner or kinds of people on both sides, you see. Anyway, these things take their course.

There followed a little more banter from Mickey before his voice started to fade out; he apologised that the power was going, which meant that he was unable to hold on any longer and in his customary fashion, he bade us goodbye, asking us to keep our chins up – double ones as well.

Six months after this sitting, following a series of encouraging results in our own home circle at Harold Wood and just a few days prior to the new Woodford Church opening, we once again had the opportunity to visit Leslie Flint for a sitting. At this time the plans for the revamped Link of Home Circles were well under way too, under the umbrella of the Union of Spiritualist Mediums (I mention this because it was raised by communicators during the sitting). Unfortunately, Leslie was not in the best of health when we visited on this occasion and some of his recent sittings had been total blanks. We hoped that this would not be the case with us and, although it took longer than usual for the voices to come – over an hour – it did turn out to be a successful sitting, albeit a relatively short one.

So on the afternoon of 10 February we were again listening to Mickey and his pals. When he first came through, he told Leslie off for talking too much (as it had been a slow start at this sitting, Leslie had chatted in his normal fashion almost non-stop for an hour or so to kill time while we were waiting for Mickey to come):

> What was he on about? [Referring to Leslie.] Gets on my wick! [Leslie responded with, 'You what?'] Well, you'd talk a donkey's hind leg off, you would! [At this point, Leslie, who was clearly hurt by Mickey's remarks, tried to explain that he was only trying to keep us interested while the voices came.] Well, I know you mean well but you do go on – you talk too much.

Mickey continued by greeting us all and asking how we were. To our question as to how he was faring, he replied:

'Well, you know, I'm all right! But I worry about 'im! [Leslie asks, who?] You, you twit!'

Leslie was rather nonplussed by this and told Mickey not to be so rude, receiving the reply:

> Well, anyway, I expect he'll be all right. But, you know, he has to ease up mate. He doesn't 'alf talk these days, doesn't he? And it's not doing 'im any good.

Mickey now switched his attention to our circle and told us that he'd been to it many times, so I asked him whether he thought it was progressing OK. This was his answer:

> Course it is! I think you're making quite good progress, ain't yer? And you're getting quite a lot of inspiration, and one or two of yer are going orf. You don't quite know where you're going, though! Ha ha! You can't 'elp laughing! You're all being used! I 'eard what you were saying about forming some sort of society [The Link]. Well, I think that that's a good idea. I know that old Zerdin, old Noah, will be pleased. 'Cos he started it, you know, and it was very good, and it helped a lot of people.

Mickey told us he'd better not take up too much time because Leslie had talked too much, then he told us:

> Well, I really wouldn't 'ave anyone else, you know. 'Cos you get some of these mediums, they give you the pip, don't they? You know, I mean, at least I know where I am with him. But some of them. I went to a meeting recently. Cor, stone the crows! The medium, she was all dolled up to the nines! Got a wig on! False eyelashes! False teeth! And she wasn't arf putting it on, you know; 'Oh, blurrss you my friends.' Ha, ha, ha! You couldn't 'elp laughing! Course, she meant well, poor old thing. She couldn't 'elp it, but I wish she'd be more natural. I shouldn't really criticise, should I? But the trouble is, when I come to speak to you lot, I come back on your level, don't I? In my own environment, you'd 'ardly know me.

Suddenly a cultured and articulate female voice broke through, loud and clear. This was our circle helper, Elizabeth Garrett Anderson who, for once, was able to get a few words in:

> God bless you all. I do not know whether I shall be able to say much under the circumstances but I can only do as one can under the conditions that prevail. Actually, the conditions as you term it are very good. It's not anyone's fault if one, at times, is not able to manifest quite in the way as one would like. But the powers of the instrument vary considerably and we have to be very careful. But I couldn't, and I know that all of us here feel this very strongly, but we couldn't *not* come, if only for a short space of your time, just to say hello and to assure you that we are doing everything in our power to help in every possible conceivable way. And we do know – and I'm sure that you must be aware of what is being done behind the scenes – that we shall achieve in time that which we have set our heart on doing. The voices, and the manifestation of the power of the spirit will, in due course of time, make themselves very much more aware and stronger. You mustn't get down and depressed, because these things, by their very nature, will take time you know. But the trumpets may be used to some extent, although I think I would be right in saying that the voices will not necessarily be used with the trumpet. It's interesting perhaps, to have the manifestation of movement, but we are more concerned

> in trying to come as independently as possible. Other souls, of course, are there. Some you know. Others you don't know. Many are they who come, you know, working away quietly, often behind the scenes. Some of us you'll get to know very well. Some you do know already but there is many another person who is not making him or herself known to you.

Elizabeth went on to tell us that she would be happy to answer any questions and I asked her to confirm her name, which she did. We are told that she was delighted that the work of her hospital, which had been under threat, was now for the time being safe and would continue. However, as she tried to give us a bit more information, her voice suddenly died out, and I commented on the fact before she told us:

> Well sometimes, probably that happens. You see, we don't always know exactly the effect we're having. For instance, I stand here and I concentrate my thoughts – and it's my thoughts that are being turned into vibrational sound. I'm aware to some extent of the reaction and response. I'm aware that I'm being as it were *heard,* as you might say, but you know, it's a very odd thing. I suppose most people think that this sort of seance, whatever you call it, that we stand there and we talk. But it's not quite like that. The voicebox builds and reproduces sound, but the thoughts that we impinge upon it are then brought to you on your particular wavelength or level of consciousness and you hear what we are thinking as sound. I, I suppose, taking it by and large, that *I* don't do too badly. But it is a fact that some people are marvellous communicators. Others find great difficulty in transmitting, and I think that this is the big problem. It depends so much on each individual and whether they're tense and over-anxious or emotional. I try to be calm and placid and that, I think, is the best way, you know. Of course, sometimes when you have family reunion or family connections, I think particularly in the case of husband and wife or what have you, that the emotional aspect is so strong, and tension has been built up, so that it sometimes inhibits the phenomenon and makes it more difficult. Anyway, I suppose partly in my professional life as a doctor, but also, I suppose, everything about me to some extent suggests that I was, and will still continue to become – I don't get unduly perturbed or excited, that would never do – not in the

> profession I had anyway. It's no good going to a person in that state, all caught up in emotional feelings, you might do terrific damage [I commented here – one slip of the knife!] Yes, well, didn't say that, but I *was* thinking it.

At this point Elizabeth indicated that she must leave to make way for more communicators and she took her leave of us, urging us to continue with our work. Sister Maria came through for a brief period to once more encourage us, and an East End character called Jimmy Hawkins, who had been killed in the First World War, came to chat to us. We had heard him speak before in our own home circle, in his happy-go-lucky, entertaining way. A faint voice was heard as he left us, obviously that of a lady, addressing us in the name of Floss – Florrie Rees – but her communication was short and faded out quickly. This was followed by the voice of Doctor Marshall, one of Leslie's main guides, in a conversation which made me feel particularly proud of the dedication I was trying to show to the subject of physical mediumship and its phenomena:

> Well, well, well! As a matter of fact, I have been trying desperately to manifest. It's always rather problematic – one has to realise, of course – one never quite knows as to whether one is going to be able to break the barrier that divides the two worlds. Actually, of course, it's not a barrier in a sense – it's something which is perhaps, well, within ourselves. Now that sounds a very strange thing to say, but it's true! A great deal depends on many factors but I always feel very drawn to coming when *you* are here, because I know your sincerity and your great desire to develop and to be of service, doing the work of the spirit so that you can help as far as possible, and wherever possible, those whose needs are many. Whether it is in comforting the bereaved or healing the sick, or whatever it may be, down whatever avenue you may be led, but I do know that your interest is very deep with regard to the physical manifestations of mediumship which have now become so, so very, very rare. And we do need people like you, who would dedicate yourselves – give yourselves to the work of the spirit and manifest the power of the spirit, particularly, if possible, as we're sure you will, eventually in a physical sense. Because we feel that if we can, and I'm sure we shall do that kind of work and manifest in that

fashion – in the direct voice, and perhaps later, who knows – materialisation.

This latter is a form of mediumship which, by its very nature, will convince many a hard-headed sceptic and give the conviction to those who, perhaps normally, would find it very difficult to accept and believe in the reality of life after death. Of course, we know there are problems – we don't anticipate that it will be smooth, you know. I'm quite sure that you realise that we've never suggested for one moment that it would be an easy path to follow. It means sacrifice on your part, along with infinite patience and perseverance, but I know that you have all of those attributes, and we shall do everything – everything that is possible – to help you.

And of course, we are very interested in this new idea of trying to bring circles together, to be able to perhaps give encouragement and to give enlightenment; and make it possible, perhaps, to bring together a number of people of like mind to yourselves, where we can perhaps have the opportunity of coming through, of communicating and in other ways serving, you know. And we shall give you all our strength and all our help and all our guidance – of that you can be absolutely sure.

Actually, of course, I was a bit worried – well, as a matter of fact, I think we all were – in the sense that we weren't going to 'make it', as you term it, today. Because the medium, bless his heart – I'm not saying anything I hope that will be misunderstood – but of course, he does talk a great deal, as Mickey says. I think that it's interesting as far as it goes, obviously, but the point is that you know that his health condition – he's not ill, thank God, but he's had the warnings – and he's got to take it easy. Shouldn't overtax himself. [Leslie was 70 years old.] He should try to be much more quiet and much more quiescent, you know. I'm not saying that he shouldn't talk occasionally. I suppose one will never stop him anyway! But the point is, it's much better not to waste energy. Of course, even when a person talks, especially at length, a great deal of energy and vitality is used up, and I'm afraid we'll have to instill in him that by all means for a few minutes, perhaps at the commencement of a circle, he can make a few remarks but he is not to go on and on, you know. I hope you'll understand this but a great deal of energy is used up in such circumstances. But he may feel that by talking he keeps himself awake. As long as he keeps you awake.

But mediums are strange creatures. However, we're very grateful to them, and we're very fortunate in this one. But like all mediums, you know, we have to accept them for – well – there are many factors in their makeup; good, bad and indifferent – but we're grateful. Very grateful! But anyway, I'm looking, and not only I, but others here are looking for new instruments, you know. 'Cause they won't go on for ever, and this one won't go on all that much longer, I expect. But we are looking to you, and not only from the point of view of your particular group – but other groups, of course, that you may well become linked up and associated with. I think that this idea that has been brought into being: a re-awakening, or a 'bringing out' as it were, what you term the Link is an excellent idea, because I think that if circles can meet, they get encouragement and help, and they can also swap, as you term it, their experiences and tape recordings of seances and things that have happened; and you can get together socially, which is also a very good thing and from time to time have some illuminating and very helpful and interesting meetings. Anyway, you know that we shall do everything we can, in every possible conceivable way.

After a few private jokes with Leslie himself, Doctor Marshall took his leave of us. Two more of our own circle helpers, White Feather and Jock spoke briefly to us – White Feather giving us his blessings and encouragement and Jock taking the opportunity to confirm to us that the circle was doing well and that we should simply continue as we already were. Mickey came back for a short final burst and Leslie, very touchingly, told him (he and Mickey had been together for almost 50 years) that perhaps he could do more work with our home circle and that if he (Leslie) were to kick the bucket, he couldn't think of any nicer people for Mickey to go to.

One of our brighter sitters asked if we could perhaps adopt him and Mickey told her, just before he had to go, when the power was fading:

'Yes. In a way I'll always help yer. But over the years I've been adopted by so many circles, I'll spend me death going round and round in circles! But we love everybody!'

And with that, he was gone.

# A NEW CHURCH, A NEW CHAPTER

SHORTLY AFTER THE sitting with Leslie Flint, on 21 February at 3 p.m., the South Woodford National Spiritualist Church opened its doors to the public for the first time. There were around 130 people present, mainly invited guests and mediums who would be likely to give their services to the church in the future.

It was an extremely happy occasion as Gordon Higginson, the then SNU President, opened and dedicated the church in the name of spirit. After the frustratingly long time of preparation by the church committee, of which I was a member, the feeling of euphoria was indescribable, as visitors sat on the new chairs, whose manufacturer I had come across by chance, but which had been carefully chosen by the committee on my recommendation, and started to browse through the church library, whose books had been lovingly restored and re-covered, and which contained a brand new copy of Leslie Flint's book, *Voices in the Dark,* presented by Sandra and me as a vital part of a psychic library.

Doris Collins gave an excellent demonstration of clairvoyance to round off the church opening and everybody was in high spirits (if you'll pardon the expression!) as the afternoon was concluded.

But for us the excitement was not quite over. During the evening, Geoffrey Jacobs had agreed to give a sitting for phenomena, and Sandra and I had been invited. While we had previously observed spasmodic movements of trumpets at our own circles, we had never before sat with a full-blown trumpet direct-voice medium. It was quite an evening we were in for when we arrived at Geoffrey's home in Chelmsford.

There were twelve sitters in all and we first witnessed an impressive demonstration of trance and transfiguration in the blue light of the seance room (unusual in itself, as most physical mediums operated in a red light). Several of Geoffrey's guides, and some personal communicators, spoke to the assembled company through Geoffrey's trance before the blue light was switched off and the physical phenomena began.

It was a short while before anything happened, but gradually, a series of very fast, light raps could be heard coming from under the medium's chair. These rapidly increased in number, intensity and speed until there was a constant rapping, apparently on the carpet or underside of his chair, which we could all hear. There were two trumpets in the room and it was not long before they 'took off', soaring all over the place at great speed – up to the ceiling, and down again to the floor; in all, far too fast and distant from the medium for the phenomena to have been produced by him. Several voices conversed with us through the trumpets and, at one point, when the vibrations 'dropped', one of these trumpets shot back to the medium, hitting him hard in the solar plexus, whereupon he was heard to have been somewhat winded by the blow.

This then, was our spectacular introduction to a sustained aerobatic display by soaring airborne trumpets of the type we had heard so much about throughout our studies into physical mediumship, and it was not to be long before we experienced similar phenomena at home ...

The next day, the Woodford church was full for its first public service. There were 177 people crammed into the church. The service (taken once more by Doris Collins) was so popular that over 20 more had to be turned away and, in Doris's capable hands, the congregation was spellbound as she demonstrated her mediumistic gift. The comments overheard by the committee that evening showed a general satisfaction with the service and the new church.

Eileen Roberts had often mentioned the knock-on effect of physical mediumship to me in the past and had related the story of how, in her own physical circle, sitters had been able to feel the power building up over several months but could not get their own phenomena 'off the ground', so to speak. The solution was to invite Geoffrey Jacobs to sit with them one week for phenomena. With Geoffrey there, the trumpets took off in the usual way, and they had a wonderful evening.

The following week, the circle sat once again, without Geoffrey. This time the trumpets flew around the room and the circle's phenomena continued thereafter without any problems.

On the evening after the opening of Woodford church, John and Joyce, as previously agreed, came round to our home to participate in a sitting for just the four of us. We could not help feeling during the sitting that we were ourselves perhaps experiencing the knock-on effect of Geoffrey Jacobs' mediumship, the only difference being that Geoffrey had not come to us – we had gone to him for physical phenomena just a couple of days previously. Our Monday sitting was a relatively short one; just one hour, in fact, but the phenomena packed into that hour was prolific. Afterwards, when I wrote up the sitting in my diary, as was my usual habit, I added the comment: 'One of the most fantastic hours of my life!'

The phenomena started after just five minutes, when one of the trumpets, which had been standing upright on the floor, fell over. Water was sprinkled on my face, and on Joyce's. Within seconds, the two trumpets shot up to the ceiling several times, ducking and weaving as they did so, performing their dance routines and aerobatics all over the room. The tambourine we had in the centre of the table also levitated several times, rattling and shaking to the music, and once or twice travelling so fast that it gave the impression of a flying saucer.

Sandra clairvoyantly saw a spirit scientist in the room in his white coat and was clairaudiently told that he was of French origin, and wished it to be known that 'these four sitters are important in the scheme of things'. Being her usual cautious and canny self, Sandra, who had not immediately passed on this information that she was receiving, mentally asked that if she was seeing and hearing the message correctly, she would like confirmation by way of the trumpet falling over again.

Hardly had she got the thought out before the trumpet did as requested, and keeled over. Once more through clairaudience, Sandra got the message that we now needed luminous plaques in the circle. This time she asked mentally for a trumpet to be lifted from the floor on to the table in order to confirm the message, and immediately a trumpet was picked up from the floor and placed gently on the table.

The trumpets, whose movement could be seen from the luminous bands around both ends, continued to fly up to the ceiling at intervals, and each time this happened, they were picked up from the floor or table, rising in a split second to a point high in the room, beyond the reach of all the sitters. They were then placed gently back on the table (which we could not see, as it had no luminous tabs on it) without fumbling or faltering. The movement was fast but strictly controlled.

The conversation between the sitters turned to our experiences of Saturday, when voices had issued from the trumpets at Geoffrey's. Without delay one of the trumpets in our current sitting took off and hovered, with its narrow end almost touching the ceiling, and its wide end hanging down a little below that level, so that the wide end was pointing at us, the sitters. An unmistakable voice, issuing from it, intoned just the one word: 'Winston'.

Naturally, we were all delighted by this result and wondered aloud if perhaps the 'wee Scotsman was around'. Once again the trumpet rose up to the ceiling and, as it hung down in the same manner, we heard three distinct words: 'It's Jock here.'

This trumpet direct-voice phenomena was followed by the bowl of water (kept in the room to assist in maintaining the humidity of the atmosphere at the correct level) toppling over, as did the table, which fell on to its side.

Interestingly, however, the table must have been restored silently to its normal upright position by the spirit helpers almost instantly, as the next time one of the trumpets soared to the ceiling for an aerobatic session, it was afterwards replaced gently back on to the table, much to our surprise, as we had assumed that having heard nothing, the table must still be on its side.

When the bedlam had died down a little, and the trumpets now rested quietly in their original positions, our spirit friend with the well-known stentorian voice spoke to us in the independent voice, the source of which we judged to be high up in the centre of the room: 'This is Winston – we don't need the amplifiers.' And as we discussed the exciting developments of the night: 'I'll get the job done.' It was clear that Winnie was listening in to our conversation as we spoke of the opening of the Woodford Church, and commented that Woodford was part of Winston's parliamentary constituency, as he told us: 'I was there. Vote for Winnie.' He continued with a few friendly words for us, culminating with his farewell for the evening, finally adding the wistful observation. 'I wish I could be organising things on your side now.'

By this time, the short sitting was almost at an end and, after some more sedate movements and levitations of objects in the room, we were asked by the guides to close the circle. The enthusiasm of all the sitters was back in abundance and we agreed to sit together as often as possible in the near future.

Our connection with Geoffrey Jacobs had clearly been advantageous to us. Sadly, however, our earthly friendship with him was to be a short one. On 5 March, Geoff gave a short but interesting talk on his own physical mediumship at the new Woodford Church, which I had the privilege of chairing.

This was followed by a brilliant demonstration of his clairaudient mediumship, when he was helped by his spirit guide, Charlie Foster. Rarely during a public demonstration have I ever heard such accurate evidence as that given by Geoffrey to the 56 members of the audience who were present that night. Even John and Joyce (who were normally very sceptical of these things) received some quite amazing survival evidence which impressed them greatly.

When the demonstration was over, Charlie Foster entranced Geoffrey and said a few words of farewell to the audience. What I did not understand at the time was the fact that he ended with the words, 'Goodbye – we're closing the door now.' In the past, Charlie had tended to say 'Good evening', or 'Goodnight'. The words sounded final and in fact this meeting proved to be Geoffrey's mortal swan song.

He was not feeling too well after the event, so his wife Brigid drove him home to Chelmsford. It nevertheless came as a great shock, to us when his friend, Bill Dragon, telephoned us two days later to tell us that Geoff had passed away at home after the demonstration.

I attended Geoffrey's funeral in Chelmsford, where he was also buried. In my mind's eye, however, I can still see him performing his party-piece. Many years earlier, Geoff had lost an eye in an accident and, when parting from friends, he would often say, 'I'll keep an eye out for you,' as he removed his false eye. His premature death was a sad loss to those of us that knew him and the movement has since been poorer without his exceptional mediumistic abilities.

It was round about this time too in our regular weekly circle at Harold Wood that we first encountered a phenomenon which was to be repeated several times over with slight variations. This did not happen in the circle proper but took place just afterwards when we had gone downstairs to make a cup of tea and prepare the refreshments.

Our dog, Ben, was still very young and excitable, and it was Sandra's habit to go down first into the kitchen after the circle had closed, so that she could let the dog out into the garden so that he did not disturb us as the beverages and snacks were prepared. Always when this was done, Sandra locked the back kitchen door behind the dog so that he would be out of the way for a little while.

One night, however, after the circle, Sandra had gone through this usual routine and one of the other sitters, Lisa, had brought down the glasses of water we had used during the evening. As she went to put these on the draining board in the kitchen, the rest of us in the next room heard a loud scream from Lisa. We all rushed out to the kitchen to see what the matter was, and we could see that the dog was now sitting in the kitchen with his wet nose against Lisa's leg. It was when she felt his nose next to her leg that Lisa had screamed.

Our first thought was that the door must have come undone somehow so that Ben had been able to get back into the kitchen, and we therefore checked the door thoroughly. It was still locked. There was no other conclusion that we could come to therefore, other than the fact that Ben had been de-materialised in the garden, apported through a locked kitchen door into the fully lighted kitchen, where he had been somehow re-materialised with his wet nose against Lisa's leg. He was sitting in the kitchen looking totally stunned, much quieter than usual after his 'experience'.

Keeping a close watch on the dog for several days, it became crystal clear to us that Ben's 'experience' had changed his personality for the better. He had definitely become much more serious and less excitable than previously, although it was obvious that apart from this subtle change in his nature he had suffered no ill effects from his adventure.

The Union of Spiritualist Mediums (USM) was planning a spring weekend seminar on mediumship at Down Hall in Essex during April, and since their National Executive Committee, of which I was now a member, had heard that our Harold Wood circle was getting some physical phenomena, the members of the circle were all asked to be the 'Saturday night cabaret', and take part in a special experimental sitting for the delegates on 25 April. Our protestations that we had not had enough experience of phenomena in the circle to take part in such an experiment went unheard and, as a circle, we were therefore 'commandeered' for the purpose. As Sandra and I were now also committee members of the USM Romford branch, we had learned very quickly that Madam President was not one to take 'no' for an answer.

Prior to this, the USM were running their annual mediums' conference, at which many matters concerning working mediums were raised and, after much joint groundwork to re-establish the Link of Home Circles, it was planned that the new venture would be announced by Eileen Roberts at this conference on Saturday 28 March but, in the event, Miss Roberts suffered a bereavement and was unable to attend the conference. The announcement was therefore postponed until April. But by now the Link was well and truly in business and was receiving a lot of publicity in the psychic press. Through this, it began to grow steadily, and quickly came to embrace into its membership home circles from all over the world.

Our own home circle in Harold Wood continued to sit with varying results throughout this period but it was with trepidation that the Harold Wood home circle members went to Down Hall to participate in the USM experiment. The room which had been chosen was far from ideal, and we were dismayed to see light streaming from under the doors. It was impossible to maintain the required total blackout and, with some 70 people in attendance, conditions were far from ideal. Despite this, however, a few sitters in various parts of the room experienced some mild forms of physical phenomena, ranging from coldness and breezes to being sprinkled with water, and encountering perfumes which were produced psychically. With hindsight, it is not an experience I would want to repeat with a circle whose sitters lacked experience and the direct instructions of their guides and spirit team.

During the rest of 1981, Sandra and I continued to sit whenever possible with John and Joyce, as well as with the original Harold Wood circle. Phenomena were often good but it also went through lulls and flat periods. For us it was an extremely busy year, holding full-time jobs down on the one hand, while working for spirit on the other. There was still the Woodford Church, plus the USM National Executive Committee. We were both now active in the Romford branch of the USM and on the committee, as well as running the USM Link of Home Circles, and attending its committee meetings. It was in 1981 too that the Union of Spiritualist Mediums became the Institute of Spiritualist Mediums (ISM), a title that was felt more appropriate for the teaching work regularly undertaken by the organisation.

The Link established itself quickly and it was clear from the outset that many of its member circles needed good sound advice to help in their development of various psychic gifts and phenomena. This was given by Miss Roberts, who was a very experienced teacher of psychic matters. Often a visit was needed – for a couple of us to sit with a member circle for the purposes of assessing their progress, and it was common for me to make such visits with Eileen. A quarterly newsletter for members was set up, the first issue appearing in October 1981, and it became my job to put this together, photocopy the result and see to its distribution to all Link registered circles. At the time that the first issue of *The Circle Link* went to press, there were no less than 58 circles registered with the Link, embracing almost 350 sitters, and including circles from as far afield as Canada, the USA, New Zealand, Australia and Israel. The list was growing fast.

Obviously, I needed to give a lot of time to the Link project and with limited time available to me, I reluctantly came to the decision to resign from the committee of the Woodford National Spiritualist Church. After all, the real hard work had been done, and the church was now open and running smoothly, with a number of capable hands at the helm. So I took off the one mantle in order to be soon saddled with another when, shortly afterwards, I was voted in as chairman of the Romford branch of the ISM, in which role I occasionally chaired for well-known mediums such as Doris Stokes and Joe Benjamin when they did public demonstrations for this ISM branch.

# TO LESLIE FLINT'S – YET AGAIN

TUESDAY, 6 OCTOBER 1981 saw the circle once again gathering outside the home of Leslie Flint in Bayswater, London, for their booked sitting. This time, there was only one sitter who had not previously sat with Leslie and we all had high hopes that the independent-voice sitting would go well. We need not have worried. Mickey was in his usual good form and 30 minutes into the sitting, after greeting circle members in his inimitable style, he told us:

> I have been to your circle. I told you I would, several times, and I have been. Things are looking up a bit, aren't they? You know, one day I'll be able to come and talk at your circle, 'cos you see, when old Les – well, you know he don't do so much now, so I've got more freedom. And I like to help people if I can. But you know, you've got some wonderful helpers and all that, but I sort of think that, well, if I can help, like! I do hope that you lot'll stay together now, not chop and change. No, I think that once a week is enough. [This was evidential, as we had been sitting on two nights, with two separate groups of sitters prior to coming to Leslie's; a fact that Leslie was not aware of.] I don't think there should be a tendency, as you call it, to try to do more than one per week. You know, sometimes people say, 'Oh well, shall we sit twice a week?' But I don't think that it's a good idea. I think you'd be just as well to concentrate all your energy for the one evening. Lou's here! [Sandra asked who Lou was at this point.] Oh, didn't you know about that? Well, sit and 'old tight. 'E's a lovely fella! Course, you don't know all your 'elpers yet, do you? [This was certainly true.]

Almost immediately, the independent voice of a male with a very strong French accent made itself heard. When playing back the tape for the purpose of transcribing the following conversation for this book, it took me several plays of the tape to be sure I had the communication right, because of the heaviness of the accent. The communicator later identified himself as Louis:

> Ah, he's talking about me! I don't know eef eet iss – err you hear me? [We confirmed that we could hear him.] I haff, err, wanted several times to come and talk with you. I am very interest, you know, in these things. There are a whole crowd of people here, souls, you know, who are verr interest in the experimontes – you know, with the meetings. Circle, as you call eet. Can you ear me? [We duly assured Louis.] When I was on your side, I did not know notheeng about the Spiritualeesm. But since I come 'ere, I 'ave made a study, 'ow you say? I want to come and experimonte. I 'ave various friends of mine 'ere – verry interest when on your side. I never knew, when they used to say about thees what they did, I used to say, 'No, no, no, no – not posseeble!' But I 'ave a verr dear friend of mine who was a scienteest. On your side, 'ee used to study mediums – used to take a verr good interest in everytheeng and he used to talk to me about it all. Still I used to say, 'No, no, no'. But 'ee was conveenced. Now, we see another side 'ere. Perhaps you do not know, but we are experimonting with you, in our circle. Course, eet iss verr deeficult perhaps for you to realise. Eet iss verr monny people there. Some you have known for a while, huh? But others you don't know. And we are verr great friends of some friends of yours 'ere. I saw a verr wonderful man who comes to your group – Monsieur Oliver Lodge – he was verry eenterest in psychic things, huh? And 'ee 'as been verr eenterest in the experimontes. And also a German doctor, here – perhaps 'ee was not exactly a doctor, but 'ee iss a verry eentelligent man who study psychic things. And take many peectures when on your side. His name is Notzing. Schrenk – Notzing.
>
> You see, what I try to tell you iss that there iss a lot of power, a lot of energee in your group. Eef you are patient, we hope we may be able to – eventually to build an ectoplasmic voicebox. Also, perhaps, experimonte in other ways. There are certain things we have tried to do with some success, but, err, I want you to know that if you are patient; don't worry too much about things, leave eet to uss. Let uss do eet – let us do thee work and thee experimontation. All we ask of you ees to be patient. Be calm, and not to be overr anxious. Leave everytheeng to uss. I was killed – I was killed in thee war – and thees go back a long time, een what you call thee First

World War, and I tell you, I knew various people in those years who were eenterest in psychic theengs. I used to make thee fun – well not exactly, but I did not take it seriously. But when I die – then I see eet all for myself, huh? But eer, then I theenk – I don't know. When I first come 'ere, I was not sure eef I was dead. I did not know. I thought it was a kind of dream; that I would wake up. One day, I'd find eet was a nightmare dream, you know. I was what you call earthbound for a leetle while, huh? But I soon realised that eet was not so. That I was err, dead, you know! And then I 'ave a cousine, who died here a few week before I was killed, and he met me. He was killed in thee war, huh? And it was a verr deeficult time. And there were thousands of men round the earth who were dead, you know. Oh, great, un'appy time, but anyway that ees all een thee past. I just want you to know I come and 'elp you, er, I am only one but there are many others that – some of them you do know. My name ees Louis.

Louis went on his way and his heavy French accent was replaced immediately by the crisp and refined feminine tones of Elizabeth Garret Anderson:

But you know very well that you have a remarkable group of souls helping you from this side. Of course, there are a few that you know by name but there are many, many other souls – and of course, there are a group of scientifically minded people. People who, when on your side, were deeply involved in scientific research, and who specialise in this aspect of things here. Endeavouring to build – as indeed they have built – the voicebox. Of course, it's very difficult for us to explain certain things. Because sometimes, when we come here, we're able to hold a long conversation. The voicebox is sustained by the energy and the power – not only from the medium but also from each and every one of you, to some extent. For you each supply a great deal; perhaps more than you know. Which, of course, is happening when you have your own circle. But holding on to that condition or power, and prolonging the contact and the communication; refurbishing if you like, or replenishing perhaps is the word, the ectoplasmic voicebox, is the problem. Sometimes, you'll get a little whisper for a few seconds, and then nothing at all, perhaps for a long period. And perhaps not at all during that session. But these are experimental days, and you mustn't be disheartened. Carry on, and know that you are being helped. All we ever ask of you is that when you come together, you come together as I know you do – in friendship, and with affection. You must be prepared to sit indefinitely, knowing that we are doing what we can from this side. All we ask of you is to be patient, leaving the rest to us. And the healing work, too. Perhaps you don't realise how much is done in that direction. Even when you're sitting quietly, you'd be surprised the amount of energy and vitality that is being circulated.

Sometimes we bring souls to you who need help. And you *can* help them! Perhaps because they're nearer to the earth than they are, in a sense, to us. Occasionally, an earthbound soul – not a bad person or anything like that. Never confuse this! Some people seem to think that an earthbound entity or soul is not necessarily a good person. The person can be a very nice person; a very kind and very good person, who temporarily can be held by earth memories – material things – to earth's vibration. They need help, and sometimes you, unconsciously, help them. Sometimes we bring someone to you for help. You may think this is rather, in a sense, unusual, because I know your one intent and purpose is to sit for the physical manifestation of the power of the spirit; that you might receive in that direction, in that way, manifestation of the voice, or materialisation which, of course, is what we're aiming at. But you must remember that we have a duty in a sense, one to another, to help each other, and we must not be too fixed in one direction, as it were. One must have sympathy. One must have infinite patience, and one must realise that we're all thrown together in loving service. It's not a wasted effort if perhaps it may seem to you that you sit for a long period with very little happening. A lot is happening behind the scenes. Always remember that. Sometimes, when it seems that nothing of consequence is happening, there really *is* a great deal happening on our side for your benefit, and for the benefit of the work that we're striving to do through you and with you – that others may be blessed, and see the light in the darkness of your world as you have seen it. Anyway, I must go. My love and blessings to you all!

With that, Elizabeth Garrett Anderson was gone. Within seconds, however, the well-known, well-loved Scottish accent of our own circle guide, Jock, broke in, obviously in an expansive mood:

> Aye, it's all right! I was not going to be polite! I made up my mind that I was going to get a word in edgeways, today. But ye know, there's such a crowd here. I don't think you'll ever realise it, and I'm quite sure its almost impossible to expect you to understand. But it's not just two or three people, or even a dozen people. Sometimes, when ye sit, there's a crowd there. Dozens and dozens of souls; and I have in fact been on some occasions – and ye may think this rather an odd thing to say – when it's really, in a way, not; well, it could be like a railway station on Bank Holiday Monday. When crowds of souls are attracted. Of course, they're not on the same vibration; they're not on the same wavelength. I mean, we who work with ye are on a certain wavelength – it's the only way I can describe it – we're on a certain level of awareness and consciousness, and we're working on that particular level for the work we're hoping to do, but there are a lot of other souls that are attracted.
>
> Ye know, you'd be surprised if ye could see, as we see. It's like in a way, looking down in the darkness; and we see a gleam of light, and this is what happens. When ye sit together, it's not only the power that's being directed. In a way, it's the thought process – and we can read, and we can know – in a sense feel things that are happening with each individual. We know that you're blending together, and you're making a good job of that. But you must remember that to us, when we enter into your material world – we get the thought processes of all manner and kind of people. Sometimes the atmosphere, on the horizon, is inclined to be rather heavy. As a matter of fact it's almost, at times, like facing a fog. And when ye sit together, the light that ensues, and then the power that's engendered by the fact that you're all sort of sitting there in love and in harmony together, is a great blessing and a great help. And not only is it the fact that *we* can come there aware of the light and the power but it also attracts other souls; you might say, in a way – on the fringe. I don't know if ye do realise that there are many levels of consciousness.

Ye know, when ye have a circle, like this for instance, or for that matter any other type of circle, the medium may work on a certain level; or the group may be on a certain level, and it is a fact that everyone that comes from the spirit realms that can get on to that level in some shape or form, will make him or herself known, if possible. But there are other souls that have not reached that certain vibration, or at least are not sharing that vibration. And, ye know, it's a very strange thing, I've just said to ye now that well, sometimes we are aware of the fact that there are a lot of other souls, which is quite true. But we're not necessarily always aware of *all* the different souls that come. They are at different levels of consciousness or vibration and the point is that sometimes we're not even aware of certain people that may well be there. And we all have to work on the right level – the same level – and the same level that you're aspiring to. The power and the energy that you're vibrating makes possible our links with ye. And when we get on to that vibration – when we get on to that connection – that's when we break through and that's when we start making ourselves known.

It might be in the form of trance mediumship at times, it may be in a psychic, clairvoyant way; or it may be that ye feel things with great intensity and ye feel 'Ah, I must say this', or 'I must say that'. Ye know, it's difficult to explain, because different individuals will sometimes use that power to manifest in a way, perhaps, that was not quite, well, what was intended. I know this sounds a bit weird but ye see, we have to, in a way, follow whatever the possibility is with that particular individual or that particular group. Now, for instance, ye take some circles where they've been sitting for months and nothing's been happening. They're getting a wee bit bored or fed up. Then of course we think, 'Well, we must try and do something on a different level,' and we change our tactics temporarily. We'll give them some impressions, or we'll give them some clairvoyance, or perhaps take somebody over in a semi-conscious state and try to manifest through that person – in a way, err, which will bring some encouragement. You see, if a circle goes on for months and nothing ever happens, we know full well that being – as they indeed are – getting sort of disconsolate and a bit despondent, they'll soon start to think, 'Ah, we're not going to get anything.' So occasionally we back ye up a wee bit, so to speak, with, like putting a 'whizz bang' in behind ye to liven ye up, because ye're sort of down in the dumps. And occasionally we do something or other to let ye know that we're there and that something *is* happening. But, of course, there may be long gaps, when we're concentrating on experimenting, and utilising the power and the energy in the process to build up – ectoplasmically in particular – to some form of manifestation that will give ye a tremendous boost and encouragement. Ye see, ye must remember these things. That there may be times when it all goes slow – as slow as slow can be – and everything seems to be 'just a wee worrd here and there'. But, although ye're no getting any strong physical mediumship; at least ye're getting an inner awareness, and a feeling that things are good – that power is being generated and that ye're on the verge, as it were. And there'll be times when it's not like that, and ye think, 'Well, it's a funny neet toneet.' Perhaps one of ye gets some clairvoyance, or ye'll get some inspiration, and give oot what ye get. But what I want ye to realise is that *we're* not getting despondent! We're getting very, very hopeful and we have reason to be much encouraged by certain events. But at the same time, I do want ye to know that we are confident, above all else, that if ye stick it oot – if ye carry on, and ye hold together in love and in harmony, if ye say, 'Well here we are, friends! Do with us what ye will, and as best ye can,' then we'll certainly do that. We may do one or two things that strike ye as a wee bit odd and sometimes ye may say to yeselves, 'What the hell did they do that for?'

But there's a reason behind most things, and sometimes we do things which, quite frankly, they really are unnecessary – to give ye a little boost. But ye mustn't get depressed. Say to yerselves, 'Well, they're doing what they can.' After all, all *ye* need to do is to just get together for a quiet hour and sit together in love and harmony; and then sit and have the refreshments afterwards. But we've got the work to do, ye know. You're the Plasticine and we're the moulders. But the circle's OK.

At this point, as Jock was taking his leave, I asked him if he was able to let us know which one of us would be used as the main medium and he replied:

Well, I don't know whether I should. Now, I don't want ye to misunderstand this, because in the first instance, I don't think it's my job to tell ye. And secondly, I don't want anyone to get any idea, within themselves. Now ye might think that this is a strange thing to say. Ye're happy as ye are, as a bunch together, and when

> the time comes, then ye'll be told. If any changes have to be made as regarding the instrument that's being used, for instance. Ye see, sometimes, it's a dual mediumship. Sometimes it's not just one person, and in a way, each one of ye is making a contribution. I don't think it matters at this stage as to whether ye know who is, or who is not. What is important is that ye're bound together in love and in harmony. And we want to keep that harmony. We want to keep that understanding that ye have, one with the other. And when the real results begin to take place and they're strong and powerful, ye won't have to ask me for the instrument's identity. The evidence will be strong enough by itself. Anyway, that's all I'm going to say on that point, so enough is enough. Goodbye!

As the voice of Jock disappeared, Mickey came back again, and spoke to us for a long time on many subjects. He spoke to a couple of the sitters on a personal level, giving them accurate survival evidence from their loved ones and relatives in the spirit world, and giving advice which proved to be correct and evidential about the safety aspect of a car owned by one of the sitters. When it was checked over later, there was a dangerous problem with the steering mechanism. He started off by telling us that our spirit guides did not always want to let us know which of the sitters they were developing for physical mediumship. He then said that he would be happy to answer any of our questions, or to try and meet any special request, at which point I asked him if our 'politician friend' (meaning, of course, Sir Winston Churchill) was around today, and was told:

> Well, I don't know. I haven't seen him. You mean Tubby? Him with the cigar bloke? [We said yes.] Well, 'e doesn't smoke over 'ere! He hasn't gone to that place where they do smoke. Not that I believe in such a place but – Old Winnie. You're on about Winnie, ain't yer? [Yes.] Well, 'e's a bit of a character. 'E's a hard-boiled egg. But 'e's a good sort. I 'aven't seen 'im here today. Perhaps 'e is around, but I ain't seen 'im. 'Cos the trouble is, you see, I s'pose it's all right with you lot, 'cos you know 'im, but some people – they're always suspicious, ain't they? When you say you have a famous person, they ask, 'How can you prove it,' you see. Well, of course, it's much more difficult to prove with a very famous person, 'cos so much has been written about them, and people say, 'How do you know?' And

> unless you happen to have people connected to them, or related to them, who can come and get something very personal that no one else knows about, it's very difficult. There are some things you have to accept on faith, you know, don't you? Not that it matters to you, in a sense, because you're convinced – and you're happy about it. But then you go and you say, 'Oh well, we 'ad Winston Churchill in our circle.' People look at you as much as to say, oh, oh! It's difficult, ain't it?

Another of our sitters, who had often been to Leslie's, inquired about Rose, the flower seller, who used to be a frequent visitor during Leslie's seances. Mickey laughed out loud:

> You mean old Rose, the flower seller that was? [Yes.] She's a card, she is! She don't come back too much these days. She got browned off with it, I think. No – it's just that she's advanced a bit. But then again you see, a lot of people come back who *are* very highly evolved. But invariably, for some anyway, they have to use the agency of somebody else, to transmit their message. But it depends – it depends.

Mickey went on to tell us a little about some of the Harold Wood circle helpers and guides who were present, speaking of an Irish priest, an Egyptian and two Native Americans, called Blue Wing and White Feather. White Feather, of course, had spoken to the circle on many occasions, including previous sittings at Leslie's. He then discussed with one of the sitters the problems the gentleman was having with his wife's disapproving attitude towards psychic matters because of her involvement in a local high church. Mickey, as always, treated the matter in a jocular fashion:

> Well, it's what it's all about, ain't it? Some people get some weird ideas, don't they? They think that just because we've kicked the bucket, we're all sort of religious! Flying around playing bleedin' 'arps! Can you imagine that through all eternity – just strumming a bleedin' 'arp and singing hymns? They don't know nuffing. 'Cos, of course, when I come down to earth to talk to you lot, I come on a lower vibration – but in my own environment, I'm very different. People are funny, ain't they? A person is no more than he or she thinks. And if they think on the wrong level, then they'll

*be* on the wrong level, won't they? Me? I don't pretend to be what I ain't! Bit unlike some of those mediums you 'ave on your side nowadays. Ha, ha. Full of their own importance they are. I went to this meeting one day, and the lady medium was all dolled up to the nines, putting it on, you know [in a posh voice] 'Bless you friends' and all that. 'How doo you doo.' Ha, ha! Silly old sausage! And I'm sure she didn't see a bleedin' thing as she gave out these posh clairvoyant messages. I thought, 'I'll give 'er a shock!' And I ran down the aisle towards 'er waving me arms about and all that. But she didn't see me. No, people don't realise just how natural we are – least, I speak for myself I am.

After a few more pleasantries, Mickey suggested I turn over my tape, or I would miss anything that came next, and this I did. He was, of course, right – when I checked the sitting back later, the tape would have clicked off right in the middle of the short communication from the next spirit visitor, Winston, who spoke clearly in his own well-known voice to tell us that he just wanted us to know he was there. He confirmed the fact that he was retaining an interest in all that happened in the circle and that he was keeping his eye on us.

This was followed by a short visit from Maria Theresa, who had spoken to us on many previous occasions. As always, she gave us much encouragement for the circle, and urged us to carry on. Interestingly, her talk continued while Leslie sneezed a few times and although his sneezes obviously affected the voicebox, and the voice faded slightly each time a sneeze took place, it was, however, still talking all the time. Just another proof (if we had needed it by this time) that Leslie and the voices were independent of one another.

As Sister Maria faded out, Mickey broke in once again to apologise that the power was going and that he would have to leave us. His voice fell away to a whisper as he took his usual parting shot:

'Keep your chins up – double ones as well!'

It was another successful sitting and a good time was had by all. Just over a year later, we were there yet again for a sitting on 29 October. Mickey came with his usual greetings and preliminary chat, before Sister Maria once more charmed us with her mellifluous French accent and told us, among other things, that our helpers were very happy about the circle. She urged us not to lose heart and get despondent but to be patient as they had very great hopes of making regular contact with us in the circle. Not only with the independent voices but also there were high hopes that we would be able to see them in a very solid way (materialisation).

Jock came next, telling us that the spirit team didn't want any changes in the circle – it was going along quite nicely. He too was full of encouragement but he also advised us not to go back to sitting twice a week. As he said: 'Better to be sure of once a week when everybody can be sure of making it, than to be no sure of twice a week.' He was aware of the fact that we had endured a number of disappointments and that, occasionally, we got a little down and despondent about the situation. He also stated, quite accurately, that we'd had a few people let us down over the years. But he was sure that if we stuck together, and were patient enough, with the large amount of power and energy that was being generated in the circle we would be bound to succeed.

Mickey made a few of his usual rude but true remarks about my putting on weight, before telling us of the presence of two Red Indian circle guides, White Feather and White Cloud, commenting on the fact of their being connected. He also spoke later of an Arab helper and an Egyptian who regularly visited our circle. This preceded the longest communication we had ever had from Sir William Crookes, who spoke to us directly. Since the content of his talk was most interesting and informative, and may be of help to other circles, I quote it here in full:

> As a matter of fact, I was waiting for an opportunity to say a few words to you. Mainly because, as you probably well know, there's a whole crowd of souls here who are deeply interested in everything that's happening and are endeavouring to do as best they can from this side of life in regard to your circle and the development. Of course, it's easier perhaps, in a way, for us to say we're doing this and doing that – which of course is true enough. But you're more concerned, and quite rightly so, with the results of the efforts that we're making. From your point of view, sometimes you sit there, and although you're inwardly aware or conscious of our presence,

sometimes it needs a little something or another to happen which you are able to perceive so that it lifts you up – temporarily, anyway.

But the point is that we *are* doing a great deal. Far more than we could explain to you. I mean, there are many things that, quite frankly, one can't put into language – one can't put into words. Things appertaining to our efforts and our work here, and there's no way really that they can be explained. All I can tell you is that the energy and the power which is generated in your little group is of such a nature that it gives us tremendous hope for the future. We are experimenting in various ways. The manifestation of the power of the spirit, I'm quite sure, will show itself to you from time to time and, of course, we're aiming for something quite extraordinary.

Not only the physical side of it from the point of view of the voices and the movement of the trumpet and objects in the room, but also to materialise, which is a much more difficult problem in itself. And the use of the ectoplasm which, for instance today, has been moving around – very much so – which we hope to manipulate and utilise, and to mould so as to make possible the physical apparition, as you would term it, of an individual here and there who is hoping to so manifest.

But it is very difficult to explain these things to people. What we have to do in a technical sense – if I can use that expression, is pretty much almost, you might say, impossible to depict or describe. Because we're dealing with substances and we're also dealing with conditions which are so far removed from your normal experience, and they're not altogether – indeed they're certainly not totally or materially or physically as you'd understand.

I mean, for instance, I come and talk to you. Now you hear what is a voice. You hear to some extent the personality behind that voice. You hear perhaps my method of speech which I hope is more or less understandable and acceptable, and certainly I endeavour – am endeavouring to put over my personality and my old self as I once was when on your side. In other words, there's a combination of several things all happening at once. You see, perhaps you don't realise this, but – well, I'm sure you do really – all communication between our two worlds, whatever form it takes, is of a mental nature and process. If I want to transmit something to you, I have to send out my thought. The vocal aspect of the whole thing is that the ectoplasmic voicebox which is temporarily built up – this is manipulated, but what lies behind it, what you're hearing, are our thoughts – or my thoughts in this case – being transmitted into sound, therefore vibrating your atmosphere.

But what we're doing is, in a sense we're not doing it in a natural way. To some extent, I would have to use the expression 'unnatural'. But what I mean by that is that we are vibrating your atmosphere by the power of our thought and personality. The voicebox, as you term it, will to some extent reproduce a great deal according to the individual's effort. Now some people are hopeless at communication. Some people are quite remarkable. Some people get over not only the message they wish to convey in a verbal sense, or at least it will come to you as a verbal thing, although basically it is obvious that it indeed must be of a mental nature. All communication is a mental process. But the point is that some people will assert themselves in such a way that not only is the content of their message evidential or helpful; but also the personality behind the message is such that even the phraseology that is used, or the method that it is being conveyed in, is such that you immediately recognise a voice as belonging to such and such a person that you may well have known.

Another time, another person who is not very good at it; who is perhaps very nervous and very apprehensive – very sort of concerned – not only will they make such a mess of it that the context of their message may well be lost by the time you receive it. It's not what it was intended to be at all. Also, they have not asserted, or cannot assert, themselves in regard to personality, and you hear, perhaps, what one might almost call a 'flat' voice, which seems to have no personality or no character, in fact has no resemblance whatsoever, in some cases, to the person that you are communicating with that you remember from the past. Of course there again, you can say that when a person's been over here a number of years – as you term time – and they've broken, as it were, their links with the material world, they have made some progress into our higher state of being; although they have remembrance of things past appertaining to their earthly existence. Of course, the links and the ties of love are so strong that they never lose the desire from time to time to return, and come and see how someone they are fond of is getting along and – perhaps even where possible – make a contact and speak or communicate.

But you must remember that, for instance, if your grandmama – she passed at 90 years old – you'd hardly expect or even desire that in the world in which she now finds herself, that she should be physically as she was when she was on earth with all her aches and pains and infirmities! That is purely a material thing. The reality; the soul; the person; the one that you really loved and cared about – though the body had grown worn-out and tired and heaven knows what else, and you were distressed to see all this – yet the personality and the spirit has not aged. And the outer expression of the real self is such that a person will go back – in appearance that is – to the prime of their life. Maybe in the 30s or whatever, and they don't see themselves as perhaps you remember them.

You see, you look at the old faded photographs of some dear old soul that you knew when you were a youngster, and you say, 'That's a picture of my grandmama,' you see. So you attend a seance and, of course, if your grandmama came back as she probably already is on this side – young, full of vitality and utterly, completely different to how you'd imagined her, or from your remembrance of her when you were a child, or from photographs you've seen in an album – you'd immediately say, 'Well, that's not my grandmother.' But if she – as she does when a person enters the material conditions of your world – they exert themselves and their personality, and they endeavour to reinstate themselves temporarily, you might say, into the old self. Sometimes, and more often than not, this is deliberately done for recognition purposes.

But you see that you must never assume that a person, although they have come through at a sitting such as this for instance, and they have given you a very good message or an evidential context in the message appertaining to themselves as you may well remember them, you must not assume that because of that, that is exactly how they are in their own happy environment over here. If you really love a person, the last thing you would want is for them in their old age to be old over here, with all the infirmities, or the consciousness of those infirmities, clinging to them. You know, it's an interesting thing – and I wish you could see this – when people come here, how they throw, you might say to some extent, overboard – even in the early initial stages of their coming – many aspects of the old self.

Sometimes these may be parts of, as it were, their preconceived notions and ideas that they've discarded. And you get some of these very religious people – this may sound very odd to you – but it's perfectly true. Some of the people who perhaps, in a sense find it most difficult to settle in the initial stages are people who have got very strong religious convictions. They often assume – possibly or rather obviously because of their very strong views in the religious sense – that they are in a sense rather privileged or special people. And you even get some who really quite genuinely are waiting for the day of resurrection. And they live in a kind of state of mind and, you see, that's another thing you must remember. With every individual, whether in your world or whether in this, to a great extent, it's just a matter of state of mind. If you think on a certain level, if you follow a certain path, whether it's religious or whatever it happens to be, you will be so affected by that that it will become your state of being. It will be your state of thought. And you don't necessarily always shake that off immediately when you pass out from your world into this.

You get earthbound souls, for instance. They're not necessarily as some people surmise; that they're necessarily very bad people, or evil people. Of course, you do occasionally get a person who has not made any progress, and hasn't a particular desire to make any progress. You may get someone who is very earthbound, and indeed on rare occasions, certain souls are brought to a circle such as yours for help. Because sometimes they're so much nearer to the material side of things that often they can be helped in the initial early stages more by people in your world than people in ours. But that's another aspect altogether.

Your circle is not a rescue circle but that doesn't mean to say there have not been the rare occasions when someone has entered into your auric emanation – that's the best way I can put this – you see, that's another thing. When you sit together, there's not only a blending, as it were, of your personalities. Not only a blending of your attitudes of mind. It's not only a blending of the desire to achieve and to accomplish things of a spiritual or a psychic nature. It's not just even what it may sometimes seem. It's much more involved than that. If you could see the auric – and I use this expression auric – emanation which is built up in your circle, and which is composed fundamentally of individual auric emanations; because even when you are closely linked and working together as a circle, which at its best is a wonderful auric state of being for us to work with and through, and so on; but the point is, that you are still individuals, of course – and I don't want to say anything that might be misinterpreted or misunderstood – but I know that you are sometimes, at times – individually at times, anyway, under some stress.

I'm not saying this happens very often. But there are times when a person can arrive at a circle full of enthusiasm, of course; but something has marred, or happened during the day which has caused a certain amount of irritation, or some distress. And it's not the easiest thing, of course, always to shake it off. You know you're due at the sitting at a certain time and you wouldn't miss it for anything. You arrive and you settle down, and you're full of hope. But there may be something very mundane or very ordinary, which has caused a certain change in the auric emanation of an individual. And if this happens, as it does and can happen sometimes in two or three people, then it *can* have a detrimental effect.

I wish I could explain this more fully. But you see, we depend – well of course we absolutely *do* depend – on each one of you. Individually and collectively. You are creating the conditions under which we will endeavour to do the work that we have set our hearts on doing. You know, this is where mediums can take some credit – and I don't wish to give a wrong impression here – but what I'm trying to say is, of course, in a sense: the less the medium interferes, whether it is consciously or unconsciously with his or her mediumship, the better that mediumship will be. I suppose the art of good mediumship is to cut yourself adrift from it. Let us – that is, we on this side – take over. Let *us* utilise to the best of our ability. And the less you assert yourselves; the less you intrude on what is happening or what we are trying to do, the better that mediumship will be.

Of course, then you do get mediums – I regret to say some – who are very bumptious, and really think they are, well, the kingpin. Which in a sense, I suppose one might say, yes, well to a point that's true. But if they assert themselves and take a lot of the – sort of – glory, as it were, then that is detrimental. Do you understand? [Leslie Flint sneezed here and the voice asked, 'Have you got a cold?']

When I was on your side, I had a great interest in this whole business, you know. I studied it and I experienced a great deal one way and another – good, bad and indifferent! [At this point

I asked who he was and he confirmed his name.] Crookes here! I suppose you've seen some of those photographs that were taken in my heyday? [We agreed that we had – mainly some of the 44 remarkable photographs that were taken of the materialised form of Katie King, through the mediumship of Florence Cook.] Well, of course, she was a remarkable instrument. Marvellous medium, you know. And, of course, like all mediums, they're under all sorts of influences – good, bad and indifferent. And that's another thing I might one day be going into detail about, I think.

I do think – I'm not expecting too much from anyone – but do think it's vitally important for everyone to realise, of course, that you will not take out of the circle, or for that matter anything else until, to the best of your ability, you put quite a lot in. You know, it's an extraordinary thing. I've been to these circles, various circles, at different times. And I'm interested in all the groups that may be sitting and hoping, and developing and goodness knows what else. But there's no doubt about it; there are occasionally sitters, and sometimes the whole circle for that matter, who frankly – I don't think they realise it, but they are not going to achieve very much. One hates to admit it, because, after all's said and done, if a group of people are prepared to give up their time and sit regularly week in and week out, month in and month out, and they are sincere in their aspect and their attitude; one could only assume and hope that things would go well, and things would happen and transpire, and that development would take place. Which, of course, invariably it does. But there are occasions when one has to admit to oneself that there is something radically wrong.

And if you try to tell – given the opportunity to come through and talk to them – tell them about some of the errors, I won't say errors of their ways exactly but of course motive is an important factor. But if they are going to sit there and think, 'Oh dear, I should be developing this,' or 'I should be developing that,' and if everyone sat thinking on the lines that it's an individual development, or an individual thing. I'm not suggesting that it isn't in a sense a good thing to hope to develop oneself in a certain way. When you've been given some experience or other. Perhaps you've had the good fortune or otherwise – whichever way you look at it – of having gone to different mediums, or been at various demonstrations where a medium has picked you out and said, 'You know, my friend, my guide tells me this, that and t'other.' Well, no one's destroying the message – at least that is not my intention – but what I'm trying to get at is this. Whatever you may have been told, whether it's individually or collectively, you must realise that if you're going to make any real headway at all, you've got to – to some extent – lose identity.

You've got to lose the 'I am'. You know, this is a tragedy with a lot of mediums. Even those who, perhaps over a period of a long time, have developed something unique – a form of mediumship – they do get this unfortunate state of mind where they think that they are really the ones who are responsible for everything. Which in a sense – looking at it from a material level – I suppose you could say it's true enough. But you must *lose* yourself to *find* yourself. What I'm trying to say here is that, if you want to find your true self, if you want to do the work of the spirit, if you want to be an instrument of the spirit – the less conscious you are of yourself, the more you are inclined to let yourself disappear, even though it's only temporary, during a demonstration or whatever it is, the more accurate your mediumship is going to be.

The more satisfactory it's going to be the less you intrude, and the less you get in the way; the less you have your own opinions – and sometimes these are very strong ones – impinging themselves on that which is endeavouring to be done by your guide or guides, or helpers – whatever they are. You must not intrude. Try to stay out of the picture when you sit together in the circle, as best you can. Completely relax. Don't sort of force any issues, or have any too strong a view. Just say, 'Well, here we are; we're all here together as one. In one accord together, in love and in harmony. Do with us as you will. Do whatever it is that you feel you can do, that will benefit not just us, but perhaps who knows in the future? Many will be helped, guided, uplifted and inspired by that which we have endeavoured.'

And you know, the tragedy of this, in a sense, is very true. There are certain mediums that I have known, who have developed unique mediumship over perhaps a very long period. And some rare cases, after a number of years, have been well on the way to losing their mediumship – because they have allowed themselves to become rather bumptious – rather stupid. Sort of elevating themselves, although this is not necessarily always their fault. Sometimes, some of the people who attend the sessions, the meetings, the seances boost the medium, and they put the medium on a pedestal. Well, I'm not going to say that's a bad thing in a sense – but it is a very stupid thing, because the medium must remember and must realise that they are the channel. They are the individual who has been given the wonderful gift of the spirit. Admittedly, they have worked on it. They have given, and to some extent they have no doubt sacrificed to become that instrument, to serve and to help humanity. But it is true – the less the medium has to do with their mediumship, the better that mediumship will be. And to cut yourself out isn't the easiest thing. I know there are mediums who go on the platform or wherever it is, they are demonstrating and unconsciously, in certain instances, they intrude. But the less they know, the less they are conscious of themselves. It's when they hear themselves saying certain things and they start to analyse it. They find themselves in a state of mind where they are saying to themselves whilst they're giving out, 'Oh dear, what is it?' They begin to doubt themselves – and of course, there *is* a human element – a natural thing.

Obviously, sometimes you cannot always differentiate between what may be coming from yourselves, or from some outside force or some influence or other. It's not until the message perhaps to some extent has been accepted or delivered that you can with any certainty be sure what you've received is correct. But, of course, we're now talking in a sense, more on a mental level, of mental mediumship. My main purpose in coming to you, my main interest, is that I do realise that you have a wonderful physical power. There is a tremendous amount of living energy which makes possible the use of ectoplasm, which is drawn from various – well, in fact everyone makes to some extent a contribution.

Admittedly some, perhaps more than another. But that's not important in a sense. It's what we achieve that matters. Not who supplies. And you do get, sometimes, people in circles who have perhaps an inflated idea of their own importance. Sometimes it's not their fault. Sometimes it's been given to them through some mediums – or perhaps it may be that they have got this idea into their head that they are the kingpin. Well, in a sense, this is all understandable, and I'm not condemning or condoning, but what I'm trying to say here is: even if you are aware; even if you are conscious of the fact that you are *the* instrument, as it were – don't let it disturb you unduly and certainly don't let it prejudice you.

> Don't assume too much. Because where would you be in your development if it were not for the rest of the company? Those who are making all your development a reality and a possibility. I suppose really, when you get down to the basics, what I am really trying to say in a nutshell is that mediums should have humility. Of course we are all proud of them; we are glad of them, and we are conscious of their sacrifices, particularly in the early stages, for the sake of their developments, etc., etc. We know that there is a great responsibility placed upon their shoulders. We know all the complexities but I do think it is so important for people to realise that if their mediumship is going to be of real value – it can only be of real value when they themselves cease to intrude upon their development. Or even when they have achieved some success, they must not be allowed to intrude upon the work that they are endeavouring to do – or rather what is being done through them. In other words, do your best, to the best of your ability! But don't make it too obvious. Don't allow yourself to become intense about it. Be patient. Sit together in love and in harmony, and just – well wait for us to move, and do the work of the spirit.

A long speech, I must confess. But what Sir William Crookes had to say was very important to aspiring circles and mediums and it will, I hope, also explain certain aspects of communication more fully and life in the spirit world.

Following this major message, there was a short visit by a Frenchman, Maurice, who was already very conversant with the work of our circle and offered encouragement, as he spoke in the independent voice. A Chinese guide, Ling, made himself known to us, and the seance was rounded off by a short but succinct communication by Elizabeth Garrett Anderson before Mickey, as MC, offered his usual farewell.

The sitting had been a wonderful success.

# GROWTH OF THE ISM HOME CIRCLE LINK

THROUGHOUT THE LATTER part of 1981 and into 1982, my connection with the ISM continued apace, both at a national and local level through the Romford branch of which I was now chairman. It is true to say that I had learned a lot about committees and committee-meeting procedure from my experiences as mediumship secretary of the new Woodford National Spiritualist Church but it was at, and through, the committee meetings of the ISM Executive, the Romford branch of the ISM and the ISM Link of Home Circles that I really served my apprenticeship in relation to formal meetings. The knowledge and experience gained here was indeed to stand me in good stead for my future psychic work, as you will see later.

Since I worked as a representative in my daily life, and thus had the opportunity to visit many and varied parts of the UK in the course of my work, I took the trouble to spend a little time during my evenings away in distributing information leaflets about the new ISM Home Circle Link, leaving them with local Spiritualist Churches and psychic organisations who I felt would be interested in the advice and help the Link had to offer and, while church circles as such could not themselves register with the Link, most of the people who attended the churches knew of home circles locally who were eligible.

Reading back through my diary of 1981, I am quite amazed – with all the leaflets I distributed – that I ever had time to do my normal work!

The main thing was, however, that my efforts, and those of other Link committee members to achieve some publicity for the new venture, paid off. The Link had been launched amidst a blaze of publicity in the *Psychic News*, at that time edited by the well known Maurice Barbanell. He had been happy to give us lead stories over a period of time in his newspaper and this ensured that we got off to a good start, with up-to-date news about the Link and its progress staying, as it were, on the crest of a wave for some time.

The original Link Association of Home Circles had been set up by Noah Zerdin and 11 colleagues on Saturday, 25 April 1931, to help with the development of phenomena within home circles, and to exchange news, views and useful information between its member circles. The organisation was very successful. Its founders had envisaged an association of perhaps some 25 circles exchanging reports but, by October 1933, it boasted membership of no less than 156 circles!

On occasions, the Link Association would organise a mass seance for physical phenomena and one of these, which is well documented, was held as part of its third annual conference, with over 300 people present, on 15 October 1933. (I am in possession of a photograph of all the participants in this 'Great Experiment' which was described in detail in Link Booklet No. 1, published in 1934.) The direct-voice seance was very successful, under the brilliant physical mediumship of Mrs A. E. Perriman.

Various instructional booklets and leaflets very quickly became a feature of the original Link and, as a consequence, many a home circle was able to form and achieve spectacular results through the association. It was not long into the life of the new ISM Home Circle Link before a number of similar instructional teaching booklets were written by Eileen Roberts and distributed to the registered circles to help them on their way. The *Circle Link,* voice of the ISM organisation, also contained a useful question and answer section which addressed the most common queries about home-circle work.

Its first issue contained, amongst other things, a message of encouragement from Mr Daniel B. Zerdin, son of Noah:

> There is no doubt that the Spiritualist's primary and secondary school is the home circle. In it the beginner learns the ABC of communication with the spirit world. Probably the first lesson is that it doesn't happen overnight! It is often a slow, sometimes boring business, and he can sit there, week in and week out, wondering if he couldn't be doing something more useful – like

watching the telly! Nobody raps, the table remains obstinately still and the only movement of the trumpet (does anyone still use a trumpet, I wonder?) is when someone stretches a leg and knocks it over. And yet, the chances are that something *is* happening and, provided you have the right blend of sitters – which means that they all harmonise, which in turn is sometimes like asking for the moon – within a few months some kind of manifestation will occur.

Slowly, ever so slowly, one sitter (possibly two) may start to show signs of mediumship. Nourish the symptoms but don't worship the sitter, or his subconscious will colour whatever happens in direct proportion to the swelling of his head. He needs the circle as much as the circle needs him and he must be discouraged from rushing out and setting up shop as a medium on his own account. It is then that the real work of the circle can begin – when, that is, some kind of communication is established.

When my father, Noah Zerdin, founded the Link Association of Home Circles in the early 1930s, his aim was to spread the knowledge of the reality of Survival throughout Britain and beyond. In its heyday, the Link boasted several hundred home circles flourishing in many parts of the world. They were the backbone of the Movement and it was no accident that in the 1930s and 1940s the standard of public mediumship, particularly physical mediumship, reached its peak.

The world today lies sorely in need of the message of Survival before it blows itself to bits and we all discover the truth the hard way. For this we need first rate mediums who are developed strongly enough to convince the sceptics. They will come only from a strong Home Circle Movement. I am sure my father would support Eileen Roberts in her efforts to rekindle this vital spark, and he would surely give a cheer at the number of Home Circles already under your umbrella; knowing his deep commitment to the Movement, he may well have been one of the unseen instigators himself!

The ISM Home Circle Link continued to grow. By March 1982, when the second issue of the *Circle Link* was published, the number of registered circles all over the world had swollen to 76. In April, the ISM weekend study course (an annual event for the parent organisation) was dedicated to the study of home circles. Sandra and I attended for the whole weekend and the event proved most enlightening, as well as providing an excellent opportunity for members of the Link and the ISM generally to get to know one another socially.

The next step was to organise an annual conference for members of Link-registered circles and the first of these took place on 5 June 1982 at the London Spiritual Mission, Pembridge Place, London W2. The day was extremely hot and humid but, despite the outside temperature, the event was successfully conducted by Eileen Roberts, who was happy to share her considerable experience with the euphoric Link members, all of whom were proud to be a part of this historic occasion. We need have had no worries about the members' enthusiasm. They came from far and wide to attend this conference in London, and I remember with great pleasure welcoming members who had hired a minibus and driven all the way down from Lancashire especially for the occasion.

That particular party was made up of members of a very privileged circle who were regularly enjoying materialisation seances through the brilliant physical mediumship of Frank Havard. Frank himself attended with his wife, along with his brother Eddie and sister-in-law – all staunch and loyal members of his remarkable circle. It was the start of a beautiful but brief friendship, as Frank and I had similar interests and he was an extremely pleasant and dedicated person. However, fate was to step in before I had the chance to sit with him. A few weeks after the first Link conference, Frank unexpectedly passed to spirit himself, and was sadly missed.

At the conference, he described the early days of his circle and how, after just a few sittings, a materialised head had appeared to all the sitters, wearing a cap, and carried on a conversation with them. From that day onwards the circle started its development proper but it was to be many more months before any other such spectacular and encouraging phenomena took place. The first experience, as often happens with physical circles, was a dramatic 'carrot' from the spirit people to ensure that the sitters kept themselves together as a group and continued their development to the point where good and evidential physical materialisation phenomena took place on a regular basis.

The conference was reported in issue No. 3 of the *Circle Link*, published in August of 1982, and by now containing an extra 4 pages.

Future editions of this publication were from then on issued every four months, instead of the six-monthly period between the first three issues. By August, the Link had 89 registered circles on its books.

At this time, having been involved with physical circles for a number of years, I had been fortunate enough to acquire a lot of specialist knowledge on physical mediumship and its phenomena. In August, when a scheduled speaker at a local ISM meeting failed to turn up, I reluctantly agreed to give a talk on physical mediumship, past and present. For me, this first lecture was a knee-knocking experience. I had not learned much about lecture techniques and I dried up after a half hour or so. I remedied the situation, however, by inviting questions from the floor. Since I had a lot of knowledge on the subject, I found the questions comparatively easy to answer, and it was not long before I actually began to enjoy myself.

The result of this first talk was that I was booked by medium Olive Giles to give another lecture at the North Kent branch of the ISM, which she ran. This was obviously much better prepared than my first effort and the talk (on physical mediumship – what else?) was repeated the following January at the Potters Bar branch, run by John and Peggy Goodwin. This was altogether a new development for me but I have drawn on these early experiences for the lectures which now undertake regularly.

The fourth issue of the *Circle Link* reported in December 1982 that we had almost reached the magic figure of 100 registered circles. During the past year there had been a number of visits by Link committee members to assess the progress of member circles and I had accompanied Eileen Roberts on some of these. Instructional booklets that had been written and distributed that year had definitely helped many circles to progress and it was planned to conduct a survey of registered circles early in 1983 to see what was happening and where.

This survey revealed that the Link had under its umbrella all manner and sorts of psychic home circles. Most were of course, run as mental mediumship development circles, although there were a few physical circles scattered amongst the rest, as well as circles for healing work – and very specialist circles for 'rescue' work. (Not to be recommended unless the members of such a circle know exactly what they are doing and are physically strong enough to restrain those spirit entities who may be disturbed and on occasions could even be violent while controlling the medium. They need 'rescuing' and counselling by sympathetic and experienced circle members to overcome their problems and make progress in the spirit world.)

The Harold Wood circle was very proud of the fact that its membership registration number within the ISM Home Circle Link was circle No. 1, although its own development went in fits and starts during this particular period, and we never quite managed to achieve that spectacular ongoing phenomenon that we had enjoyed in the Romford circle.

By April 1983, more than 100 home circles had registered with the organisation, and things were looking very healthy. At the end of this same month, the ISM once again ran its annual study weekend at Down Hall, near Hatfield Heath in Hertfordshire, and since the theme for the weekend was physical phenomena and as Sandra and I were Link committee members, we were in the forefront of the action.

May of 1983 saw the second annual conference of the Home Circle Link, once again held at the London Spiritual Mission. It was well attended by members and every bit as successful as the first conference the previous year.

1983 was certainly a good year for the Link. I was privileged to meet a number of Finnish Link members when, in the course of my work (I worked for a sales agency selling Finnish paper in the UK) I made a routine visit to Finland, and was able to stay on over the weekend to talk to and advise these very pleasant people.

On a holiday visit to Israel later in the year, Sandra and I also had the opportunity to meet and talk to the main sitters in an Israeli member circle. They were lovely people and made us most welcome. We returned the compliment when one of the sitters and her husband visited the UK the following year.

In July, we decided that we would have the holiday of a lifetime and, along with another couple who were sitting in our circle at the time, we planned a three-week trip to Israel and Egypt for September. In view of the fact that I spent my fortieth birthday amongst the tombs in the Valley of the Kings, near Luxor, it also turned out to be very memorable. Before we got to Egypt, we had been given the telephone number of a psychic society in Cairo who welcomed visitors and, as a consequence, when I spoke to the gentleman who ran the society, we were invited to meet a number of the members at one of their regular events – a development circle in the Cairo suburbs. I must confess that none of us were quite sure what to expect on that visit – and wondered if perhaps it was an omen that the taxi driver could not find the address for what seemed an eternity. But we did eventually arrive to discover the people involved to be wonderful hosts. They even insisted on cooking us a meal before we left.

Although the setting was not quite what we were used to, the circle itself was a worthwhile experience and not too different from the average development circle back home, although the participants were all real characters in their own right, and we made some outstanding friends, despite the fact that most of them, with the exception of our host, could not speak a word of English, so that much of the conversation during the evening was conducted in sign language. As I remember it, the circle was held in darkness but with the curtains flapping at the open window in the breeze. Sandra and the other lady who was with us took off their shoes for the sitting and felt little furry animals running over their feet during the whole duration of the circle. Only this time, we were all pretty sure that these mice and/or other creatures were not materialisations, but the real thing.

On this same holiday, in Israel, Sandra and I also had the opportunity to meet and talk to the two main members of a Link registered circle in Tel Aviv (this meeting had been arranged some time in advance) which was an extremely enjoyable experience too, and the lady leader of the circle entertained us royally. Since we had been in contact with these people by letter, in this case for a couple of years, we felt that we already knew them well. It was therefore quite a thrill to meet them face to face, and to discuss psychic matters with people of like mind in such a far-off country. Although I resigned from the ISM National Executive Committee later in 1983, due to pressure of work and the inability to attend meetings regularly, the involvement of Sandra and Myself with the Link continued for about four years, by which time the organisation was well and truly established, with some 200 home circles involved. In 1985, Sandra and I were running our own meetings on a regular basis in a Scout Hall at Harold Wood. These were popular non-religious clairvoyant demonstrations to introduce the subject to members of the general public, and all of this was in addition to my necessarily more important commitment to my fulltime work. The mixture of all these activities took up a great deal of time and effort and since the local branch of the ISM and the now well-established Home Circle Link were both running smoothly without any problems, we retired from both committees to concentrate our efforts elsewhere, although we did continue as registered members of the Link until our Harold Wood physical home circle broke up in 1986.

Aspiring 'Likely Lad'. Robin Foy, 2nd from left, at RAF Hornchurch Aircrew Selection Centre – June 1960.

Newly commissioned
Pilot Officer Foy, aged 18.
Early 1962.

Elmer J. (Bill) Browne – leader of the author's first physical circle. Photograph by courtesy of Psychic News. Date unknown.

Outstanding independent voice medium Leslie Flint, aged about 50. Photograph by Bram Rogers – actual date unknown.

Robin and wife Sandra on their wedding day – April 1979.

The Harold Wood house where Robin and Sandra held their own physical home circle for many years.

The late Mrs Maud Gunning of Westcliff-on-Sea. In her day, she was a remarkable materialisation medium. Photgraph by Robin Foy, 1980.

Interior of the new Woodford National Spiritualist Church, February 1981, looking towards the rear of the building. The author was the mediums' secretary of the church at this time.

Trumpet direct voice medium Geoffrey Jacobs, 1981 – as the author knew him – shortly before he passed into spirit.

The author in Egypt, September 1983. Posing by the Sphinx as his father had done fifty years previously in the 1930s.

Physical medium Leslie Flint, as Robin and Sandra best knew him later in life during the 1970s and 1980s. Exact date unknown.

The author's friend Archie (left) and other roommates on the Arthur Findlay College physical mediumship week, Stansted Hall – April 1984. Photograph by Robin Foy.

Physical medium Colin Fry, also known as 'Lincoln', early 1994. Photograph by courtesy of Psychic News.

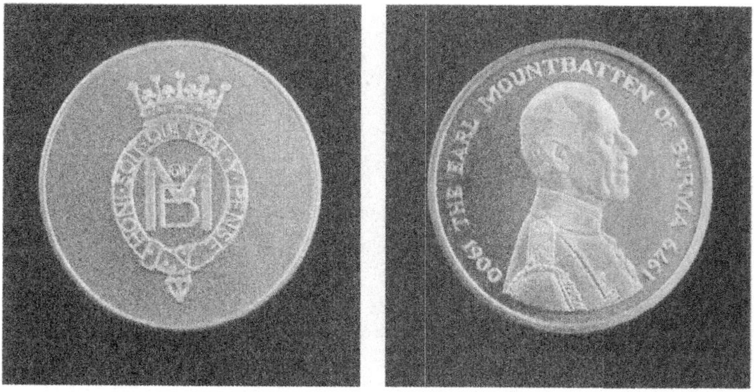


The two sides of the apported memorial medallion received during a special experimental sitting with physical mediums Stewart Alexander and 'Lincoln' in the Scole cellar – 30th May 1994.

Robin and Sandra Foy's current home and location of the Scole cellar, which today is the scene of wonderful physical phenomena every week during sittings of the Scole Experimental Group.

A recent view of the interior of the specially converted Scole cellar. The dome in the centre of the table is where the spirit 'team' store the creative spiritual energy they use for the production of spectacular physical phenomena.

'Lincoln' (seated centre), with other members of the 'Swift' home circle, Gaunts House, near Wimborne, Dorset – May 1992. He had just been presented with an engraved tankard by the committee of the Noah's Ark Society as thanks for his mediumistic services.

# THIS AND THAT

THE HAROLD WOOD circle, in the meantime, was making only slow progress. Following the sitting we had enjoyed with Leslie Flint earlier in 1981, we cut out one of the two circles per week we were then running. It was, however, a difficult year for the circle in that there were constant problems with the harmony of the sitters. Some sitters left, and were replaced by others, some of whom were not really suitable. Sometimes John and/or Joyce from Romford would attend, and sometimes they would not. When they did, we were always optimistic that we would get some phenomena, but it was not always the case, and our sittings around this time were all 'hit and miss'. Even without our Romford friends we often had movement and levitation of trumpets, plaques, table, tambourine and water bowl. But there was no sustained pattern to these phenomena. We would get them for a couple of sittings and then nothing for weeks on end. We occasionally got whispers, raps, taps and thumps around the room and the odd word or two of independent voice when John and Joyce were there. But the phenomena generally showed no real sign of developing into a regular thing.

As 1981 slipped quietly into 1982, little changed. Early in the year, a series of sittings which included John and Joyce produced some results. There were the usual independent voices but no sustained conversations. On one occasion, we were told that a materialised rabbit scampered round the room. (We could hear it and feel it as it ran through our legs and over our feet, but since we were still sitting in total darkness, we were unable to see it.) On a subsequent evening we were aware of the beating of the wings of a large bird, which had apparently been materialised, as it flew around the room.

February of 1982 showed more promise, however, as a sitting on 8 February, which included John and Joyce, produced several short independent voices, as well as a long conversation in this fashion with Sir William Crookes. Jock and Winnie also managed to speak at some length. I was touched by solid materialised fingers on my left knee and Sandra was aware of ectoplasm pouring down her front. This exuded a typical strong, musty smell which was apparent to us all, and a heavier animal than previously – possibly a dog – was heard scampering around the room.

The sitting on the following Monday was also excellent and, of course, we all started to get excited again about the circle. But it was not to continue. John and Joyce, for whatever reason, decided to pull out of the circle for good – something that seemed to happen all too frequently with John as soon as we got close to a good and positive sustainable result. We never sat with them again and shortly afterwards they left Romford to live in Lincolnshire.

As you might imagine, this left us with somewhat of a problem in the short term and we closed the circle for a few weeks to take stock and change sitters once again. When we restarted once more in March, things went very slowly, although psychic power could be felt building up in the customary coldness. There was often a smell of ectoplasm but we had little happening, other than the odd touch by a materialised hand.

By the end of April, a reasonable harmony seemed to have built up between the new sitters. We were getting the odd flashes of light. Most of us were touched, and we had raps, clicks and lip-smacking noises indicating the presence of our spirit friends. Once again, a small animal was felt scampering round the circle room. In May we had gone forward again, as a few words of independent voice were heard by all. One of the sitters had his trouser legs pulled by a solid spirit hand; lights were seen. Raps, clicks and voices, plus the strong smell of ectoplasm were witnessed by all.

As the year wore on, the results waned once more, and we seemed to be back at square one. We brought in one or two new sitters, and frequently changed our positions in the seance room to try and overcome the stalemate situation we found ourselves in but to little avail during the summertime sittings. We suspended the circle over the holiday period, with the intention of resuming it at the end of August, when we felt that we could approach the circle once more with a fresh attitude, and maybe go forward again.

Fortunately, that is precisely what happened. During the first sitting we attempted on 30 August Sandra felt solid rods and sheets of ectoplasm attached to her. This was accompanied by the now familiar smell, extreme coldness, clicking, rapping and lip-smacking noises. As the group sang one particular rousing song, a spirit person was heard stomping their feet in time to the music, so loudly that it was heard clearly in the room below.

Interestingly, when Sandra had been at home on her own on several occasions over the previous two weeks, she had heard footsteps and other noises around the house. After this first sitting following the break, the circle did quieten down for a while, but there was another excellent sitting on Monday, 27 September 1982, when we had all the phenomena witnessed at the August sitting, plus whistles, hissing noises, and the sound of a watch being wound up.

The next morning, after breakfast, Sandra felt psychically compelled to return to the kitchen. Normally her daughter's pet hamster was sitting in his locked cage, high up on top of an old fridge/freezer. This morning, however, the hamster was running loose on a kitchen worktop, three feet below that. As she returned the animal to its cage, Sandra realised that the cage was still locked. There was no possible way it could have escaped by itself from a locked cage, or even got on to the work surface without sustaining major injury to itself, but there it was, happily playing. This was obviously a bit of a mystery to us, but we solved it the very next week.

After the circle on 5 October, which itself proved very lively, we went downstairs to discover that the hamster was no longer there! Its cage was again empty and there was no sign of it anywhere. For any stranger walking in at that moment, it would have made quite an amusing sight, with all the sitters on their hands and knees, searching the lounge and the hall for the hamster, but the search was in vain. No sight or sound of the hamster was discovered, despite a very thorough search. Sandra suggested that it must have been dematerialised and been taken somewhere by the spirit people, so she went into the kitchen and asked them out loud to bring the animal back, as she knew that its full disappearance would upset her daughter.

Then followed the most amazing thing! In full light, and in full sight of Sandra, the hamster reappeared on the work surface he had been found on before. Sandra described the experience as being just like the 'Beam me up, Scotty' sequence in the science fiction series *Star Trek*. One moment there was nothing there, then a faint shimmering outline appeared, gradually becoming more and more solid – first transparent, then translucent, then opaque, and finally quite solid. The animal did not seem any worse for its experience and lived quite a long life afterwards.

Prior to this happening – the evening before – the whole circle had had the opportunity of sitting in at a demonstration of apport phenomena which was held at Grays Church, Essex. The personable young medium involved was well known to the president of the church, who for a long time had helped him develop his gift, and on many occasions the church president has himself testified to the wonderful phenomena he witnessed over a long period of time through this mediumship, including seeing sheets of ectoplasm hanging from the ceiling. I know this church president personally and can vouch for his own integrity. Later on in his career, the young physical medium was to be the subject of controversy, and to have accusations of fraud levelled at him through the pages of a national newspaper. I can only speak for the one occasion that we sat with him but can state quite categorically that I am convinced to this day that what we witnessed could only have been genuine.

The sitters, some 20 in all, sat in a semi-circle around the medium. The sitting took place in darkness but we were instructed by the medium's guide that when the medium, who was walking around in trance, squeezed the hand of a specific sitter, that sitter was to call out 'Lights!' – at which point the subdued room lighting was to be switched on momentarily so that all sitters could witness the arrival of an apport from the medium's mouth. The sitting started with the entranced medium's guide speaking about philosophy and there was a display of small 'spirit lights' around the medium's face and mouth.

Then the apport phenomena began. Several of the sitters called out 'Lights!' at various times in the sitting and the subsequent room lights revealed the medium, standing open-mouthed as a number of apports appeared in his mouth, falling out into the cupped hands of the particular sitter. The items were mainly flowers but one sitter, who was coughing badly, was informed by the guide, 'Something for your hoarse throat!' as he watched a horse chestnut (conker) mysteriously appear from the medium's throat.

Then it was my turn. When I felt my hands squeezed, I called out the customary instruction and the lights came on immediately. I could see that there was nothing in the medium's mouth but then I suddenly saw a dark red rose form in front of my very eyes and drop out on to my outstretched hand! Shortly afterwards, another sitter received two separate roses on separate stems (albeit of the same variety). He was instructed to examine these and as I was sitting next to him, I also had the opportunity to examine them well. The medium then put these two stems and two roses back into his mouth. A split second later the two roses re-emerged, but *joined together* and growing naturally on *one stem!* Needless to say, both the sitter and I examined the roses quite closely again and we were absolutely certain that they were exactly the same roses.

As a finale at the end of the sitting, we were told that something would be brought for those few sitters who had not been fortunate enough to receive an apport earlier. As the lights went on at the end, I watched in amazement as I saw about twenty blooms materialise in mid-air about a foot below the ceiling, and drop to the floor. There were tales amongst church members present at Grays of previous occasions when locked cars and coat pockets in the cloakroom (under lock and key) had been discovered to be full of apported fruit at the end of similar seances.

This same week that we had the second incident with the hamster, there were other signs of activity around the house. Some days earlier, a new tube of toothpaste had gone missing in the house without explanation. At the end of the week it appeared again, back in its original place under the sink, and still in its new packaging. There was the sound of footsteps on various occasions, both in the light of daytime and at night – heard by all of us. We also had the distinct sound of marbles being played on the wooden stairs and lots of unexplained raps and taps in the house at all times. There was certainly a lot of psychic power around and we were hopeful that it would transfer itself into the group, so that we could enjoy lots of good physical phenomena but our hopes were once again short-lived, as the circle went quiet for several weeks afterwards.

In fact, despite our dedication in sitting regularly, we never did achieve much more in the Harold Wood circle than we were getting towards the end of 1982. As before, the harmony varied considerably between good and pretty awful. It was never 'excellent'. There were times when we got so fed up with our poor progress after the wonderful results we had earlier enjoyed, that we suspended the circle for a few months to try to recapture the enthusiasm and vitality of the sitters.

We were continuing meanwhile with the local clairvoyant meetings which we took pride in organising ourselves at the Harold Wood Kingsland Scout Hall and since we took care only to book mediums of excellent standard, whom we knew personally or who had been recommended by word of mouth, we always managed to get a full hall. Through these monthly meetings, many people who might otherwise never have come into contact with psychic matters were able to learn much of the basics of mental mediumship and communication with the spirit world. We placed a lot of emphasis on showing the public that such things were quite natural and involved nothing to be frightened of. Many who did attend went on to become involved in other aspects of psychic work.

We also believed, rightly or wrongly, that there were not enough opportunities at that time within other psychic organisations for social gatherings and get-togethers for people of like mind to swap stories and experiences; so the members of the Harold Wood circle resolved to do something about that. It was decided that we should hire a large hall and put on a half-day event, with three mediums demonstrating clairvoyance/clairaudience in the afternoon combined with a dance and social event in the evening, at Kim's Hall, Hornchurch, Essex on 22 January. The tickets, which we sold to the general public for a nominal amount (we weren't looking to make a huge profit), were snapped up very quickly indeed. The demonstrations, by the late Arthur Clarke of Hornchurch and two other local mediums, were extremely evidential and successful, and the 'knees up' hosted by a lively DJ went down a treat. We hoped that we might be able to repeat the success by putting on more events like it, but regrettably, we never had the chance.

We continued to visit Leslie Flint from time to time to renew our inspiration, usually getting excellent independent voice seances there, and spent many an hour around this time having private sittings with various clairvoyant and clairaudient mediums, which had the same morale-boosting effect. There was constant encouragement in both ways for our involvement with physical mediumship and its phenomena. So whilst the Harold Wood circle seemed to have very little hope of reaching its full potential, we never actually gave up hope that eventually, somewhere, somehow, in some way, shape or form, it would all come together, to provide for us the cream of physical phenomena on a regular basis. Our faith has since been rewarded many times over!

In April 1984, I had the opportunity to take up a cancelled booking for a place on the trance and physical phenomena week at Stansted Hall and since it was in a four-bedded room for men, Sandra was unable to accompany me. I was glad, however, that I had gone, as I had the chance to have my trance work assessed favourably by Gordon Higginson, the principal of the Arthur Findley College. As well as making a number of good friends, some of whom I am still in touch with to this day, I did learn an awful lot about trance and physical phenomena that I had not previously known and as was the custom during such weeks, the course culminated in a mass seance for physical phenomena, with Gordon Higginson as the physical medium.

Gordon wore a simple black top and pair of trousers and prior to the sitting, at his own request, underwent a strip search in another room by two of the male sitters, who were able to testify that nothing of a fraudulent nature had been found during this procedure. They then led him back into the darkened library at Stansted Hall where the assembled delegates were already sitting (some 70 people in all). At the front of the room stood a 'cabinet' – a three-sided box of plywood, about six feet tall and four feet square. The front of the cabinet had a curtain across it which was drawn back at first, so that the interior could be seen. It contained only the medium's chair. Slightly in front and on top of the cabinet was a dull red light, shining downwards, which gave off sufficient illumination for sitters to dimly make out what was happening at the front of the cabinet.

The medium took his place in the cabinet as the sitters (who were placed in a sort of horseshoe formation around it) started to sing lively and well-known party-style songs. As I recall, it was not long before the medium (who had drawn the curtain across the front of the cabinet) went into full trance and his guides (an Irishman named Paddy and a little girl called Cuckoo) began to speak to the sitters. It was explained that they hoped to show us a display of ectoplasm (one aspect of physical phenomena that I had not previously had the chance to witness), and with it to build up one or more materialised forms.

Half an hour or so into the sitting, a pool of dazzling blue-white substance (despite the red light shining on to it from above, which should have reflected red under normal circumstances, the colour of the substance remained this same blue-white, and the impression I gained was that it was almost self-luminous) began to spread outwards into the room from under the curtain. I was watching visible ectoplasm for the first time. The substance, which only advanced some three feet or so from the cabinet, seemed to have a life of its own as it billowed upwards and appeared to pulsate. The spectacle could be seen for several minutes before the substance receded into the cabinet once again. As we continued to sing softly, the cabinet curtain was drawn partly back, and we watched as the ectoplasm inside the cabinet formed a mound, which gradually extended itself upwards to a height of about three-and-a-half feet. This mound fell back to the ground on a couple of occasions, then built up again, finally remaining stable for several minutes at the approximate shape, size and form of a small child, albeit covered in drapery. No face or limbs were visible, and the form did not speak at all, simply remaining there while the sitters craned their necks to get a better view. This apparition eventually collapsed back on to the floor, and the substance was drawn back into the cabinet as the curtain closed once more.

It was a matter of minutes before anything else was seen, then suddenly the top part of the curtain was moved to one side and a fully formed face, with drapery atop and at the sides, moved forward so that it was protruding out from the front of the cabinet. The features were well-defined, and a number of the sitters recognised the face as belonging to Jack Wakeling – a lifelong Spiritualist and husband of another physical medium, Betty Wakeling, who was sitting at the side of the cabinet that night. This was the only recognisable materialisation of the evening, and it did not venture forth from the cabinet at all. Nor did it speak.

Following a few more apparently abortive attempts to build up further forms, the ectoplasm receded altogether, the medium came out of trance, and the sitting closed after about one and a half hours. I understood, from several delegates who were present and had witnessed the mediumship for many years, that this was not one of his better sittings in that, following illness and advancing years, the phenomena of the medium were limited to preserve his health. On previous occasions, materialisations had actually walked out of the cabinet.

I was to witness more ectoplasm in the future, but in somewhat different circumstances.

# ARCHIE'S STORY

One of the other delegates to share my room at the Arthur Findlay College trance and physical phenomena week was a very tall, typical sandy-haired Scotsman in his early sixties, by the name of Archie.

Archie was vehemently Scottish in his outlook and was exceptionally vociferous if any of the assembled company should take the mickey out of Scotland or the Scottish people. Despite his nationalism, he was an extremely pleasant and generous man and it was not long before we became firm friends on that Stansted week. It soon became apparent that this was his first excursion into the world of physical phenomena and he was desperately hoping to contact his late wife, who had passed to spirit some months previously from cancer.

Having spent his life working hard in the teaching profession, the income had not been enough for him to see the fruition of his plans and to assure the long-term security of his family, so in order to guarantee that his children had a good private education, the best that could reasonably be provided to give them a head start in the harsh real world, Archie had spent most of his spare hours running a series of businesses in addition to pursuing his calling as a schoolmaster. Needless to say, he and his wife had been amply rewarded when they finally saw their children settled into good professional jobs. At this point, with retirement looming, the couple were looking forward eagerly to spending more time together, both at their lovely home overlooking the sea in a town on the west coast of Scotland and also following their first love of roaming the beautiful islands, hills and glens of their native Scotland.

Imagine, then, the enormity of the catastrophe that was looming over them when, just at the time it seemed they might most enjoy one another's companionship, a routine medical check-up revealed the first signs that Archie's wife was suffering from terminal cancer. He loved her dearly and could not bear to see her suffering as he helped nurse her through those last desolate months. He never really came to terms with the death sentence that had been passed on her by fate and constantly felt that his own life would be pointless without her physical presence.

Here was a man who had been absolutely devastated by his wife's passing which, although now expected, had nevertheless come as a great shock to him and, despite the fact that some time had elapsed since the sad occasion, he was finding life too difficult – in fact, almost impossible – to carry on without her. It occurred to me from the very first moment I met him that Archie was pining for his wife and, all these years later, I have no reason to change this initial view of his pressing problem.

The first instinct that Archie had after the funeral was to seek solace and the answer to all his questions as to whether his wife would survive after her 'death' from the minister of their local conventional parish church only to find that, although the cleric was well-meaning, the sympathy gained consisted of a number of rather unsatisfactory generalities, because the minister did not have any of the answers himself and so could not give Archie the assurance he needed.

Archie knew nothing about Spiritualism but was willing to try anything to attain the answers he was so desperately seeking, so he eventually plucked up the courage to attend his nearby Spiritualist church, where the medium of the day was able to give him an evidential message from his wife, the content of which nobody present on that occasion could have known, and this helped to convince him that his wife was really still alive in a spirit world and able to contact him.

In the weeks and months that followed, he read as much as possible about the subject, visited several Spiritualist churches and psychic institutions in Scotland, and started to have a number of private sittings with various mediums who were recommended to him by his new contacts. He came to realise very quickly that the reality of survival was the only possible explanation for the wealth of messages and evidence of his wife's continued existence that was speedily building up around him.

But the messages Archie was receiving from his wife through mental mediums (clairvoyants and clairaudients), although welcome and comforting to him, were just not enough. He longed for her physical presence, or a physical contact of some kind and it was this desire that brought him to the Stansted Hall trance and physical phenomena week.

Sharing the four-bedded room at Stansted with us were an elderly chap from the East End of London – a larger-than-life character who was a laugh a minute – and a young man who was developing a promising trance mediumship. This young man was a really caring person, as was reflected by the job he did in civvy street and, between the three of us, we made a real effort to ensure that Archie got a lot of attention and help that week to bolster his confidence and lift his spirits (if you will pardon the expression).

During the Stansted week, Archie had access to a number of top mediums and like us, was able to witness the materialisation seance held at the end of the week by Gordon Higginson. In his private sittings, Archie's wife made herself known several times and during a couple of private late-night trance sittings we arranged in the bedroom, she was actually able to speak to him through the trance mediumship of our young colleague, albeit with difficulty. He had hoped, however, that he might have had the opportunity to see her materialise at the physical seance and in this he was sadly disappointed. But through his long conversations with us, and the general experiences of the week there, our Scottish friend was convinced that he must find a way of contacting his wife direct and he resolved to try to join a circle where he hoped this would happen.

Since we had become firm friends during this Stansted week, Archie and I kept in close touch after he returned to Scotland and we would speak to one another regularly on the phone. He did soon manage to find a circle which had the potential for physical phenomena and started to sit in it on a regular basis. But the progress was not fast enough to satisfy his yearning for a contact with his wife and he started to look in other directions too.

Convinced that he might stand some chance of witnessing physical phenomena if he came to London, Archie came down to stay with

Sandra and me in Harold Wood for a few days during July. I booked a sitting with Leslie Flint for our circle, but was unable to get a date before November. This was usual for Leslie, whose seances were often booked up for six months in advance, and it was agreed that Archie would be able to come along with us to that sitting.

In the meantime, however, I took a few days off work while he was staying with us and we toured many of the places around London where good mediumship could be witnessed. One of these, the London Spiritual Mission, had a demonstration of clairvoyance by Albert Best, which we attended, allowing us to witness Albert's excellent mediumship at first hand. Needless to say, Archie was one of the recipients picked by Albert for a message and once again he got some firm proof of his wife's continued existence and of her constant concern for his health and wellbeing.

A few weeks after Archie's visit to us, he called us to ask if we would go and stay with him for a few days. It would be the last opportunity that we would have to see his lovely home, as he was selling it – the place was too large for him to run alone and the children had all now left home. It also held a number of painful memories connected with his wife's passing. His intention was to buy a small flat in the Edinburgh area, where he would be much closer to the circle he now attended, and to the Edinburgh Spiritualist churches and centres.

Sandra and I jumped at the chance, as I have always had a great affinity with Scotland, and the prospect of a pleasant few days away from home in the company of a good friend appealed to both of us. In the event, we were not disappointed. Archie delighted in showing us all the lovely places that he and his wife had frequented regularly. The islands, the highlands and the glens. Their favourite place, Glen Lyon, was a joy to behold, and the scenery we witnessed through the good offices of Archie was breathtaking. Many of the places we visited we would never have known about without the specialist knowledge of somebody local to guide us.

During our trip, it did become increasingly evident that our host was still very much preoccupied with his wife and her new life in the spirit world. The pain of her passing had clearly not receded for him over the months, and she occupied his every thought. I found myself wishing that November would come along quickly, and that he would be fortunate enough to get a contact with her at Leslie Flint's.

By invitation, we went along with him to his weekly circle and were introduced to his fellow sitters. One, who was running a pub at the time and in whose home the sitting was held, has since gone on to develop definite signs of physical mediumship. Another young man was scientifically minded, and going through a stage of intense investigation into Spiritualism.

After Archie moved to Edinburgh, he became a close friend of this young man. They clearly had much in common in that they were both seriously investigating the ins and outs of psychic matters. As their friendship progressed, they would sit together regularly with a Ouija board, through which Archie was able to form a contact with his wife. I knew nothing of this, however, until all was revealed at the Leslie Flint sitting of 2 November 1984. Archie had asked permission to bring the young man to that sitting and they attended together, along with the members of the Harold Wood circle. Leslie had a friend from America staying with him and asked if we would mind if the friend sat in. We did not, of course, but that was how we came to meet the amiable American who, years later, was to become a good friend of ours, too.

This time, we had to wait much longer than usual before Mickey came along with his unique blend of humour. As we were beginning to fear that we might have a blank sitting on our hands, we decided to sing a little to raise the vibrations in the hope that it might help the communicators to get through, and we started to sing to the strains of 'Roaming in the Gloaming'. As we got to the bit that goes 'that's the time that I like best', Mickey's voice chipped in 'that's the time to change your vest'. The sitters dissolved into spontaneous laughter and we were off and running.

This led to Mickey reminiscing about the days when, as a newspaper vendor, he used to get into the local music hall during a matinée where it cost fourpence to sit right at the top of the Bedford Music Hall in Camden Town, giving him the chance to see many of the old stars, like Florrie Ford.

Mickey went on to give us some excellent evidence of the things he had witnessed when he visited our circle at Harold Wood. As always, he was spot on!

Next came a bit of teasing. Mickey asked if the two new people (meaning Archie and his friend) were windy? On being assured that they were not, he said:

> I bet them two new people don't know what to make of me! Are they Scottish, then? [We all chorused 'yes' to this question.] I thought they probably was! Does he play them awful bagpipe things, then? [Referring to Archie – to which we answered that he didn't but his son was an expert player.] His son does? Well, I suppose they're all right if you get used to 'em! They're like a squeezebox, ain't they? Does he wear them skirts and things? [Referring to the kilt.] Hee, hee – I bet he don't know what to make of me.

Archie was being unusually quiet for once when faced with a little teasing but knowing of his strong sense of national pride, I rather hoped that there would not be much more along these lines. I need not have worried, however, because Mickey now started to get down to the job and put on his 'serious face':

> There's several people here for that Scottish fellow and that boy. [I asked here if Mickey could describe them at all.] Just a moment – you leave it to me.

Mickey broke off and we could hear him whispering to his other spirit friends in one of his fascinating asides, obviously intent on helping someone through. And then it happened. A lady's voice, speaking with great difficulty, addressed Archie. It was his wife! Despite the fact that the voice was rather weak, he recognised her immediately, and an intimate conversation took place which left us in no doubt as to the fact that Archie had found his ultimate evidence. A direct contact with his beloved wife, for which he had been desperately searching ever since her passing. There was not a dry eye in the house as we all sat in silence witnessing this loving and touching conversation between husband and wife; the one in this physical world, with the other speaking from the world of spirit.

Their tender words continued for several minutes before her voice cracked with emotion and faded out but Mickey was on hand to help out with more evidence:

> The lady's a bit emotional. She's terribly excited! And anyway, you've got a ring belonging to her, and I think if it were possible for it to fit, she'd like you to wear it. [Archie had had this special and unique ring made for his wife many years before but explained that he was reluctant to wear it as it was delicate and easily got broken.]

A very unusual connection followed, in that there seemed to be a strong psychic link between Archie and the young man who had accompanied him to the sitting; not just in themselves, but also by way of a linking of guides and helpers attached to them both, for the common aim of communication and development of their psychic faculties. Mickey referred to this as he continued:

> Who's Peter? [No response from Archie.] She's called out 'Peter'. No; there's some man here who's a beautiful soul and his name is Peter. She's met him over here, and he's helping her. But he is no relation or nothing. And do you know anything about guides? [Archie did.] Yes, well, there's a beautiful man here who, when he was on the earth, he was a very spiritual man, and he was a Roman Catholic priest. They call him Brother Peter and he is helping in the connection today, to help the lady communicate with you.
>
> She's also very interested in that fellow with you today, and she comes a lot to see you when you're together. That boy; he's very psychic. He has a lot of energy and power and I think she tries to link up and contact you regularly – and all of it is due to his energy and power. Does he sit with you, then? [Archie and the young man answered yes in unison.] Well, this is what it is, you see. But she is so anxious for you to know of her presence and she's never far from you in your home. But you've made some alterations there, haven't you? 'Cos she says it's not where she used to be. [By this time, Archie had moved to Edinburgh.] She says she understands the situation, of course, but evidently you're living in an entirely different place. Anyway, she comes to you where you're living now. Hold on.

[At this point Mickey broke off to speak to Archie.]

> If you want to ask anything, cock – then I'd be pleased to help in any way. I'd like her to speak better, but she's a little bit emotional, and it's difficult.

Archie responded by asking Mickey if his wife found the method of communication which he and his young friend Michael were using to be satisfactory, to be answered by Mickey thus:

> Well, she's very interested in what you get up to – and she's particularly interested in him [meaning Michael] because he's obviously very psychic. You're using some method of contact, and evidently she tries to get messages through it. Did you go through the alphabet? [Both of our Scottish friends answered in the affirmative.] As well as that, she's telling me about the thing that moves to different letters [evidential – they were using the glass and alphabet method] and she says she does the alphabet through his hand during your sittings. She moves the thing to different letters and gives various messages [evidential].
>
> She says sometimes you doubt – but you shouldn't, because she says it is she. By the way, who is this Margaret? There's a lady that's referred to – another lady whose name is Margaret, though she's not often called by this name. [Archie asks if Mickey means in this world, not the spirit world, and is told yes. Archie then says it is his wife's sister, and confirms that she isn't called by her real name normally.] No, that's right, but Margaret is her proper name, and we ask them to give their proper names in messages. She wants you to give her sister her love.

Mickey then turned his attention to Archie's friend, and proceeded to give him some evidential information, before handing the floor over to a very cultured male voice belonging to Brother Peter, the young man's guide:

> I wish, for a few moments of your valuable time, to come and speak to our young friend Michael … I thank you. You do not know me, my son, and yet it is my hope that eventually you shall become fully acquainted not only with myself, but with others here who are most anxious to be of service. When I was on your side of life, I would not have acknowledged this truth, as you understand it, of

communications. I suppose, looking back on my life, everything that transpired was a consequence of my early formative years and my background. I was almost forced you might say, by my parents, to enter into the ministry. I look back on that life of mine with some happiness of course, but at the same time with some despair. I was for many years in a holy order – and it is my desire and my wish that at some times it might be possible for me to come and communicate with you. You do not perhaps yet, my son, realise your full potential as a medium. But you could be a remarkable instrument in service, in love, and in bringing forth comfort and joy to those who need it. I sometimes have regrets about my own life inasmuch as, looking back, I feel that I confined myself to four walls – admittedly, perhaps in some sense, I was able to serve others. But I want to work with you and through you. If you will have faith and patience and persevere in your efforts, then I and others here will manifest with you and through you.

The dear lady who was endeavouring to contact your friend [Archie] sends her love and blessings. She came here today full of excitement and although, perhaps for the moment, she has not been able to manifest as well, obviously, as she would have wished, she wants you [Archie] to know of her love and her presence. She watches over you and endeavours to help you and to do everything in her power that is for your good.

And as for you my friend [addressing Michael], be of good faith. Be of good heart. Continue your experiments and know that in the days that yet lie ahead I, and I hope others, will be enabled to serve, to work, and to do the things that will be a blessing unto many. My love and blessing, and peace be with you and all your friends. Goodbye my son.

And with those last words, the gentle communicator was gone, leaving much for the young man to mull over in his mind. Mickey took up the reins once more:

That's your guide, or one of them. That's the one who was referred to as 'Brother Peter', and he was a monk in a Roman Catholic Order. But have you been sitting long? [Michael told him 'not long'.] Well, long enough to get an idea of things! But if you wanted to, and if you persevered, I think you could be a very good instrument. But you've got to give yourself to it! It's not always the

> easiest thing, and I don't want to go into personal things. I don't want to stick my neck out, but I think you're in a bit of a muddle.

As usual, Mickey just went on to do exactly what he said he didn't want to do and he proceeded to give the young man many evidential details about his personal life, and to give him sound advice which he hoped would help him sort out his life and his problems. Mickey continued:

> I don't know why I'm saying this, but I think you're very much caught up with that bloke you're with [meaning Archie]. There's a strong link between you, and it's a link that will strengthen, or should strengthen, although it's up to the pair of you as to how it will work out psychically. But the lady who comes with such a sweetness – she just wants you both to understand that she wants to help you.

Archie asked Mickey to thank his wife for coming, and was told:

> Yeah, I'll see to that. But she loves you, you know, mate! You probably get a bit down in the dumps [an understatement from Mickey] or a bit depressed and all that, but she's never that far from you. [Mickey went on to give lots more evidential information about the illness Archie's wife had suffered, and the hospital she had been in before she passed.] I like you, you and that lad. I think you've got a lot in common. And I hope that boy will stick by you and continue to sit for you and with you; because I think you need each other, perhaps more than you realise [both acknowledged that they helped each other]. Have you got a flat? [Archie agreed that he had.] 'Cos your missus here – she's telling me about the flat, and the fact that she comes to the pair of you there in that flat. [Archie answered yes.] And that's where you experiment, isn't it? [Quite correct.] And also, you made an awful mess there the other day, when your missus was with you in the kitchen. You dropped something. [Archie answered that he may have done.] Listen, mate, you did! You may be Scottish, but you still break things! Why is it that the Scots are considered tight-fisted? [Archie told Mickey that only the English thought that, at which Mickey dissolved into hoots of laughter.] I suppose your china bounces, being Scots! But I'm only pulling your leg, mate. Of course I do know really that Scottish people are more generous than most – no one's that tight-fisted …

Mickey gave some final evidence to the two Scottish sitters before going off at a tangent on another subject. Shortly afterwards, his voice faded as another communicator – a young girl – made herself known to us. She didn't give a name, but we were pretty sure that it was Beth, one of the helpers in our home circle, as she addressed herself, giggling, to Mr Robin Foy and Lady Foy. Once again, we were given encouragement for the circle. Mickey returned to talk generally about mediums – that they should be seen and not heard! He greeted the American visitor, and told him that his missus – 'Madame Butterfly' as he called her – was there. (His wife had been Japanese.) Shortly afterwards, Maria Theresa spoke to us in her now familiar rolling French accent, once again, offering encouragement for the Harold Wood circle, and giving good advice as to the way forward. This was followed by the distinguished voice of Sir Arthur Conan Doyle, who addressed us all:

> Arthur. Arthur speaking. Hello Conan Doyle here. Arthur Doyle. Conan Doyle. I'm not quite sure as to whether you can hear me [we assured him that we could], but I just want you to know that although I'm not a regular member of your group exactly, from the point of view of often being present, I am aware, to some extent of the possibilities there. I do hope you'll continue and not lose heart. I hope you'll go on, because everyone here who's closely linked and associated with your group is very hopeful. And my goodness me – we *do* need instruments. We need the mediums, and I think there's tremendous positivity with your group, so *do* carry on. As a matter of fact, I was very interested in the communication that came earlier for the young man there. I do hope he continues too, and is not put off – because we do need youngsters being able to develop their gifts and be of service. I only hope you continue, my friend. [Michael answered yes.] Good ... Good. Anyway, I mustn't take up your valuable time. Goodbye!

There followed more shenanigans by Mickey, who gave some more evidence to the assembled company amidst fits of giggles, before making way for the voice of Madame Butterfly, the Japanese wife of our American friend Bob, who was sitting in. For some time, yet another husband and wife were able to converse intimately across the barrier called 'death', and none of us could help but be moved by their touching endearments to one other.

A rough diamond who called himself 'Mason', but who was unknown to any of us there, then came along to talk a little of his own life and times before he passed over to the spirit world and amused us with stories of how he didn't believe in survival before he 'died'.

Mickey rounded off the sitting on this occasion by giving Sandra and me some sound advice about a business venture (shop) we were thinking of buying. Basically he was saying that we should only run a shop such as this if we were both prepared to put enough time into it and he rightly said that because I wanted to continue with my full-time job at the same time as we had the shop, it was unlikely that we would succeed. We subsequently dropped the idea but I should have listened harder to Mickey! When we *did* go into business with two shops in 1986, just as Mickey had warned, it proved to be nothing like the success that we had hoped for!

The sitting was over when Mickey told us:

> Sorry, but the power's going. When are you coming again? 'Cos old Flint, he ain't getting any younger. And he might not be 'ere – on your side, I mean – you never know, do you? You might as well get one in before he kicks the bucket, mate.

It had proved to be yet another memorable sitting, but most of all I was delighted for Archie, who had so desperately hoped for a direct communication from his wife, and had been fortunate enough to enjoy exactly that.

Our contact with Archie continued for a while before it suddenly ceased for no apparent reason and it is only comparatively recently that I learned he is now in the spirit world himself. I like to think that he and the wife he loved so much are now together again – something Archie had longed for ever since her passing.

I wish him well in his new life, and I shall always remember him with affection – resplendent in his green tweed jacket, and sporting a mop of tousled, sandy hair – looking for all the world like an eccentric professor.

As for the young man, Michael, who accompanied Archie to the Flint sitting, I regret to say that we have not maintained a regular contact but I do hope he has followed the advice of the spirit world and his guide Brother Peter and gone on to develop the obvious mediumistic potential which he possessed. Although much is asked of good mediums, they do derive a tremendous amount of satisfaction from reuniting sitters with their loved ones in the spirit world.

# TWO FINAL SITTINGS AT LESLIE'S BAYSWATER HOME

DURING THE LAST days of the Harold Wood circle, and following Mickey's advice to 'get some in before old Flint kicks the bucket', we managed to enjoy two more sittings before Leslie retired to the seaside and went to live in Hove, near Brighton, a few years later. I now include some highlights of those two sittings, which took place on 21 June, and 8 November 1985. By this time, Leslie had ceased using his blacked-out lounge as a seance room and was instead using his private cinema.

For many years, Leslie and Bram had run a small film club for pensioners and people interested in old silent films, of which Leslie had a unique collection gathered in the main from his many well-known friends and contacts in America's Hollywood. The cinema had a distinct advantage over the lounge for Leslie's seances in that it was self-contained and sitters could wander down the garden to it without needing to walk through his flat first. Leslie had also noticed that, with his advancing years and the increasing number of blank sittings which were now occurring through his mediumship, he seemed to get better results in this room which opened directly into his garden.

The two seances were totally different in their content. To the June sitting, for the very first time, we invited more outside people than members of the circle, so that they could have the opportunity of sitting with Leslie before he retired. This turned out to be the longest period of constant communication from spirit in all the time that I had visited Leslie – a solid one-and-a-half hours packed with independent voices. Yet, perhaps partly because of the way that the party was made up – many of them strangers to us and to Leslie and most with little or no previous experience of physical mediumship and partly due to the fact that we were accustomed to visiting Leslie as a circle with spirit communicators being on the whole our own circle guides and helpers, it was the most difficult seance for Mickey, Leslie's guide, that I had ever known him to undertake.

During the afternoon, Mickey worked like a Trojan, trying hard to keep the atmosphere relaxed and light, while doing his best to behave like an 'agony aunt' for several of the new inexperienced sitters so he could bring them excellent evidence of the survival of their loved ones.

Apart from Mickey, who spent most of the seance chatting to us himself and relaying messages from loves ones, the majority of the communicators were personal relatives of the guest sitters, and were positively identified by them. We did however enjoy some brief conversations with old faithfuls, such as Sister Maria, Jock, little Beth, and actress Dame Ellen Terry.

One of the sitters was Polish in origin and, after initial difficulties, her father spoke to her for a while in perfect Polish, although Leslie Flint had no knowledge whatsoever of that language. There was some confusion and excitement among this lady's other relatives in their efforts to communicate, which resulted in their voices fading out from time to time in frustrating fashion, and this was the cue for the real highlight of the seance when we were addressed at length by Cosmo Lang – a former Archbishop of Canterbury, who told us in his cultured voice:

> I suppose it's to be expected in the communicators, when they're excited to be there. The desire to make contact, without perhaps realising it, when their dear ones are close – it's very difficult to be cool, calm and collected on such an occasion.
>
> But, you know, the experience has been interesting for me. Indeed, more than interesting – fascinating! When you come here; and not only when you come here, but when you gather together in your homes, or wherever it is that you hold your sittings as you term them, innumerable people are attracted. Not necessarily always the people that you'd expect.
>
> Of course, there are always those that you do expect – guides and helpers – but quite a lot of other people are attracted. I wish I could explain this to you. To us, in a sense, your world is, as it were, in a kind of mist – due to the thought forces emanating from the world, and of course I don't have to tell you that the circumstances

of your world are causing a great deal of concern. The heartache over here is getting used to it! There's so much going on that we never expected, and we feel rather helpless – and have to, in a sense, stand aside. There's very little that often we can do.

We cannot make people think and act differently. Of course, if they've shown a psychic inclination that they would like to be different – or change their attitude to thought, or attitude of mind and action – then we can reach them. But what I was really going to say was that whilst your world is in a kind of mist or fog; and it's when people like yourselves, who have some realisation and knowledge of these things, when you gather together – there is an illumination.

It's rather like the hymn, if you remember it: 'You in your small corner, and I in mine'. What was the hymn we used to sing? 'Jesus bids us shine – like a candle in the darkness'. I can't remember the exact terminology of the words, but I remember that the boys – the two youngsters – used to like that hymn. And 'you in your small corner, and I in mine'. In a sense, there's some truth in that.

We see you – as it were – as a light in the darkness of materialism. Of course, we have great ideas for you; individually and collectively. And in a way some of you are certainly opening up your consciousness and are doing certain things appertaining to the spirit. And you're doing as best you can under prevailing conditions and circumstances. Of course, some of you are in a sense on the threshold. You're just, as it were, peering in and wondering how deep or how far you will become involved.

But I can only say this: that if you are seen as an illumination to the view of those of spirit, let that illumination lead you and guide you into the fuller light, and the fuller realisation of the great possibilities that lie within each one of you to develop the powers; and the force of the spirit that is naked or dormant in emotions and things within. Some of you have already expanded your reason. Others are seeking, endeavouring to find an assurance perhaps, about the whole subject of communication; but I can assure you that if you are patient – and persevere in your efforts and sincerity of purpose into the aspect that you have of going ahead or forward in this realisation – we can link up with you and help you. The higher you lift yourselves above material things, the most easy it is obviously, for us to link up with you.

I realise, and you realise, the difficulty of living in a material world, and that the conditions around and about you are to say – well – so appalling at times. Very frightening and very distressing! I know you try to keep yourselves, as best you can, out of the darkness of things – but it's very difficult, because all around and about you, these things are happening. You are being bombarded as it were, daily, with all these tragedies. All these terrifying things that are happening through man's stupidity. Through the various aspects of his thoughts.

Religion has a great deal to answer for! Although I was myself very caught up with religion all my life. And I look back on my life now, and I realise that if I had only *known* – what I know now – I could have done so much more! And there's so much that one might say in regard to religion. I suppose if a person who's sincere in their attitude of mind tries to put into practice those things that are truly of God, then things would be very different. If that were repeated on a large scale, then change would take place. But, unfortunately, often religion separates people in reality. Each religion has its own creeds and beliefs, and you get this attitude of mind where people get set against people. One considers that their religion is right whilst everybody else is wrong. But at the end of the day, we're all part of the same spirit. And if only humanity could realise – irrespective of origin, colour and creed – that we're all part of the same spirit; that unifying spirit which really is the animating force that gives life to every human being, and even to the animal kingdom. You see, where there is life, there is spirit. The truly great spirit of Universal Harmony; of life, and of love. We're all animated to some extent; some more than others, by this force.

But you know, a lot of people have strayed away from the realisation of truth. Take the basic truth, and build on it. Make use of it. Expand your vision. Give us an opportunity to break the barriers between the two worlds and let that little candle become a flame in the darkness of your world. Each one of you here is vital and important to us – and the work that we hope to do with you and through you. Some of you are pointing the way as you go your separate paths but, nevertheless, each path has its own destination, in respect that some may be called to work in a different way to others.

That is as must be, but where there is a possibility of your working together – then call out for us together. Develop the powers of spirit, unifying your souls mentally and physically and of course, spiritually. We shall not fail you! The work that we endeavour to do through you is greater than ourselves. We are the means – as you are. Indeed to us, whilst we are in a sense working collectively as spirit and whilst we are a part of each other, we are still to a certain extent individuals – and we want each one of you to realise, individually and collectively, that you can come together in love and in harmony and serve, by doing the work of the spirit.

I only wish to goodness that I had realised more about these things when I was on your side! I was a little afraid of it. I mean, I had some experience, it's true. I read of course, the books and things that were appertaining to psychical research. I was very interested in what Doyle and Lodge and others had to say ... I wasn't perhaps ... well, I certainly wasn't enamoured.*

I wish now that I might have been enamoured with the subject. I did have an opportunity once to attend a seance but I suppose in a way that I got cold feet. In fact, I turned it down. But it might have been a great revelation. Who knows?

Of course, in all these things, you'll find that there's good, bad and indifferent. And you get some mediums I've been with since I arrived over here ... quite frankly ... I mean, I made a point actually, of going to different seances and watching people do the work of the spirit. Some do extremely well. Others not so well – and I have had one or two shocks with some of the mediums who, quite frankly, I mean – if I could help them in some way – I would, but I don't think I, or anyone else, could do much for them. It's about time they helped themselves a bit; to get on a different level of consciousness.

You know, it's really important – and people don't always realise this – that in the manifestation of the spirit, there are many levels. And I'm not saying you should ignore the lower levels; but one should always strive for the higher ones. But often, on those lower levels of consciousness, there are conditions of existence on this side which are very interwoven with your material world. Let me tell you; there are people who – I suppose you could say they were earthbound. That doesn't necessarily mean to say that they're bad or evil people – in fact there's always a wall of protection built around you when you gather together. But occasionally, someone will be brought along to your meetings, who's in some need; though perhaps because they're so near the earth – in a sense that their consciousness is so materialistic – that in a way, perhaps you can help them more than we can. But the situation is more rare than common.

But you know, I just want you dear people to *know* that all of us here are doing everything in our power to help you – individually and collectively. Don't get depressed. Don't get despondent. These things are not going to happen overnight – some of you will make progress quicker than some others. And of course, the human element – being what it is – some of you may think, 'Oh dear, what's the point? I'm not developing. I'm not seeing. I'm not experiencing.' And some of you will, of course, in time get very depressed about it. And I've heard many a time; people in the past at seances I've attended from this side, where everything's going along pretty well; the one or two getting, as you might say, a little fed up. They have started to make excuses and then they didn't turn up for several evenings, then eventually they dropped out.

And yet you never know. Often the slow developer eventually turns out to be the best instrument. A lot of people don't realise that. It's not those who seem to develop their mediumship quickly – before and way ahead of the others – who are necessarily going to be the best instruments. Of course, a lot depends on which way they develop, and exactly what they're developing.

What I mean to say is that some people develop clairvoyance, and some clairaudience. Others develop a form of trance mediumship. I've heard people, and in fact I've known individuals who've developed a trance mediumship and everything quite excellently. They've been taken over by the controls; and I've tried to do that on certain occasions myself – I have even succeeded on some occasions – but often, of course, the instrument … the medium … has been aware of what's being said through them, and they have their doubts. They think, 'Oh dear – was that someone outside of myself communicating – or was that me, unconsciously creating, as it were to life, some character that has no existence in fact.' But, of course, this is problematic. Because what you have to say to yourself is 'All right!' You are taken over temporarily, and you lose to some extent your identity. You're partially conscious of what is being said; or perhaps very conscious, and yet you have no control over it. And the entity which is endeavouring to use you has none of your personality. They probably speak in an entirely different way – use a different way of speech, and perhaps even discuss things, or say things that are completely foreign to yourself, under

> normal circumstances. You see, when you sit together – don't worry if sometimes you are aware, or you are conscious. That is when your own mind starts to intrude. Let whatever happens happen! And let it find its own level. Analyse it after the seance is over, and not before. But we're very pleased with your group. Keep up the good work.

All in all this Flint sitting, which was closed by Mickey in his usual cheeky style, had been a mixed bag, but nevertheless a great success. Several of the sitters had enjoyed their unique opportunity to speak directly with their mothers, fathers, wives and loved ones. We had even been treated to a Polish song complete with Polish words by one of the communicators. An extraordinary number of the guest sitters had arrived with material problems of differing sorts which, with the patient help of Mickey, they had been unburdened of during the course of the seance. If he were still of this earth, Mickey would have gone home with laryngitis but many had their reasons on that day to be thankful to him for his efforts, which at the time seemed to fall into a category above and beyond the call of his duty.

On Friday, 8 November 1985, we once again took our places in Leslie's seance room, only this time the sitters were drawn just from the ranks of the Harold Wood circle, as had been our usual practice in the past.

Mickey did not take too long to greet us and he initially brought some personal evidence for one of the circle who had not previously visited Leslie. The Cockney guide was always a bit of a stickler for correct seance procedure and on this occasion (as had often occurred before when we were present) he admonished one sitter for crossing his legs (this prevents the correct flow of power in a physical seance). However, none of us owned up to having our legs crossed and we began to think that perhaps, for once, Mickey had got it wrong.

Not so! Sheepishly, Leslie himself owned up to having had his legs crossed and rectified the situation. Obviously Mickey could still see in the dark.

Mickey's opening comments went on for some time before he took a break and Leslie was clearly upset as he told us that he himself needed some advice from Mickey and that he could not understand why Mickey had not said a word to him about it as soon as he came through when so many things were going on around him at the time. Mickey obviously heard what Leslie had to say, and countered:

> You keep quiet! You're going to do all right. We've got an eye on you, and we're looking after you. Everything will work out – you'll be surprised. You keep quiet now! Just let me get on with it.

Leslie knew then that he would be OK. (This was the time he was looking to sell his Bayswater house and move out of London.) His health was not good and he was clearly getting anxious about selling his home and finding a new one for his retirement. Mickey chuntered away in a good humoured manner, though:

> Honestly! Mediums! Not that I wouldn't 'elp 'im – but I want to work at the moment. Old Flint – 'e's getting old. He'll soon be over here with us. Anyway, when 'e comes, then I can pack it all in. I ain't coming back again. I'm sure I've done my bleedin' work.
>
> People get funny you know, and you can't 'elp laughing. Some of them 'ave said to me [he used a posh accent for this], 'I suppose when he goes, you'll come back and help someone else? Perhaps you'll come to *our* circle?' And I say to them, 'Not on your Nellie!' My work will be finished when 'e's kicked the bucket. I reckon I've done my whack over the years.

Maria Theresa then came to converse with us, and to offer encouragement for the circle. In all the visits I had made to Leslie's, this communicator, apart from being a delightful and loving soul, and one of our own circle helpers, had never failed to come through to talk to us. I took the opportunity to ask her about the circle, and she replied:

> Well, that iss verr' – 'ow you say – eet iss on the up and the down, huh? Eet iss verr' good, and there are many theengs 'appening. There iss a lot of power there – a lot of energee, and the physical power, you know. We 'ave great probabilities in that direction but you must be patient you know, weeth eet. But don't worry about anytheeng. Eet will continue. *But not quite in the same way.*

Needless to say, Maria's comments got me thinking. She had not expanded on her prediction that the circle would not be working in 'quite the same way' but it had sown a seed of curiosity, and I wondered if this sentiment would be confirmed elsewhere. Mickey now had more to say and kept up his banter with one of the sitters, a gentleman who was a bit of a character, but who had much to offer the circle. He was given some excellent evidence, which culminated in an exchange with his father, who managed to come and speak to his son. Another sitter had the opportunity to converse with her mother in much the same way. There was also a short visit by Sandra's uncle Ronnie, which proved to be evidential.

This was followed by a visit from Rose the flower seller, who had in the past been a regular communicator at Leslie's seances. It was pleasant to hear her again, however, as it had been several years since we had heard her talk. We need not have worried. Rose remembered us well, and we were greeted as old friends.

Our Scottish friend and circle guide Jock who, in addition to his regular visits to the circle, rarely missed the chance to pop in and say hello at Leslie's, did so again, and our Red Indian helper White Feather did likewise. Another of our circle helpers, previously unknown to us, announced himself as the 'Reverend Charles Edward Ellish'. He spoke encouragingly of the potential that there was in the circle and expanded a little on his earth life when as a minister he had preached the gospel – although he added somewhat wistfully that he didn't then have the same knowledge and experience that he now had.

Reverend Ellish went on to explain and discuss some of the technical aspects of communication via the independent voice and the practical difficulties arising from the use of an ectoplasmic voicebox such as that he was currently using. (It is not necessary to cover this conversation in depth, as most of the information is already given in this book through other communicators at Flint's.)

At this point the power began to fade and the voices became fainter. By way of a last burst, however, there was a short communication from the Frenchman, Maurice, who was connected with our group and had spoken before at Leslie's. Amongst his other pleasantries and words of encouragement, he said:

> We are very thrilled, you know; very happy with the circle. *There will be a change,* but don't worry 'bout anything! It is alright. It has to be.

So we now had the *confirmation* of Maria's earlier words; things would be changing but for the better and strictly within the scheme of things. However, what we did not yet know was exactly how radical that change was going to prove to be. As the power went, and the voices faded, Mickey said a brief farewell. We would not be sitting with Leslie at this address again.

# THE IN-BETWEEN YEARS

IT WAS NOT long after the November 1985 sitting at Flint's that the Harold Wood circle broke up once and for all. Throughout its existence, the hoped-for development never seemed to be forth-coming on a permanent basis. The circle had been struggling on for some time, meandering along without proper direction until, in the early days of 1986, the harmony between sitters fell apart completely. Bearing that in mind, as well as the fact that we had been told during the Flint sitting that the circle was going to change, we reluctantly decided to suspend it indefinitely, to give us time to think the situation through.

At the same time, we made a conscious decision to go into business, in the hope that in this way we might become financially independent. The thinking behind our decision was that this scenario would allow us to work full time for spirit in the future without the need for a regular wage.

It was therefore with this in mind that we bought a fish and chip shop in Walthamstow, situated right on the North Circular Road. I had been brought up in Grimsby, Lincolnshire – the world's premier fishing port during my childhood. My grandfather and uncle had been fish merchants there and my father was involved in the manufacture and sale of fish meal, which was used as animal feed. His family all came from Scarborough, Yorkshire, and I knew that area well, too. In both locations, one could always buy excellent fish and chips, and I had known nothing else until I moved to London.

Regrettably, the quality of that produce left a lot to be desired all over London, and I missed my favourite meal considerably. I therefore reasoned that if I offered a product as good as that I had enjoyed regularly in the north of England, there would be many more Londoners who would appreciate such excellent fish and chips so, in mid-1986, we were frying in style. The business did well at first and the turnover grew quickly to a respectable amount at The Yorkshire Pride, in particular as a consequence of our advertising campaign on Capital Radio. The following year, however, we were in for a shock, as it was decided to widen the North Circular Road, and we discovered that the work would go on constantly for three years.

From the very first day that this North Circular project started, the roadworks took over our parking area, and customers were unable to get to us. All the heavy traffic passing our door was unable to stop and just carried on going by. We had never realised that our trade would be so badly affected and as a consequence – in order to survive – we had no option but to find an alternative way of keeping the takings up. We figured that if the customers couldn't get to us – we would have to go to them, and the solution would therefore be to set up a fish and chip home delivery service. Thousands of colourful leaflets were subsequently distributed to local homes and we started to deliver orders within a five-mile radius. This measure achieved what we had set out to do but the hassle we encountered in organising motorbike couriers to deliver the goods persuaded us that we should consider selling the shop.

As a consequence of these problems, 1987 was not a good year for us. To complicate matters further, my father's terminal lung cancer, which had been diagnosed several years earlier, finally caught up with him, and he was taken into hospital for the last time. I mention that because his illness and passing triggered two more psychic experiences for us. When the Grimsby hospital called us to tell us that he was fading fast, Sandra and I dropped everything and headed northwards to visit him. Sandra's daughters were still young and we had arranged with them that when we arrived in Grimsby, we would telephone to let them know we had arrived safely. After a short visit to the hospital, we returned to my father's home to make the telephone call back to Harold Wood. The youngest daughter answered the telephone and a few words were exchanged.

Then, quite inexplicably, the voice of Sandra's daughter faded out and was replaced by a noise which appeared to be caused by static interference. Within seconds, however, a lady's voice came on the line, saying simply, 'We are waiting for his death.' It was just six hours later that my father passed into the spirit world.

Sandra has on occasions experienced vivid bouts of clairvoyance, when she has seen spirit people as quite solid beings but when my father 'died', this had not happened for several years. At his cremation service, we were sitting on the front row of the crematorium when, part way through the service, Sandra saw my father. He did not seem to be totally solid but appeared as a misty, semi-transparent form. He was not in the slightest bit interested in his coffin but stood right in front of me, watching my reactions in a way I found to be a rather touching and typical gesture, when Sandra told me afterwards.

Following the problems we had experienced at The Yorkshire Pride and to increase our chances of success in business, we reasoned that we should perhaps diversify into another type of shop, and we purchased in addition a high-class delicatessen in Brentwood, Essex, called Crackers. It turned out to be an appropriate name, for we *were* surely crackers to have bought it! We carried a number of exclusive lines and again, at first the business appeared to do reasonably well.

That was before the storms, and the floods. Within a short space of time we were twice flooded out, and had the shop canopy wrecked by freak storms! Within months, many of our exclusive lines were exclusive no longer, as the large grocery superstores which were then being built in various locations all started to install comprehensively stocked delicatessen counters and we discovered that we could no longer compete. In this case, we turned to an additional sandwich delivery round from the shop to keep us afloat.

We began to feel a little paranoid, surmising that perhaps 'someone upstairs' didn't like us any more. Whichever way we turned, it seemed that everything we tried was being blocked. In 1988, therefore, we reluctantly came to the conclusion that our two shops had to go. Matters were not helped when within 12 hours one weekend, both the fish shop and our home were burgled, despite the fact that they were 15 miles away from one another. The loss of a week's takings nearly finished us off altogether.

Despite the problems, however, I am convinced that we actually did get more than a little help from the spirit world in selling our troublesome brace of shops as going concerns. Once we had finally taken the decision to sell, we found buyers for both very quickly at a time when businesses were not selling well.

The Harold Wood house never quite felt the same to us after the burglary, and we felt that we ought to move away from the area – at least for a time – to give ourselves a breathing space and a change of scenery. It was now ten years since we had first occupied the house, during which time the area had deteriorated somewhat.

After the demise of the businesses, we really did not feel that we wanted to get back to running a circle again for a while and a complete break therefore seemed quite attractive. My job selling paper from Finnish mill to paper merchant now involved my travelling not just around London, but also in the Midlands and East Anglia areas.

We began to take a great interest in tracing our family histories as a leisure-time activity and consequently spent some time in East Anglia where Sandra's father had been born and raised. Also, when the pressures of life had become too much over the last three years, we went to East Anglia for short-stay breaks at hotels and one of our favourite boltholes was the Scole Inn, a picturesque seventeenth-century coaching inn which was reputed to be haunted, where we would stay in one of their roomy four-poster bedrooms and pamper ourselves.

I remember vividly looking out of the window of our room on to a large old house which sat almost in the car park of the Scole Inn. We admired it greatly and wondered who lived there, assuming (as it happens, incorrectly) that it was perhaps the house of the hotel manager. We loved the area, and wished that we could be living there. Today, we *are* – but that's another story!

Since housing costs in East Anglia were lower than in other places, we decided in principle that this was the direction in which we should head. Both of Sandra's daughters were now old enough to be independent and were happy to stay in Essex while we moved away to another location. Since we would only be renting a property, however, the dilemma was to find a suitable unfurnished house which would provide us with enough space for a separate seance room, once we had settled down in the area and had regained our tranquillity.

Neither of us had forgotten our desire to find an old rectory to live in – we felt that such a property would have the right atmosphere of love and spirituality about it to give a new circle a head start.

After giving the matter some thought, we reasoned that it was just possible the Church of England might have a rectory to rent somewhere, due to their recent policy of merging a number of parishes under one rector or vicar, which was giving rise to redundant church houses.

Cheekily, I therefore set about contacting the various Church of England diocesan housing departments within the East Anglia area to see if they had any rectories to rent but without any success in the Cambridge, Peterborough, Chelmsford and Ipswich areas. At this point I almost gave up but something inside me urged me to try just one more.

When I phoned the housing manager of the Norwich diocesan area, I was quite amazed to hear him say, 'Well, as a matter of fact, I *do* have one which I may get permission to let.' This was in a little village to the east of Norwich, called Postwick, and was a very modern four-bedroomed rectory, right next door to the village's picturesque old church. The house did not look much from the road because its best aspect was from the large garden behind but it was beautifully built with solid oak parquet flooring in the hall, lounge and study. There was solid wood everywhere, in the doors, cupboards and built-in wardrobes. The lounge and dining room were large and functional, and the study, which had a lovely spiritual atmosphere to it, would make a perfect library and circle room. (By this time, I had gathered a large and unique collection of psychic books, many of which were rare and out of print.) Above all, the rent was very affordable. Needless to say, we were over the moon at the prospect of living in this lovely house and we were happy to take a two-year lease on the property, from 1 August 1989.

Early in April, however, whilst still living in Harold Wood, I was beginning to feel rather restless at not having been involved in a physical circle for so long, and my thoughts once again began to turn towards that 'Holy Grail' of physical mediumship and its phenomena.

Right out of the blue, I spotted a rare advert in the *Psychic News* one week, seeking sitters for a physical circle in Ilkeston, Derbyshire. Despite the considerable distance that I would have to travel to sit in such a circle, something within me told me that I had to reply, so I answered the advert and sent a resumeé of my psychic CV.

It was a rather clandestine affair initially, as the advertiser wrote back suggesting that current members of the circle meet up with me for a chat at a pub north of Loughborough and, in fact, that is exactly what happened. It transpired that the circle was sitting monthly on the Saturday closest to the new moon for the development of physical phenomena through their medium, Stuart, at Ilkeston in Derbyshire, although the same members of the circle also sat weekly as a general development circle. My application was duly put to the circle guides for their approval and I was then invited to join this physical circle on a trial basis.

Without realising it at the time, the Ilkeston circle was to have a profound effect upon my life but when I started to sit there, it was just another physical circle. I recall being rather impressed with the medium's trance and the usual signs of early development of physical phenomena were there: the coldness, the breezes, raps, taps and whistles. Despite the speedy addition of table phenomena by way of movement and levitation when a wooden table was introduced into the circle, development appeared to be rather slow due to the fact that the circle was only sitting monthly, but the following year heralded a more promising situation with the development of the phenomena showing definite signs of acceleration.

During the last sitting we had attended at Leslie Flint's Bayswater home in November 1985, we had been given to understand that he was going to retire completely from giving private sittings after he moved away from London. Since we had not been in touch for a while, we did not have any idea where he was now living but we had in the meantime made a good friend of another medium called Keith, who was running a psychic bookshop in Walthamstow, close to our own shop. It was in fact from Keith that I had acquired many of the out-of-print psychic books now in my collection. After we had sold The Yorkshire Pride, I remained in close touch with him. Keith knew of my intense interest in physical phenomena and was aware that in the past I had often sat with Leslie Flint, as he had himself.

It was when visiting Keith's bookshop during July 1989, that I discovered not only did he know where Leslie Flint was now living – in Hove, Sussex – but also that he was once again taking bookings for old friends to have private sittings. Keith himself had a sitting booked for a group to go to Leslie's on 7 August and offered to include Stuart and his wife Val from Ilkeston as well as me in the group that day. As always, I did not need any second bidding to attend a Flint sitting and we were there at the appointed time at Leslie's lovely new house.

Since it was not actually our booked sitting, the content was mainly personal messages, most of which turned out to be very evidential, and Mickey was on excellent form, although the sitting was a short one. But the three of us from the Ilkeston circle were specifically addressed with exceptional clarity by Florence Marryat, the Victorian novelist and leading Spiritualist of her day:

> I do not have to tell you how very anxious we all are to break the barrier between the two worlds. I was very interested indeed in regard to the reference made earlier to your circle. Because I do think, in fact I am quite sure if I say to you that if you are patient enough – and I'm sure you are very patient – to continue, then you will achieve results. You've had indications [true]. You've had several odd things happen which have led you to have confidence in what may yet transpire. But these things do take time. You must not lose heart!
>
> You know, when I was on your side of life, I was deeply, deeply involved in the things of the spirit. I was very much indeed caught up with the development of mediumship, and I attended many functions and many various places where people were experimenting. And I tried to help as far as it was in my power to be of assistance. But you know, looking back, I suppose one should say it was not necessarily easier, but I don't think that we had the distractions that you have today. I think the conditions around your world are such that it becomes more and more difficult – it really does – and I mean, all right, I can come and talk to you from time to time via the agency of the medium, but there must be many, many

occasions when we try desperately to break the barrier between the two worlds, and it's not easy at all.

But you know, you'll probably not even remember me – there's no reason that you should. I've been here many many years, but I was deeply, deeply, deeply involved in this subject, you know. My name is Marryat. Florence Marryat. [At this point we assured the communicator that we knew who she was.] Well, I've no doubt that if you are deeply involved in the Spiritualistic work, that you would have heard about me.*

But the point is, it's not the past that matters. It's the present. We look to people like you – each one of you – to be as patient and as persistent as it's possible to be; to open up your awareness – your consciousness; and above all, the physical power that you possess, so that we can break the barriers that lie between our two worlds. But there is a tendency, I regret, for people to get disillusioned, and to get discouraged. Which is really sad, because you – dear people – we look to you. You are the ones we look to to carry on the work. To hold aloft the banner of truth. Everybody has the power of the spirit to a greater or lesser degree. Everybody can – in some shape or form – be used. But there are several of you here who I am told have very strong physical power, which means that you could either develop materialisation or direct voice – or some other manifestation of the spirit.

But try to be patient with us because there will be times when you get a little disheartened. We do as best we can under whatever the prevailing conditions are. I was asked to come and talk to you because you are all deeply rooted, and deeply serious in the things that are of the spirit. Some of you are already doing the work of the spirit; going out and about – encouraging and enlightening people who are in the darkness of material things. We bless you and are thankful to you. Please carry on, each one of you – individually and collectively.

Just over a month later, I was in a position to return the favour for Keith, as I had by now been able to book another sitting with Leslie in my own name. On Monday, 11 September 1989, we were once again in Hove, with a mixture of sitters from Ilkeston plus Keith and his friends, and one or two personal friends who came along for the trip.

As before, there was a lot of good personal evidence for several of the sitters, some of whom had parents and relatives speak to them direct.

Most of the communications semed to be of a general nature, owing to the mixed bag of sitters who were present but, as always, Mickey proved to be worth his weight in gold as he dished out a stream of remarkably accurate information from spirit people behind the scenes who were not able to speak in person. Two interesting communicators, however, stood out from the rest. Both were most encouraging about the work of the Ilkeston circle and their talks were calculated to spur us on in our efforts on behalf of the spirit world. Sir Arthur Conan Doyle was the first:

> Arthur speaking. Arthur Doyle here. Arthur Conan Doyle. I'm very interested, of course, when I make a contact – to find certain people who are endeavouring to develop the powers of the spirit, so that they can become used for you – mankind. We do look to each one of you to do as best you can, and to develop the powers you have dormant there. I know some of you are doing the work in one way or another. And some of you are hoping to develop and become, as it were, instruments. I was very blessed when I was on your side in finding the truth of life continuous. Your circle is very much, often indeed, in our thoughts. We may not always – some of us – be able to be permanently around, obviously. But we come as best and whenever we can, you know. Carry on your good work. Don't get disheartened. Know that there are always some that are constantly around you; advising, guiding, uplifting and endeavouring to do whatever it is possible to do through the agency of your powers. Be of good strength and good heart. Know that we shall not fail, for that which we do is greater than ourselves. We are instruments, as indeed are you, of the power of the spirit. Be of good heart, my friends. Bless you all!

As Sir Arthur took his leave, his voice was immediately followed by that of a very cultured lady. This was slow and articulate and the clarity of the independent voice was quite amazing. It belonged to Dame Ellen Terry. She spoke of several things, and rounded off her talk by returning to the importance of developing psychic gifts:

You may feel sometimes, after a session, that well – very little happened, and it was perhaps a little disappointing. And no one felt particularly, as it were, caught up with the power of the spirit. I know there are these moments when you get disheartened. But try to remember that while you are gathered together in love and in harmony, and are at peace with each other and the world, that a lot is happening behind the scenes. When you least expect it, no doubt, something will transpire.

Something will happen that I know will give you such cause for joy. Because I do know there are various groups of spirit souls here who are working with you individually and collectively to bring about a certain form of mediumship. It may not necessarily be always exactly what you wish for or anticipate, though every effort is made to open up for the certain gift that has been promised. And that gift will, in time, be brought into being in such a way that you will then say, 'Well, it was worth the waiting and the patience, and the perseverance we had – one with the other'.

... You know my dears, each one of you is important. You may not feel it so and, in a sense perhaps, not fully realise or understand. We see you much more completely than you realise. Much more than you can dare, indeed, hope to see yourself as we understand you. We know you better than you know yourselves. We know of your potential, we know of the spiritual vitality and the spiritual realisation that shall and will come – in some instances while you're still yet upon the earth. Do not think – any of you – that you are not important to the work of the spirit, because you are. You may not be fully conscious or aware of it. You may not feel that you're particularly psychic – as you term it. But everyone is. You *all* have the psychic gift. The psychic power. The energy! You have that power of immortality which goes far beyond your comprehension. While you sit together, many souls are standing around you; waiting and hoping that they may sooner or later be able to manifest – if not in one way, in another. Each one of you who sit together are as important, one to the other, and to us. You know, words are really inadequate for us to try to depict to you, or to explain, or indeed to show the realisation of the spirit that we now happen to be blessed with.

Dame Ellen went on to describe some of the gifts of physical phenomena which may be available to us should we choose to develop them. As she took her leave, Mickey popped back to tell us that the power was going and that he would have to close the sitting, telling us:

> Don't worry about old Les. He'll be all right. 'E ain't going to kick the bucket yet! I've got enough trouble already. Don't want 'im here! Ha, ha! He's all right as mediums go, and I love him really, but of course, it takes more out of 'im now. I suppose it will do as 'e gets older. Poor old sausage! Anyway, bye bye!

From the time that Sandra and I signed the two year lease on the Postwick property at the beginning of August 1989, we spent some four months getting the rectory ready for our occupation, during which time we spent a week's holiday cruising around the Norfolk Broads (something I had wanted to do since childhood).

We actually moved in during early December and found that not only was the house quite superb to live in but also that the villagers and parishioners (the latter had a tradition of parking in our front drive when they attended a service or funeral at the small church, which of course we didn't mind putting up with) were friendly and I even found myself enjoying the odd opportunity to attend Church of England services next door. (As a boy, I had attended church regularly.) Sandra's name even appeared frequently on the voluntary church cleaning rota while we lived there – a duty we tended to share. Interestingly, early on in our tenancy, Sandra twice spotted the 'ghost' of an old fashioned priest or rector on the private path between the rectory and the church, but he never bothered us in the house.

After we moved, I continued to travel monthly over to Derbyshire to sit with the Ilkeston circle, which by now had further indications of developing physical phenomena. Early in 1990, the wooden table in the centre of the circle was put aside at the request of the guides, and the medium's chair was moved into a makeshift cabinet comprised of curtains strung on a wire across the corner of the seance room. The seance room itself was a special room at the very top of the house which had been set aside for circle purposes and was permanently blacked out. It was used for no other purpose, so that the atmosphere was not disturbed between sittings, and this helped create the necessary conditions for physical mediumship to blossom.

In the January, 1990 copy of the *Psychic News,* there appeared another advert seeking sitters for yet another physical circle, this time situated on the south coast, in Hove – within a few streets of where Leslie Flint was living. This was a weekly circle and it seemed totally illogical that I should even consider making another long journey on a regular basis but I felt somehow drawn to the advert and replied.

John and Gerry (short for Geraldine) were a very pleasant couple who had been involved in the Spiritualist Movement for many years. Like so many of my other connections, they had often sat with Leslie Flint in the past and, before their retirement to the coast, had lived close to Leslie in London. It came as quite a surprise for them to discover that they were once more living just a short distance away from him. They had been involved in physical circles for some time, with varying results, and were then trying yet again to get their physical circle off the ground. I felt that I might be in a position to help them by supplying a little advice and some physical power, and it was agreed that I should start to sit with them on a trial basis on Tuesday 13 February.

Just before that date, however, I had another private sitting booked with Leslie Flint. The group this time included the whole of the Ilkeston circle, my wife Sandra and one of our ex-sitters – Lisa, from the time of the Harold Wood circle. We were not to know it at the time, of course, but this sitting turned out to be the very last *successful* seance we ever enjoyed with Leslie.

# LESLIE FLINT – A REMARKABLE LAST SEANCE

MONDAY, 5 FEBRUARY 1990 proved to be a very special day, with everybody arriving in good time at Leslie's. Leslie himself seemed in good health and there was an air of anticipation as we all climbed up to the top of the house, where Leslie had his seance room. Bram Rogers, his secretary, busied himself with ensuring that the blackout was complete and, with Leslie in the chair, the sitting began.

Mickey came through comparatively quickly and was loud and clear as he greeted us in his inimitable humorous style, often shouting to demonstrate his ability to communicate independently. He asked me how I was.

After assuring him that I was fine, and inquiring as to how he was, he continued:

> I'm all right. I'm ever so pleased to see you all – but only if you can hear me?

We told him he was loud and clear, and Leslie commented that even *he* could hear him. Mickey then said to Leslie:

> You're getting deaf, ain't yer? [Lesley agreed.] And old as well! Poor old Les!

Before the sitting proper started, Mickey also had this to say about the Ilkeston circle:

> You know, it's extraordinary really, because I would have thought that with the power that your group give, you'd have got more results in your own environment. [We told him that the results *were* starting to come.] Well I hope so, because they *are* experimenting, and I know they're trying to do physical things. There's a lot of power among you – all of you – here, quite apart from old Les, you

> see. And I'm hoping that in your own private circle like, you'll get a lot of manifestations as a result of their experiments.

Mickey was followed immediately by a male communicator with a strong French accent who had spoken to us before, and announced himself as Maurice:

> Hello! I don't know if you hear me? I'm trying, you know, to man – to manifest. It is a little complicate, you know. I think it take a little time to be able to manage to speak properly. But I will try. Maurice speaking. I have want you to know that I have very much interest in everything that is happening. And we know there are problems, but hah! They go. And we are doing everything in our power. We have great hope of the group. You must not lose heart, you know. These things will take time, huh? But already we have been able to achieve certain things. And that is only the beginning. Many things yet to come. Please continue – we *will* be successful.

Maurice was followed by the dulcet cultured tones of Florence Marryat, who once again talked to us at length about the need for the spirit world to develop physical mediumship at the moment, as it had become so very rare. She was encouraging and enthusiastic in her attempts to keep us motivated to continue the efforts of the Ilkeston circle and reiterated the fact that, although she was not in the strictest sense a permanent helper within that circle, she was a frequent and interested visitor with specialist knowledge in the subject of physical mediumship.

As this communication faded out, there came the voice of one of our Native American circle guides, White Feather, who had spoken to us many times before, both at Leslie's and in various of our other circles. After many years of practice, it seemed that he had learned much more English, which helped him with a more sustained talk on this occasion:

> White Feather. White Feather come, bring blessing Great Spirit to children. I happy come talk to children. White Feather very thrill – very thrill – how you say, frilled? I learn more words so that I can come. Speak good English – yes? I want you know. We want you to be happy, but everything you know, this circle make good progress – and the power is good. And you not get down in what you call

> the dumpses. But I want to say one thing. And I don't usually tell futures! But there's going to be big change. There's some hope – how you say in English – I don't know. But there is some change, which at the time you think, 'Ah, maybe.' You don't know. But I say to you it is good thing. Don't be upset. Don't be worry. Don't be sort of – how you say – depress. Because it is good. What is to happen is for the best. And you find it will lead – as it were – into something that make you very happy. But you think I talk in the riddle? But I know you do the work of the spirit and that there is a little problem at the moment. But I says there is things that are going to change and you're going to be much happier. And much more settled in your mind when things develop in the way they have to go. But there will be something that when it come to pass will be something like a surprise probably, you say. But I say to you don't worry! Everything good.

Little did we know it then but this prediction of White Feather's was amazingly accurate in that it foretold of a momentous event which occurred two-and-a-half months later and was to have worldwide recognition; sparking off a chain of events that was to turn my own life upside down in a very short space of time and have massive repercussions in the world of physical mediumship and its phenomena. At the time of this sitting with Leslie Flint, physical mediumship throughout the world was gradually becoming extinct. In the UK, there were now only a couple of mainstream physical mediums left that we knew of who were demonstrating to the public. Leslie himself was one of them, and the other was Gordon Higginson. In both cases, the mediums were elderly, and their powers of physical mediumship were no longer of the strength and calibre that they had once been. While there were a scattering of private home circles sitting for phenomena – a few of which *were* enjoying positive results, these tended to operate as closed circles (closed to visitors) with only the regular sitters and a handful of personal guests witnessing the phenomena. Very few new groups sitting for physical mediumship were starting up, and when they did so, most had little or no knowledge of how to proceed in order to develop the phenomena. It seemed that contemporary physical mediumship for the benefit of the public had little going for it, and might be destined to go the way of the dodo when Leslie and Gordon Higginson finally kicked the bucket, as Mickey would put it.

Several factors had contributed to this decline: physical mediums and potential physical mediums were, and still are, extremely rare, often needing to possess a particular property within some of their genes and chromosomes to activate their mediumship. Good physical mediums tend to be *born* with their potential gift and they also need the *desire* to develop such mediumship for the good of mankind.

In addition, physical mediums of the past sometimes took 20 years or more to develop their gifts successfully. With the increased pace of modern living and distractions of this technical age such as television sets, video recorders and hi-fi equipment, the majority of people would be reluctant to devote such a large part of their lives to the development of physical mediumship, and not only the medium, but also a suitable group of dedicated sitters would need to give the same commitment to spirit for the development of *only one* physical medium.

A further factor is the very real fear of injury to the physical medium caused by inexperienced and ignorant sitters behaving in an irresponsible way during the production of ectoplasm by the spirit operators (the failure of sitters to stay in their allotted places, or the sudden introduction of light into the room without warning during seances, can cause the ectoplasmic substance to fly back into the body of the medium at great speed, often causing him or her painful burns or even internal haemorrhages). Also the harsh, almost sadistic treatment meted out by the so-called researchers of the day, such as being sewn into a mailbag for a couple of hours or being forced to hold a measured quantity of coloured water in the mouth for over an hour, helped considerably in driving physical mediumship underground ... But I am digressing again! Let us return to the February Flint sitting.

Mickey returned once more after the communication by White Feather, to give a certain amount of personal evidence of survival to several of the sitters. He trotted out fact after fact, name after name, and all turned out to be accurate. He spoke of a boy who was present who had committed suicide, and named the street in Derbyshire where the boy had lived, as well as the fact that one member of the Ilkeston circle had been trying to help him advance from the earthbound position he had been in to the more spiritual realms of the afterlife.

Interestingly, part way through Mickey's chatter, Leslie was seized with a coughing bout and, while Mickey kept on talking throughout, his voice became weaker each time Leslie coughed. Mickey once again told us that when Leslie kicked the bucket, he (Mickey) would be finished with this communication lark. Touchingly, Leslie asked him, 'How much longer, Mickey?' To which he got the curt reply: 'Can't answer that! And even if I could, I wouldn't!'

Suddenly, Mickey told us:

> Winston's around. I don't think he's very happy, though! Well, he's happy of course, in a way – yes, of course he's happy. But he's not happy about the set-up on your side. Well, the state of your world. Although a lot of things are happening that are good, but there's also a lot of unhappiness and misery. A lot of hatred and malice, ain't there? And Maggie's got herself in a twist, ain't she?

This was followed by the familiar tones of Winston Churchill, who came to talk to us:

> Hello, hello, hello! Well, I'm not quite sure whether you can hear me? [We answered in the affirmative.] This is like most things, you know. You get into a state where, quite frankly, from time to time – conditions being what they may be – one's never quite sure as to whether one's going to be able to manifest. But anyway, I'm trying to do my best. Well you know, I do come to your sessions, and I keep a great interest in everything that's happening. I'm quite sure that if you're patient and persevere, we shall achieve a great deal with you. But you mustn't lose heart, you know. I shall always be around. I'm around with your group, and I'm around in other directions too. Particularly with the Conservative Party, but I'm not going to make any statement on that. I only hope and pray – well – that things will change for the better. There are certain things that I'm not happy about. But then again over here – in a sense – there are no politics. But if you've been a politician and you've been very much to the fore – when on your side – you don't lose, as it were, interest. And if you feel you can be of some help and some value – then you do try and bring certain influences to bear wherever possible.

> Not necessarily just with Spiritualists and mediums. I try to influence in other directions, as indeed do many of us here. Of course, we're very, very happy with the way things are changing in Russia. And not only in Russia, but in other places as well – other countries. But you know, I'm a bit concerned about being over-anxious, I think, where Europe is concerned in particular. It's got to be a slow reunification. I mean I don't wish to be pessimistic, or I certainly don't want to say anything that's in any way detrimental, but we've got to learn and experience things – which by their very nature could open up, well, complexities, and could open up doors which are best kept closed. But I don't want to say too much. By all means, things are improving. And the European aspect too is – I think – much better than it once was. But I'm very concerned about my party that once was. I hope it's not putting too many pressures on people, as I feel that is detrimental not only to the people but also detrimental to the party. But there again, perhaps I shouldn't go into politics too much. But I do hope and pray that as far as your little group of souls is concerned, you will realise that not only I, but innumerable souls here are doing everything in their power to help and assist. Just be patient with yourselves, and be patient with us. Anyway, I mustn't stay. Can't stay in any case! All my blessings. May God go with you! All the best, and if I may so say – and if these days I don't see it in years – all the very best for the year. Goodbye. Make it a spiritual one. And I don't mean out of a bottle.

Mickey seemed fascinated by what Winnie had had to say, and commented:

> Cor, he's got a sense of humour! I mean, you lot don't hit the bottle, do you? No, I'm only kidding. There's no 'arm in 'aving a drink! When I was on your side, and I was a nipper, like, my mum and dad used to knock it back. Cor, stone the crows.

This whirlwind of a Cockney guide went on to give out a further myriad of messages which involved many individual pieces of accurate evidence on a personal level for various of the sitters. He also told us a little about himself as he really is before the power gave out:

> Ha, ha! You can't 'elp laughing! Everybody assumes when I come, like, that I'm a kid. Well, I come back as I was, like – mentally I reproduce, if you want to put it like that, aspects of the old self as

I once was. But away from you lot, I'm on an entirely different level, you know. I don't say I'm so highly evolved and all that – I don't mean that. But the point is – I'm happy in my new environment over 'ere. But I always look forward to coming down and chatting – doing me job and all that. 'Cos, of course, when old Les kicks the bucket, ha, ha! 'E's got a bit longer to go yet I expect but anyway, when the old body's disposed of – and they'll 'ave a job with that – I don't know that I'll bother to come back. But the power's getting down now. You see, it's my medium. He's getting worn out, and so am I. I can only do me best. Anyway, carry on the good work. I can't 'old on. Bye bye.

After the sitting, Leslie seemed totally worn out, and had to take his leave quickly before going for a nap. Bram gave us another date in June but that turned out to be a totally blank sitting. We had just enjoyed our last chat with Mickey and the gang through Leslie Flint's excellent mediumship and the sitting had been a good one.

# I BECOME THE FOUNDER OF THE NOAH'S ARK SOCIETY

AFTER THIS LAST excellent Flint seance, I continued my monthly sittings with the Ilkeston circle and in addition started to sit weekly with the Hove circle. At Hove, there were some definite signs that physical phenomena could develop, despite the fact that it took a while for the membership of the circle to settle down. After I joined there were some other new members commencing to sit, with other members leaving but, provided that this personnel situation was stabilised, I felt very confident that the harmony would build to a degree where some good phenomena might take place. Little did I know how good! During late March, John and Gerry decided to buy a new carpet for their lounge and a young man from a local carpet emporium visited to measure up the room.

He turned out to be a young man who had been blessed with a natural psychic ability from childhood, although he had no practical experience of formal psychic matters. Right out of the blue (and he has no idea to this day why he felt compelled to say it), he blurted out, 'I know what you use this room for – seances.' You could have knocked John down with a feather. He was, to use a modern expression, gobsmacked! Well, one thing led to another, and after a long chat on the subject, the young man departed, with an order for one of his firm's carpets under one arm, and a book on physical mediumship he had borrowed from John under the other. This resulted in his being invited to join the Hove circle, where he started to sit towards the end of April. At a later date, I suggested that he worked under the pseudonym of 'Lincoln' to protect his true identity as a trance and physical medium, which he has ever since done although, having gone on to make quite a reputation, he now also works under his own name of Colin Fry. The

Hove circle I dubbed the 'Swift Circle', as it was run by John and Gerry Austin, and there had once been a car called the 'Austin Swift'.

Back at the Ilkeston group, things were also speeding up, as the medium's development became more obvious. On 21 April 1990, just after Easter, the sitters were pretty much taken unawares when, for the first time, a spirit entity spoke to us in the independent voice. In fact, it was not until the entity had finished speaking that we all realised just exactly what had taken place. While the spirit voice was speaking, we had all clearly heard loud lip-smacking voices simultaneously coming from the medium's own mouth. But it was the content of the communication that I recognised as being particularly significant.

The communicator introduced himself as Noah Zerdin, and he told us that spirits wanted us to form an educational society for people of like mind for the development, promotion and safe practice of modern physical mediumship, to ensure its survival so that current and future generations could witness its wonders for themselves. We were also asked to create a newsletter for regular production and distribution, so that people of like mind could be linked together on a firm basis. Shortly afterwards, it was discovered that this special communication had come within four days of the 59th anniversary of the inaugural meeting of the Link Association of Home Circles, on 25 April 1931. That meeting had also been held on a Saturday, in Wimbledon, south-west London, and the Link had subsequently been run successfully for many years by Noah Zerdin.

Needless to say, I was filled with excitement at the prospect of creating such a society for what was clearly a worthy purpose. I spent the next week in a daze, working out in my mind what sort of committee structure would be necessary to undertake such a massive task; mulling over too the potential of involving other physical circles; the types of meetings that should be undertaken; the practical help that should be offered to those who were seeking to start up a group for the development of physical mediumship; the possibilities of providing demonstrations of physical phenomena for members to witness; the educational information about physical mediumship that should be imparted to members of the society; the funding of the project (most important) and, above all, the supplying of a suitable name for such a society.

The initial reaction from the other members of the circle was not so enthusiastic but with a lot of cajoling, and a small amount of bullying, I managed to get a blanket agreement for them to join me in making such an important society a reality. Within a week, I had come up with the name – the Noah's Ark Society for Physical Mediumship. The name came to me one day in a flash of inspiration, and it turned out to be very apt for the following reasons:

1. The reference to Noah was a tribute to the late Noah Zerdin, who had delivered the message.

2. Noah's Ark in the Biblical stories was created to save the animal population from extinction. The Noah's Ark Society would surely save a form of mediumship – physical mediumship – from the same fate

3. Again, in the Biblical sense, the Ark of the Covenant was a repository for Psychic Power and Spiritual Knowledge, and it was hoped that these attributes would also be found within the Noah's Ark Society.

It was as if I had at last discovered my own true destiny as to what I was meant to do in this life. I felt very exhilarated and extremely privileged to be one of the people who had been selected by the spirit world to get the ball rolling, and I lost no time in launching myself wholeheartedly into the project. I found myself doodling away to try and come up with an appropriate logo for this new society that I had just named, and eventually put my ideas to a small company of graphic artists in Norwich who brought the current logo to life, as well as designing letterheads and other necessary stationery. This whole operation rapidly became so important to me that I never stopped to draw breath until everything was in place for a low-key launch of the society.

In the early days, since there were not as yet any members, it follows that there were also no funds in the new organisation with which to support its launch. However, since I was already fully committed psychologically to the success of the project, I did not allow that to stand in our way, and personally covered all its initial expenses, so that it did not start its life at a financial disadvantage.

The first committee meeting was held in Ilkeston on 3 May. Since there were no formal officers at that point, I chaired the meeting of seven delegates (all members of the Ilkeston circle). It was proposed that a society for physical mediumship be set up immediately and that such a society be called the Noah's Ark Society for Physical Mediumship. The motion was carried unanimously.

It was further proposed that an advert be placed for two weeks in the *Psychic News* inviting inquiries and membership applications 'to test the water'. This motion was also carried unanimously, as was the motion calling for the preparation of suitable literature and application forms.

I therefore put together a broadsheet, setting out the aims and objects of the society as we saw them, which was prepared, along with a membership application form, for sending out to interested parties. I also placed the following advert in the *Psychic News:*

THE NOAH'S ARK SOCIETY

FOR PHYSICAL MEDIUMSHIP

A new worldwide social and teaching organisation invites inquiries and mem-bership applications from individuals and home circles of like mind.

We have been founded by the inspiration of NOAH ZERDIN speaking from spirit in the "independent direct voice" to counsel, instruct and promote the development, growth and safe practice of PHYSICAL MEDIUMSHIP TODAY, as well as the informal exchange of relevant ideas and experiences.

For membership forms and further details of the aims and activities of the society, please write enclosing a large SAE to:

The Membership Secretary,
Noah's Ark Society

The first inquiry generated by this *Psychic News* advert arrived on 21 May and the initial trickle of inquiries soon turned into a steady stream. One of these, which arrived on 31 May, came from a northern businessman called Stewart Alexander, who wrote:

> Kindly send details. I have been very active in respect of physical mediumship for over 20 years with my own circle. I am involved in lecturing and have had articles published in magazines in both this country and America. I correspond with many people all over the world regarding such mediumship, and I have many unique recordings – most made many years ago at circles for the direct voice and materialisation. At the present time I am in close contact with an old time Spiritualist who was a neighbour and close friend of Noah Zerdin.

On 5 June, Stewart Alexander also became the very first associate member of the society and was allocated the membership number AE1. It had been decided that we would offer three types of membership: associate membership for individuals who were interested in physical mediumship, corporate body membership for churches, societies and organisations who were interested in the subject and circle membership for a circle who were sitting for and/or getting physical phenomena. I devised a simple system of reference so that these categories could be easily identified by the initial letter of their membership number which ensured that associate members had an 'A', corporate body members had a 'B' (this type of membership was later restricted to overseas bodies only), and member circles were identified by a 'C' prefix.

The second letter, or group of letters, identified the geographical location of the member; so that 'E' stood for England, 'S' for Scotland and 'W' for Wales. 'NI' was for Northern Ireland, 'U' for the USA, 'FIN' was for Finland, 'AUS' for Australia and so on. The Ilkeston circle carried the membership number CE1.

On 11 June, as agreed, we once again went to visit Leslie Flint for a sitting. This time the party was made up of sitters from both the Ilkeston and the Hove circles but we were all to be disappointed when the seance was a total blank. Apparently, by this time, Leslie's results had become more blanks than successful seances, and his recent sittings had nearly all been failures. While we were there, however, I took the trouble to explain to Leslie what we were trying to achieve with the new Noah's Ark Society and he was invited there and then to become an Honorary Vice President of the NAS, which he accepted – much to our delight.

Although Bram gave us another booking for 1 October, it was less than two weeks after this abortive seance that we had a standard letter to say that sadly, owing to Leslie's poor health, his advanced age, and the present state of his once-flourishing mediumship, he had reluctantly been forced to retire from private sittings. To us, it seemed that it was definitely a case of one era ending as another one began. Over the years, I had enjoyed many wonderful sittings with Leslie, and could appreciate how he must be feeling himself. The loss of regular contact with his guides and helpers, especially Mickey, would be like losing all the members of his family in one fell swoop and, despite the fact that such guides and helpers were already 'dead', to use layman's terms, such a loss of contact must set off a grieving process akin to a normal bereavement.

The second committee meeting of the society took place on 14 June, when the formal appointment of a caretaker committee took place. I was installed as chairman and membership secretary, as well as editor of the proposed newsletter. It was agreed at the meeting that the formation of the newsletter and its production should be set in motion at once, as this instruction had formed an integral part of the original message from Noah Zerdin. Stewart Alexander, the only non-member of the Ilkeston circle to be appointed to the committee at this stage, became the archive officer, as he had for many years been deeply involved in researching the physical mediumship of many veteran and pioneer mediums within the Spiritualist Movement. By now, there had been 26 inquiries from our initial adverts, which had yielded 5 associate members and 1 member circle.

Meanwhile, sittings of the Ilkeston and Hove circles continued apace. At Ilkeston, there were further instances of independent voice occurring regularly, in parallel with the normal trance communications. It was requested that a special cabinet be designed that could be converted quickly from rectangular to triangular configuration, so that it might also be used across the corner of some rooms, as well as centrally in others. I applied myself to this request and took my appropriate designs to a local joiner to have it built. The cabinet could certainly be altered quickly, which was the object of the exercise – just a few minutes, a change of standard roof from rectangular to triangular, and the adjustment of a few bolts and wingnuts – and it was transformed from one shape to another. Unfortunately, however, I had got a bit carried away with the dimensions and sitting in the cabinet became like sitting in an indoor garden shed. There was literally room for three. But the thought was there, and it did the job for which it was intended.

At the Hove circle, matters were becoming even more exciting. Within a few weeks of the young man Lincoln joining the circle, it became increasingly obvious that he was a natural deep-trance medium and his mediumship gradually began to unfold. Very quickly, a myriad of different communicators spoke through him. I recall very vividly being present when a spirit person who identified himself as Liberace (the piano-playing American entertainer and star) spoke through Lincoln in this way. Remembering his voice from his past television shows, I was absolutely sure that the voice of this communicator was identical to the 'real thing', and the list of spirit people communicating in this way grew steadily. The sustained voices were most impressive and included entities from all walks of life.

Gradually the main guides and controls made themselves known in this way and the serious development of physical mediumship within Lincoln and the circle itself started to take place. In the beginning, it was not always strictly controlled, which is one of the normal problems of early development in this field. The very first instance of physical phenomena as such was the apport of a 20p coin, which was ejected forwards with some force from the solar plexus of the medium, coming to rest on the floor a few feet away from him. It was accompanied by a message from a deceased relative for one of the circle members to the effect that he needed the cash, but it caused a furore amongst the guides and helpers since the spirit entity who caused the apport to be brought had not been given permission to use the medium in that way. Sitters were told that such an uncontrolled demonstration of phenomena would not be allowed to happen again and that much stricter control would be exercised by the spirit group who were working with the circle from now on. Thereafter they kept to their word and the controlled development of the medium began to accelerate at an amazing rate.

The Noah's Ark Society continued to grow from its humble beginnings. As editor, I completed production of the first edition of the monthly *Noah's Ark Newsletter* (which was dated August 1990) and distributed copies to members, as well as to those who had inquired about the society. This first issue was in A5 booklet format and consisted of 16 pages of script, typed by my own fair hand on a 'steam' typewriter, before being photocopied and supplied with a blue cover carrying the NAS logo. It was, however, well received by all, and the appearance on the streets served to boost the membership of the society.

During August, in addition to the creation of a newsletter, I realised that it was important from the beginning to provide as much help and practical advice as possible, both for existing physical circles and for those groups of people who wished to form and run new physical circles. Some of this educational information could be imparted to members by the society in the course of teaching seminars but that was not yet a possibility – so urgent action was needed in order for inexperienced sitters to know exactly what they were doing in their circles. I believed then as I believe now, that the necessary production of the right harmonious conditions in which the spirit people are able to develop good physical mediumship is the joint responsibility of *all* the sitters in that circle and not just the responsibility of the medium. The answer was to educate the sitters in a circle as well as the potential medium and I set out to do just that by writing a 16–page teaching booklet for physical circles. I then distributed a free copy of this to all the members of the society. Today, through using the booklet and adapting the basic information for personal use, many physical circles all over the world have achieved positive results – a fact of which I am very proud.

Not everybody within the Spiritualist movement welcomed the advent of the Noah's Ark Society, which came as something of a shock to me at the time. There was mixed reaction from the Spiritualist 'Establishment', some of which bordered on open hostility. One Spiritualist organisation even went to the expense of placing adverts in the psychic press, publicly distancing itself from the NAS. Once, when I made a special journey to Stansted Hall, the manager would not even allow me across the threshold to discuss the possibility of the Noah's Ark Society running a week's course there. I was told curtly to 'write in'. Regrettably, when I did so, my letter was ignored by the college – I never received a reply or an acknowledgement.

The society continued to grow regardless, and we were all quite amazed to discover that some 60 per cent of the inquiries about the NAS were being converted into firm membership. A further service offered from the outset was for a visit by one or more representatives of the committee to member circles for assessment purposes. In the early days, I undertook most of these visits myself, and I remember clearly the first of these taking place on 10 September (which also happened to be my birthday) when I sat in at the inaugural sitting of a new physical circle in Watford. The circle showed great promise, as did others I assessed subsequently at Romford, Basildon, Ilford and Forest Gate, East London. At the last of these venues I witnessed the most superb demonstration of transfiguration proper, involving an ectoplasmic mask over the medium's face, which changed according to the communicator. In one case, I was able to see the completely moulded image of a Roman centurion, complete with helmet and plume.

Because of his previous business commitments, the first monthly committee meeting that Stewart Alexander was able to attend was the meeting on Thursday 18 October and we arranged to meet up beforehand at the Trowell motorway services for a coffee, so that I could show him the way to Ilkeston. While we were sitting in the cafeteria, he dropped a bombshell, in the form of a confession that he was a deep trance and physical medium who had been sitting in his own home circle for 20 years, in addition to acting as the medium in a special experimental circle at Elton, near Chester, which sat once a month. He told me too that his physical mediumship had recently been stopped by his guides till further notice for reasons known only to themselves but that he was continuing sittings at Elton and in his home circle where he was still being used for deep trance work. Out of this conversation came an invitation for me to sit in the next monthly experimental circle at Elton, which was ratified by the circle leader of this Noah's Ark member circle. This sitting took place on 30 October and I was extremely impressed by Stewart Alexander's excellent deep trance mediumship. I received some wonderful personal evidence of survival from my first father-in-law who, to be honest, was the last person I would have expected to communicate with me there! There was also a confirmation of the genuineness of the coin which had earlier been apported through Lincoln, this being his first physical phenomenon.

The sitting at Elton fully confirmed the superb quality of Stewart Alexander's trance mediumship. In addition to being able to converse direct with my ex-father-in-law, it included a 'book test' (a form of evidential communication concerning books at the home of the sitter which the medium would have had no knowledge of. This was previously made famous by the medium Mrs Gladys Osborne Leonard, through her child guide, 'Feda'). At Elton, it was conducted by Stewart's child guide 'Christopher', who was able to describe my home (the rectory) in minute detail accurately. I might add here that the medium had never in his life visited this house. During this 'test', Christopher clairvoyantly led me correctly through the various rooms of the rectory, giving evidential details of them all, until he arrived at the library. I was then directed to a certain bookcase and told to go down to a certain shelf where, so many books from the left, I would find a certain book with a red cover. I was told to turn to a certain page, and was accurately given the passage of words that appeared there.

Naturally, until I got home after this sitting, I had no way of knowing if the information about the book was right or wrong. Imagine my amazement then, when I discovered that everything that I had been told was absolutely and 100 per cent true.

By November 1990, two members of the Ilkeston circle had left both the circle and the NAS Committee and two members from Leicester, Janet and Roger, were co-opted on to the committee to replace them. The society was becoming well established by this time with almost 50 individual members and 18 member circles. The production and distribution of the monthly newsletter was getting into a steady routine and, despite the hard work involved, was running smoothly, with regular articles by me and by Stewart Alexander as archive officer. We were considering a venue for a weekend residential seminar the following spring and had already booked a meeting room for 70 at the brand new Sleep Inn on the nearby Nottingham/Derby junction of the M1, which was to be used for our first one-day seminar on 20 January 1991.

Alan Crossley, leader of a member circle, was appointed an honorary vice-present of the society in recognition of his 40 years' experience in the field of physical mediumship. Alan knew Helen Duncan and Maud Gunning well and had sat with Alec Harris, Leslie Flint and most other prominent physical mediums of the day on a number of occasions. His book, *The Story of Helen Duncan,* is still in print today and has become a psychic classic.

In late November, I once again visited the Hove circle, which had by now started to get regular levitation of the trumpet through its medium, Lincoln. During the visit, they experienced their first totally independent voices, one of which belonged to the son of John and Gerry. A psychic rod of ectoplasm was produced which proceeded to rap out Gerry's full initials, despite the fact that her middle initial was unknown to all but John, the circle leader. Interestingly, Lincoln stayed conscious while this phenomenon was taking place but was rendered temporarily paralysed. At one point, however, he *did* move a hand to his front and touched the rod, from which he appeared to almost suffer the effects of an electric shock. The result of this – seen after the sitting – was a painful blister on his finger similar to one which might have been caused by a burn.

Early December saw me visiting a member circle in Essex, which had been running for about six years, and had just recently changed its venue to a small coal cellar. During my visit, the physical phenomena commenced quickly when the table started to lift and tilt by itself without being touched by any of the sitters. This was done in a lively fashion and the movements could be seen in the darkness because of an ingenious system of small red LED lights on the four corners of the table. Each only came on when its respective corner of the table was off the ground. So for instance, if the table was right off the ground, all four lights came on, while one corner off the ground gave rise to just a single light. At one point in the seance, two diagonally opposite legs of the table were off the ground together, as indicated by the lights. Think about it – that is a physical impossibility – but it *did* happen in my presence!

There was also the rolling of toy balls and budgie bells across the floor. During the sitting, a heavy brass handbell was rung. There was an apport of a 2p piece, discovered after the seance on the central table, and undisturbed by the table's movements. To cap it all off, a man's voice was heard to speak independently from near the ceiling, bidding us 'hello', and this had been captured on the recording of the session as we later heard. The circle certainly showed great promise.

Back in the Noah's Ark Committee, final preparations were taking place for the one-day seminar to be held at the Nottingham Sleep Inn. The meeting room was ideal and we were proud to be the first organisation to use it since the hotel was built. The only problem on the horizon was the fact that the hotel's restaurant facilities were not yet completed, so delegates would have to eat elsewhere at lunchtime. We solved the problem by taking a block booking for a set-price lunch at another hotel a quarter of a mile away. The programme was now in place, and we were ready to go. All we needed were the bookings, and I must confess that I was not absolutely sure whether we would be able to fill all the available places. In the event, I need not have worried.

The Park International Hotel at Leicester had been chosen and booked for an NAS weekend residential seminar from 10 to 12 May. For the first time, we were including an experimental sitting for physical phenomena to be attended by all the delegates present. The development of the young physical medium Lincoln had so far been amazingly fast and he and the Swift circle at Hove had agreed to help with this experimental sitting, during which Lincoln would act as the medium.

By the time that I visited the Hove circle again on 26 February, Lincoln was, at his own request, sitting in the circle each week in a restricted state, tied to his chair by his wrists and his legs. While he was happy to sit in this fashion, the restriction took nothing away from his mediumship. During my visit, the trumpet was seen to rise and stay aloft for a full 35 minutes, with clear spirit voices issuing from it. A tambourine was shaken, levitated and moved around the circle at the same time. I was able to confirm at the end of the seance that all the medium's bindings were still intact. These advanced phenomena, which had actually been developed over a relatively brief space of time, were now nothing short of spectacular.

# NOAH'S ARK SOCIETY SEMINARS

The inaugural seminar of the Noah's Ark Society was held as arranged on Sunday, 20 January 1991. Starting at 9.30 a.m., it proved to be a full day for the delegates until 5.30 p.m. The caretaker president gave an introductory talk and expounded on the 'State of the Ark'. There was a talk by Stewart Alexander on the history of physical mediumship; then I spoke about its mechanics, owing to the fact that through ill health, Alan Crossley was unable to attend to undertake this particular lecture. After an excellent lunch at the Nottingham Post House, Tom Harrison (founding manager of the Arthur Findlay College at Stansted Hall, Essex, who also happened to be the son of famous materialisation medium Minnie Harrison as well as a member of an NAS circle) gave a superb and very entertaining talk and slide show on his home circle experiences of many years ago when, through his mother's mediumship, circle members were able to experience materialisations on a regular basis. I followed this with a further lecture on the development of physical mediumship as a guide for those present who wanted to set up and run their own physical circles. The seminar was rounded off by an overview of how we saw the Noah's Ark Society evolving in the future and an open forum where a panel of committee members was available to answer any questions. From this point onwards, it seemed that I was well and truly launched on a lecturing career and I have since given many lectures on the subject to churches and interested groups throughout the country in addition to my regular talks at NAS seminars.

This was also the first occasion that my wife Sandra had helped out at an NAS event and a couple of weeks later she went on to join the committee as treasurer of the society. The seminar itself went down extremely well with the delegates, although at this stage not all of those who attended were actually members of the NAS.

The running of the seminar had, however, been an eye-opener for the committee as it had spelt out exactly how much work and commitment was necessary to stage even a one-day seminar. Shortly afterwards, the Ilkeston circle broke up. The caretaker president and many of the committee members decided to go their own way in future and we found ourselves having to find extra committee members at short notice to continue the work of the society.

Alan Crossley, as honorary vice-president, was approached to take on the presidency and despite his poor health, he agreed. Over the next few weeks we added a separate membership secretary, a technical officer and a publicity officer to the committee. We also appointed area representatives of the society for Scotland and Wales.

In February, Sandra and I started up our own weekly physical home circle once more, for which purpose we used the rectory study – one room in the house which had a very spiritual atmosphere about it. We had great difficulty in finding suitable sitters in the East Anglia area and initially ran the circle as a low-key affair.

The Swift circle at Hove continued in its dramatic development of Lincoln's mediumship; when I visited again in 19 March, a new guide made himself known to the circle. He introduced himself as 'the Mandarin' and explained that his was the task to get the circle on a proper footing, ensuring that the future work would concentrate on the more important phenomena. The child guide, Charlie (in his lifetime a distant relative of the medium), who had been responsible for trumpet and other physical phenomena, would on occasions be able to appear as an adult. Lincoln had started the seance as usual, with his arms and legs secured. During the sitting, there was a loud thud, and it was discovered afterwards that one of his leather wrist straps had been completely undone and thrown across the circle. However, the plastic cable tie which bound it to the arm of the chair was still intact. Cable ties had been chosen for use in his binding because they are so designed that they are impossible to undo once secured and it was therefore the normal practice of the circle members to *cut* them off at the end of a seance in order to release the medium. For the plastic cable tie to have remained intact in this way would have required it to pass through solid matter in the course of the phenomenon which *had* occurred. This was pretty clever stuff from the spirit operators, and would have been totally impossible for the medium himself to accomplish.

On 26 March I was again privileged to sit with the president's experimental circle at Elton, where we were once more treated to a wonderful display of evidential trance mediumship by Stewart Alexander, which rendered up a considerable amount of survival evidence to the sitters present. One of Stewart's guides, White Feather, spoke to us at length, giving detailed instructions for the residential weekend seminar in May.

The date of the first Annual General Meeting of the Noah's Ark Society was 6 April and for this, we found ourselves back at the Sleep Inn. All of the committee were returned unopposed, under the presidency of Alan Crossley. My positions of chairman of the society and editor of the newsletter were ratified by the membership, as was Sandra's appointment as treasurer. With this behind us, it was 'full steam ahead' to prepare for the May residential seminar with the bulk of the work, consisting of bookings and organisation, being undertaken jointly by Sandra and me.

It had been suggested by a member that since there was currently an offer on specialist video cameras for filming in total darkness, the society should purchase at least one. I travelled to Harrow for this purpose and, with the agreement of the committee, bought two, which we were sure would be extremely useful to the society in the future. I also had two wooden stands made so that they could be adapted for circle work. At a later date, the leader of one of the society's member circles, who suspected that not all the phenomena which were occurring in his circle were genuine, secreted one of these cameras during a sitting of the circle and afterwards spotted on the recording that a particular sitter was creating phenomena fraudulently, while sitting there with a big grin on his face. Even later still, a person who professed to be 'one of the leading physical mediums in the world' allowed one of his sittings to be filmed in total darkness by another of these special video cameras. Suffice to say that the resulting video recording showed very little that could be attributed to genuine physical phenomena, as the medium concerned had failed to realise with what clarity the camera could function or the fact that it was fitted with a wide-angled lens. The society would never, therefore, have endorsed his mediumship.

When I visited the Hove circle on 9 April, there was again levitation of the tambourine and trumpet. Indeed, the trumpet stayed aloft for 45 minutes this time, during the course of which it performed various manoeuvres and aerobatics. It was obvious to us all that the movements were precision controlled in the dark to an exceptional degree and the voice of the Mandarin, speaking clearly through the trumpet, continued to issue instructions and comments throughout. On more than one occasion, his communications were prefaced by a crackling noise similar to static electricity coming from the ectoplasmic voicebox (a typical feature of this type of phenomenon).

The spirit operators had previously asked the Hove circle to place a bowl of salt within the circle before each sitting. During this particular seance, there was a grating sound as objects were moved over the hardboard flooring, and it was afterwards discovered that the salt had been sprinkled over the floor. The medium was wearing dark trousers and sat with his legs tied to the chair in the usual manner. Afterwards, although his legs remained tied, there was a trail of salt on his socks and trouser legs – left by the retreating psychic rods and pseudopods, which had been seen clearly by all the sitters earlier as they crossed the luminous bands on the trumpet in the process of picking it up.

Ever since the circle began, the sitters had put out a piece of paper every week which was taped to a small hardboard drawing board, together with a tiny piece of pencil, about one inch long. The week prior to this sitting, they had for the first time ever had the single word 'Hallo' written on the paper. When I sat the next week, we afterwards discovered much more writing and some small drawings on the paper which, with its board, had been moved four feet from the hearth to the middle of the circle during the seance.

Keen to receive any last minute instructions from their circle guides about the imminent experimental sitting at the Leicester seminar, I sat additionally with the Swift circle at Hove on 30 April. Lincoln's mediumship was developing in strength and quality all the time, and by now there was never long to wait before the phenomena started. As well as the salt previously mentioned, the circle had now been instructed by the Mandarin to put out a saucer containing half a teaspoon each of the following six crushed vitamins and minerals every time they sat: vitamin C, vitamin D, riboflavin, iron, calcium and magnesium. All of these plus the salt, it was stated, would help to improve the phenomena enormously and prevent the medium's own system from becoming drained of its vitality when he was being used for physical phenomena.

A heavy brass handbell was levitated and rung as it moved all the way round the circle. At one stage, the voicebox for the independent voice was actually built up *inside* the handbell. Throughout the evening, circle guides the Mandarin, Charlie and Daphne (a well-spoken lady who attends to the personal aspect of communication within the circle) all spoke quite clearly in the independent voice giving important advice for the Leicester experiment. A sweater had been supernormally removed from the medium during the sitting and one of his legs had been moved through the arm of his chair in such a way that to have achieved that result, either the chair arm or his leg must have been temporary dematerialised.

The day of the first residential seminar finally arrived and no less than 95 delegates gathered at the Park International Hotel in Leicester. After an evening meal, the seminar started on 10 May with a lighthearted experiment of table tilting, in which everybody took part, and which I organised. It was soon apparent that much psychic energy was being generated during this experiment, with tables all over the place suddenly becoming animated to perform the most amazing gyrations.

For everybody present, the seminar proved to be extremely successful, and I can honestly say that never in my life before had I been a part of anything like it. For me, and for many of the other delegates present, the whole weekend was the most intensely emotional experience that I had ever enjoyed, and even today, it would take some surpassing. At times, there was hardly a dry eye in the house as intense emotions and an incredible feeling of love swept through the 95 people present. 'Touched by angels' is the expression that springs to mind and that is indeed the feeling that many of us had for the whole of the seminar. Archive officer Stewart Alexander wrote after the event:

> Upon arrival at the hotel in Leicester on that memorable Friday evening, it very quickly became apparent that everyone in attendance were brothers and sisters, not only in respect of sharing a common interest, but also by being linked spiritually together as one. In total harmony we lived together, worked together, laughed together, and yet at times, we cried together. One simply had to be present to appreciate what happened that weekend but I have not the least doubt as to the fact that the hand of spirit was upon us all.

Naturally, the focal point of the weekend was the experimental sitting held on the Saturday night but, in addition, I ran a workshop for EVP, as well as lecturing on the history of physical mediumship and talking about the 'State of the Ark'. Tom Harrison again lectured on his mother's mediumship, and NAS president Alan Crossley spoke of his '40 Years Amongst the Physical Mediums'. Stewart Alexander lectured on the mediumship of Margery (physical medium Mina Crandon), which he had studied in depth for many years. Anthony Harris (grandson of Alec Harris the materialisation medium) spoke on his grandfather's mediumship, while the publicity officer gave a talk on psychic surgery. There was ample time put aside for questions and the final event of the seminar was an 'open forum' for discussion of anything and everything relevant to the seminar and the society itself.

There was a special session of instructions prior to the Saturday evening experimental sitting and this was also always a part of future seminars as it was felt that it was so important that delegates had some idea of what they might expect to experience during such a sitting – and of how they were expected to behave in the sitting itself. In addition, the practice of searching delegates prior to such an experimental sitting was introduced. While this might sound drastic to the uninitiated, one must remember that every time a physical medium whose phenomena involved the use of ectoplasm sat in such a large experimental seance, he or she was literally putting their life on the line (because of the physical damage which could be inflicted on them by someone doing something silly during a sitting, such as smuggling in and using a torch. There had been several instances in the past of mediums actually being killed or physically incapacitated on a permanent basis). So the responsibility of the organisers to protect the health of the medium concerned was colossal.

The *Psychic News* headline for their front-page article on this NAS experimental sitting, as reported in the edition of 25 May 1991 read 'Spirit voices heard at dramatic test seance', and I would have suggested that such a headline was an understatement. The seating for the seance was pre-arranged by me and consisted of an inner circle of 16 people, including the medium, who were very experienced in physical mediumship. The middle circle contained 32 delegates, while 47, who were comparatively new to the subject, sat in the outer circle. For security reasons, the outer doors of the room were locked during the sitting. It was an extremely large room and we were not allowed to turn off the emergency lighting. Every effort was, however, made to black out the room to the required standard for physical phenomena, by covering up these lights with thick cardboard boxes. As the seance proceeded, one of the boxes slipped slightly so that some light was indeed visible throughout the seance. While this did not hamper the phenomenon itself, it was possible for most of us present to observe the top of the medium's head throughout the whole of the sitting, thereby confirming conclusively that he never moved at all for the duration of the experiment.

On the day of this remarkable seance, Lincoln had been sitting in the Swift circle at Hove for exactly a year and a day for the development of his physical mediumship. At Leicester, on this occasion, just three members of his home circle accompanied him. Test conditions were adhered to in that at his own request, he was tied to the chair by his wrists (using cable ties) and legs (using simple ligatures). In the centre of the inner circle were placed two trumpets, complete with luminous bands around both ends, a tambourine, pencils and paper, water and a saucer of vitamins and minerals.

A prayer, which I delivered, opened the proceedings, and then the delegates all began to sing rousing songs. As soon as the singing started, the phenomena began to happen. One of the trumpets levitated from the floor, quite clearly tapping the tambourine in time to the music. It then rose up into the air as if conducting – tapping out the beat. At the end of the singing, the trumpet dipped as if someone was taking a bow.

The other trumpet levitated and everybody could see that both were up in the air at the same time, while the tambourine was being shaken in time to the music. One of the sitters asked that the tambourine might be levitated further into the air, which resulted in its being instantly waved about high over the heads of the sitters, before being thrown into the air to land with a crash under a seat in the back of the second row. One delegate was able to see dimly an ectoplasmic rod protruding from the medium's body.

The first voice communication was by the Mandarin, speaking in the direct voice through the trumpet. He explained the significance of the vitamins and minerals which were placed in the circle and also outlined his role in the Swift circle as a teaching communicator. He told the assembled company that, as a matter of interest, a baby with the potential to be a physical medium had been born that very day in Leicester 11 May, 1991.

The medium's young Cockney guide, Charlie, was the next to speak. He suddenly announced that he was not going to use the trumpet, which he threw into the centre of the circle, as he began to speak independently through the agency of an ectoplasmic voice-box which, on this occasion, owing to the unusual conditions and the unplanned influx of light from the partially uncovered emergency light, was constructed close to the medium. They were unable to move it about as usual for these reasons. He proceeded to answer a number of questions from the floor. At the same time, we could hear paper being torn off the pad – one piece landed in the lap of a sitter. Charlie jokingly told delegates that he could not find the pencil, so he would have to write the messages elsewhere and apport them into the circle.

These messages would be found at the end of the circle, and he promised that they would be evidential to the recipients. Just as predicted, after the seance, two screwed-up pieces of tissue paper were found in the area of the circle. There had definitely been no tissue paper brought into the sitting; and these had certainly been apported. One of the messages, when opened, bore a message for a woman present from her ten-year-old son who had passed to spirit. It read 'Mummy X X X Richard'. The other message read 'Annie, I still love you'. The two recipients were able to confirm that their messages were evidential. In both cases, the words were printed on the tissue in the form of little dots, very similar to Braille, or the print from a dot-matrix printer.

The third communicator of the evening was the guide, Daphne, who is a regular visitor to the home circle, whose role was to convey personal messages. She was a rather more serious character than Charlie and, in the spirit world, her job was to help young children who passed over at an early stage, as she told us following a question from one of the delegates.

Despite the fact that the lighting conditions were less than perfect for this sitting, all the spirit voices had been loud and clear. Afterwards, the medium was discovered to be still securely bound to his chair and he had to be cut free. It was also observed that the bowl of vitamins and minerals had been disturbed and obviously utilised during the course of the sitting.

There was no doubt that the seance had been a resounding success and the resultant publicity it brought in the *Psychic News* went a long way towards bringing in new members for the Noah's Ark Society. While we had been at the Leicester seminar that weekend, we had our 100th associate member join the NAS, and two months later this figure had grown by almost 50 per cent, with over 50 member circles, too.

The seminar had been a momentous and historic occasion. To a certain extent, we had put the future of the society in the hands of spirit as we undertook this important event and I am delighted to say that they did not let us down when we needed them. We were extremely thankful to the young medium Lincoln and to his circle for their participation, which had gone such a long way towards furthering the aims and objects of the society. What an immense relief it was in, addition, to complete the experimental sitting, knowing that the medium of the day was safe. Whenever we put on seances of this type, there was always a considerable amount of stress involved until we knew that everything had passed off safely. On occasions, I was known to ease this somewhat with the help of a couple of Rusty Nails (an alcoholic drink) in the bar afterwards.

The seance itself had produced a tremendously emotional effect within Stewart Alexander, as a trance and physical medium. Under normal circumstances, when he was sitting in his home circle for phenomena and trance, he never had the opportunity himself to witness the end result of his mediumship, staying, as he did, in trance throughout his seances. His own physical mediumship was quite remarkable but he only knew that because he had been told so by others who sat with him. This time, he had the opportunity to witness excellent physical mediumship for himself at the experimental sitting. After doing so, he realised fully the wonderful uplifting effect it had on others. At the Leicester seminar, Stewart therefore realised that his destiny lay to a certain extent in demonstrating his physical mediumship to others. In the June newsletter, he wrote:

> What I must say is that all I, and everyone present, was privileged to witness will live on in my memory forever. Quite simply I cannot possibly convey in words the effect that seance and indeed the extraordinary weekend had upon us all. For almost 48 hours the two worlds were blended together, such that I and many others now *know* beyond any doubt exactly what we must do in the future. Those loving, understanding and patient people from the world of spirit look to us all to help them prove the great truth to a disbelieving world! That one weekend transformed my very being, and those who know me well will know exactly what I mean.

With Stewart having therefore made a conscious decision to work for spirit as a physical medium by demonstrating his gifts outside his home circle whenever his spirit guides wished him to do so, it came as no surprise to any of us that at a sitting of his experimental circle shortly after the seminar, Stewart's guides announced that his physical mediumship was henceforth to be restored and would be further developed. I rather hoped that I might get the opportunity to witness it before too long.

# FURTHER PROGRESS OF THE NOAH'S ARK SOCIETY

THE WIND OF change was again blowing as the historic NAS seminar in Leicester ended. While Sandra and I had hoped to take a further two-year lease on the rectory at Postwick, the church had other ideas. They needed the rectory once more as accommodation for a churchman who was about to move to the area and so we had a notice to quit the property at the end of July 1991. At first we were devastated to learn of this development but we got used to the idea and, with a certain amount of trepidation, started to look around for alternative accommodation. We wanted to remain in the Norfolk area, as we had grown so very fond of it but with our own physical home circle now up and running again, we needed premises that would prove large enough for us to devote one room entirely to our sittings. This posed another problem, because properties that were large enough tended to be offered at a rent that was beyond our means.

Several houses for rent did come to our notice and we viewed them all. We preferred the idea of a village, however, rather than a town or city, as it would provide for a quieter life and a friendlier community. The houses that we did see were generally too small and too modern. Those older properties we saw (with more atmosphere) were generally too expensive. So we were in a bit of a Catch 22 situation. Finally Sandra spotted an advert in a local paper for a four-bedroomed period farmhouse to rent with a contact number for Thelveton Estates. We responded accordingly and discovered that the proposed rent, although a little more expensive than we had been paying on our rectory home, was actually affordable. We were not told specifically where the house was, but were sent an application form for a one-year lease, along with a comprehensive questionnaire designed to fully ascertain our suitability as tenants.

Having filled in and returned the forms, and been approved as prospective tenants, we were then told that we could at last view the farmhouse. As we followed the car which was guiding us there, we suddenly realised that we were being led into the village of Scole, which we already knew reasonably well from our previous visits to the Scole Inn. Imagine then our amazement, as we were shown into Street Farmhouse – the very house next to the Scole Inn which we had gazed upon with admiration from our room at the inn in the past!

As we approached it and were shown around the building, however, Sandra's jaw dropped a mile. The garden was severely overgrown and the decor of the house was in extremely poor condition, not having been renewed for many years. The house itself, which had previously been occupied by an elderly tenant farmer, had not been lived in for over two years and consequently had a decidedly damp feeling to it. There were two cellars below the house which were in a dreadful state and the single toilet could only be reached by crossing the kitchen. I had a horrible vision of having to run through the house and down across the kitchen every time I needed the toilet in the middle of the night. Apart from a number of open fires downstairs, there was also no modern heating.

But despite all these initial disappointments, the farmhouse had a wonderful atmosphere to it. The dwelling itself dated from about the same time as the Scole Inn next door as far as we could ascertain, which made it about 350 years old. We fell in love with the original carved wood fireplace surrounds in two of the rooms, which both bore a carved motto; one of these read 'After Work – Rest and After Rest – Work'. The other declared 'Welcome Ever Smiles'.

We could see the potential of the property clearly: the cellars below the house, which had once been used by the farmer to dispense milk daily to the villagers, would make wonderful seance rooms if they were renovated. The state of the place explained the reasonable rent but the property *had* been rewired throughout. We were interviewed by the landlord, who proved to be very kind to us in that he agreed to turn the small bedroom adjoining the bathroom into a second toilet and to install electric storage heaters and convector heaters. This gesture really clinched the matter for us and we moved from Postwick to Street Farmhouse in Scole on 1 August where we have since lived happily ever after.

The move itself was a little like an episode of the Crazy Gang. The house had two spiral staircases up to its first floor, too narrow to take the bedroom furniture upstairs. There was, however, a 'coffin trap' located near the kitchen. This is a section of boards on the first floor which are designed to be removed in order for coffins to be lowered down to the ground floor and is typical of many of the old houses in the area. In our case, all the upstairs furniture had to be lifted bodily through this trapdoor and the antics of the removal men had to be seen to be believed.

Shortly afterwards, on 10 August, there was another Noah's Ark Society one-day seminar, which we held at the Wimbledon Spiritualist Church. Since it was open to the general public, there were no plans for an experimental seance to be included. The format was similar to that of the inaugural one-day seminar of the previous January and the event was intended to act as a promotional and recruitment seminar. Lecturers and speakers were drawn from the committee ranks, with the exception of Tom Harrison. I gave a talk and chaired the meeting which, with over 100 participants, was very successful and resulted in a number of new members for the 'Ark'.

Following this, and having finally settled in at Scole, we re-established our physical home circle, sitting once a fortnight initially in the large room we had designated our library, although it is fair to say that at this stage there was little sign of phenomena of any significance emerging. Ever since the Leicester seminar, the guides of the Hove circle had closed it entirely to visitors so that they could get on with the necessary development of Lincoln's mediumship and the circle's phenomena without 'let or hindrance'. Later on, however, they announced that members of the Noah's Ark Society committee would be allowed to visit the circle on a two-at-a-time basis from the middle of September onwards. The first of these visits was to take place on 19 September, with Alan Crossley and me attending.

The occasion was exciting, and right from the time that I picked Alan up from Euston Station in London to drive down to the South Coast, we chatted incessantly about the Noah's Ark Society – our hopes and plans for it and about the sitting we were driving to at Hove.

Lincoln was already starting to 'go under' as he was taken into the seance room and tied to his chair by leather straps and cable ties to the arms and by two old neckties to the legs. As we entered the seance room with its red light, we could see the medium's eyes rolling, and he appeared to be transfigured by an entity who clearly resembled the physical medium, Jack Webber. Although the circle was by then often allowed to use some red light in their sittings, and had been allowed to see some materialised phenomena in that light, the recent poor health of the medium prevented us from being allowed to use it on this occasion, and the seance was therefore held in total darkness.

The medium was sitting outside the cabinet, which was itself formed by a curtained-off bay window, and it was not long before the action began. The trumpet levitated and was whirled around at high speed, demonstrating the perfect control which Lincoln's child guide Charlie had over it. The tambourine also moved around and then Charlie started to chatter away in the independent voice in his boyish way. He was obviously in solid materialised form as he walked around the circle, touching sitters at random with his warm and apparently natural hands.

As Charlie withdrew for a while, an Indian guide (one of many facets of the group of guides in this circle who described themselves as 'The Diamond') spoke to sitters at length in the independent voice. He invited questions about the Noah's Ark Society, which were all answered logically, helpfully and speedily, and it was obvious that spirit had been 'listening in' on the conversation that Alan and I had been having on the journey southwards, because without any prompting, matters from that conversation were referred to in depth. Advice was also given generally about the conditions we must all provide for spirit when sitting for phenomena.

The speech was interrupted by a loud swishing to and fro of the cabinet curtains, followed by a second, third and fourth. We were told that four materialisations were with us and sitters could feel their presence as they moved about the circle. Noah Zerdin announced himself with difficulty in a voice with a strong accent, then Helen Duncan, who signed the name 'Duncan' with a flourish, right across the hardboard floor. Harry Edwards and Jack Webber, also present, managed a few words with difficulty. Helen Duncan promised to telephone the president again shortly, as she had done on several previous occasions. The pad and pencil were heard to be moved, with the pencil scribbling away. These were then dropped into Alan Crossley's lap. At the end of the sitting, we discovered four names clearly written on the paper – NOAH, HELEN, JACK and HARRY.

Daphne, another of the Swift circle guides, spoke to the assembled company for a short time giving personal and general advice via the independent voice. Just prior to the end of the seance, there was a lot of rustling and bustling activity heard, coming from the direction of the medium, which lasted for some time. The end of the sitting came, signified by five loud raps from spirit, and after the closing prayer the lights were turned up. The medium's sweater had been removed and placed in the centre of the circle, together with his shirt (buttons still done up), although he still had his necktie on his now bare chest. His arms had been released (though the straps were still done up and intact), as had his legs. His trouser belt had been used to manacle his hands (I had great difficulty in releasing them afterwards) behind his knees, which were up near his chin! The phenomena that evening had been quite amazing.

By November, the society had acquired a sophisticated new copier machine, on which we were now producing the newsletter, and this was installed at Scole. The membership, which had been increasing steadily, now stood at 232 associate members, with 77 member circles and 2 corporate body members. We had also appointed area representatives for Australia and the USA.

The next society seminar was a one-day affair, which had been booked at the Edinburgh Spiritualist Society in Albany Street, Edinburgh, for Saturday 16 November. Originally planned without an experimental sitting, this was later amended to include a seance at which it was intended for the first time to use Stewart Alexander as the medium. In the event, owing to his wife's illness, Stewart was unable to attend, and Lincoln, who was present, stepped into the breach for us once again at the last minute. We travelled up to Edinburgh by car on the Friday and, although it entailed a long journey, the drive all the way up the A1 was pleasant and scenic. We stayed at the private hotel Bill Anderson, as Scottish representative of the society, had booked for us. While it was a bit of a shock to discover that Stewart was not able to attend the seminar after all, Lincoln agreed that we should hold a private sitting for committee members on the Friday night, at which we could ask his guides if they would allow him to officiate as the physical medium for the Saturday night experimental sitting. This we did and were given the relevant permission but, as it happened, we nearly made headline news at this short seance for physical phenomena. The president, Alan Crossley, collapsed in the middle of the sitting, which then had to be abandoned as the guides withdrew. Alan was taken to hospital by ambulance for a check up and fortunately recovered enough to rejoin us later. At the time, we thought he had had a heart attack and were already visualising in our mind's eye the next week's headlines in the *Psychic News*: 'NAS president passes to spirit in the middle of physical seance'. What a commotion that would have made!

We hastily changed the Saturday programme around to cover Stewart's talk on the mediums and the researchers of the past, and off we went. Talks and lectures were delivered by Bill Anderson, Alan Crossley, myself and the rest of the committee as usual. It was a truly interesting meeting and proved to be very successful, with 111 delegates in all attending the event. Just prior to the experimental seance however, poor old Bill Anderson had to partake in some unforeseen exercise. We were in the habit at these sittings of doing a 'dry run' with the lights out prior to the seance proper. The idea of this was to ensure that all the delegates would feel happy sitting in total darkness. The darkness required for a physical seance is absolute and total, and not many people realise just how dark and black that can be. So the 'dry run' gave those who were not too sure how they might react during the real thing the chance to leave if they felt they could not cope with the inky blackness.

For absolute safety, we removed the electric fuses, but the box was three flights of stairs down from the seance room. Two people said that they wanted to leave, and Bill had to go down to the fuse box and up again. Having once more seen to the lights, even more people decided that they would not stay, so he had to do it again. In all, Bill was up and down the stairs five times that night.

The experimental seance was held on a raised wooden platform at one end of the room. Following an opening prayer and some rousing singing, the materialised form of the medium's guide, Charlie, could be heard running round the platform. (The medium was bound hand and foot as usual.) The trumpets were levitated slightly, followed by the levitation of a small handbell and luminous plaque, which rose 15 feet up into the air. Some of the sitters could actually feel Charlie brushing past them as he moved around the platform. Bill Anderson felt two hands being placed on his shoulders, and a voice said 'Billy' into his ear. Although he could not say definitely who the voice belonged to, he noted the fact that he had not been called 'Billy' since he was a very young boy. This was followed by a warm, materialised hand taking his right hand, and raising it to his left shoulder. Many other people present at the time were able to witness various other physical phenomena that occurred at that sitting – and in several cases these were the very first physical phenomena that they had ever had the chance to experience.

Towards the end of 1991, we started to renovate one of our cellars at Scole – partly so that we could enjoy the opportunity of having a permanent home for our own circle, and partly because we felt that it would be beneficial for the NAS if we donated its use as a seance room from time to time to the society, so that we could hold regular experimental seances there for members to attend, thereby witnessing phenomena. The committee were also keen on this idea and the new membership secretary, Alf Winchester, volunteered his own services, along with those of his son, to undertake the majority of the necessary heavy work. It was a huge job, involving laying a new concrete floor, as well as repairing the steps down into the cellar, plus the installation of a large amount of woodwork and a new door.

For his dedication, and his hard work on behalf of the Ark, Stewart Alexander became the NAS vice-president during December 1991 – a role which he took on in addition to his position as archive officer, and at the same time I produced an *Introductory Booklet* for the society to use.

We also introduced a system of monitoring the success record of the member circles on a regular basis. I devised a questionnaire for groups to answer every six months, which quickly identified the strong and weak areas within a physical circle, so that the society could offer assistance and advice to those member circles who needed it, in order to enhance the progress of their development wherever possible. If groups chose not to fill this in (it was not compulsory), then we endeavoured to contact them by telephone from time to time to ascertain if there was any way the society could help them with their circle work.

We undertook yet another one-day seminar on Saturday, 18 January 1992 – this time without an experimental seance – at the Wilton Spiritualist Church near Salisbury, which proved to be a similar occasion to the one-day seminar we had held the previous year in Wimbledon. It was open to the general public, and was aimed at recruitment. In that respect, it was certainly successful as it brought in a number of new members for the society.

By the start of February, the renovation work on the main Scole cellar was complete and it was ready to be used for seances. We felt that a proper dedication sitting should take place there, so a special meeting for that purpose was arranged for all the NAS committee, with Stewart Alexander as medium being fully supported by the Elton experimental circle.

Committee members from all parts of the UK – some from as far afield as Scotland and Wales – converged on Scole for this historic sitting on Saturday, 15 February 1992. Perhaps the reader can imagine the scene. Picture if you will a spacious cellar with Roman arched roof, which is totally secure. The room easily accommodates 25 or 26 people at a time and was then painted throughout in matt black paint (walls, ceiling, woodwork – the lot) although today that has been changed to a sort of dark plum colour.

One by one we filed into the cellar, and took our places. Last in was the medium, Stewart Alexander, who insisted on being tied into his chair in full view of all, further ensuring that the ends of the knots were sealed with tape. Restful music was played after the room had been sealed. In front of the medium, sitting on a small seance table, stood three metal trumpets, a heavy brass bell and two wooden drumsticks. As the lights were extinguished and the medium slipped into trance, the luminous glow from the three trumpets was easily visible.

White Feather – one of the medium's main guides – was ready for the job that had to be done. As he spoke through Stewart in trance, he blessed the seance room in the name of the Great White Spirit. Like later spirit visitors that evening, he confirmed that the venue would become a real 'Mecca' for those of like mind throughout the world to visit – and where they could and would witness a whole collection of wonderful physical phenomena, a prediction which has since become a fantastic reality.

Two more of Stewart's guides, Jack and little Christopher, also spoke at great length – the latter acting as a cheeky MC. Speaking via Stewart's trance, Christopher brought through much personal evidence for those present. The father of one of the committee members communicated too and made a brave attempt to actually speak himself in an evidential way.

Then the fun really started, with Christopher organising the physical phenomena that followed. The three trumpets all levitated in unison and proceeded to perform synchronised aerobatics together, before splitting apart from their formation and moving to different parts of the room. Never before had I seen such control of three trumpets at the same time. Remember, it was pitch dark in the cellar. One of the trumpets came straight to me, touching me lightly on the tip of my nose before 'dubbing' me quickly on each shoulder and tapping me lightly on the head. My hands were then gently stroked by the trumpet, which finally spun rapidly round – all the time maintaining light contact with my hand. The brass bell rang loudly, and the drumsticks beat a noisy tattoo on the seance table.

There was a most encouraging direct-voice communication from a spirit announcing himself as the Reverend George Vale Owen. The seance lasted for about one-and-a-half hours in all. At the end, after we had closed in prayer, the medium was observed to be sitting in the same place as he started – with all the ropes still tied, and all the seals intact. The next morning, one trumpet showed signs of an ectoplasmic residue within, which vanished as soon as it came into contact with full light.

Throughout 1992 and beyond, I became heavily involved in giving talks to churches and interested groups on the subject of physical phenomena, showing how its development, promotion and safe practice throughout the world was growing fast as a direct consequence of the work of the Noah's Ark Society. These talks took me all over the country and many of the people I met in this way went on to join the society as their interest in the subject grew.

By March, the NAS had 310 associate members, 99 circles and 5 corporate body members. A one-day seminar was held at Faverdale Hall, Darlington, at which I officiated – this being a joint venture between the NAS and the educational sub-committee of the Northern District Council of the SNU. It was organised by Hylton Thompson, a chartered engineer and publicity officer for the Northern District Council. I quote here from Hylton's own report of the event:

> The event began on the Friday evening when those lucky enough to be staying overnight were treated to a trance sitting with physical medium Stewart Alexander. One of Stewart's guides, White Feather, gave an introductory talk and then introduced the young child Christopher who held everyone spellbound with his quick wit and humour, coupled with accurate evidence of survival for several of the sitters. Just before concluding, and with Stewart deeply entranced, Christopher invited us to switch on the lights, and asked for a set of tweezers which one of the sitters promptly provided.
>
> Alan Millichamp MSNU was then invited to test the depth of Stewart's trance by nipping his forearm with the tweezers. The medium did not respond but the mischievous Christopher was not satisfied and called upon a committee member of the NAS to 'have a go'. With the skill of a master butcher, the committee member concerned set about his allotted task – much to the horror of those nearby, he nipped, sliced and screwed the implement into the medium's flesh but to no avail. On returning from trance there was not a mark on Stewart's arm and he was not aware of what had happened until told later in the bar.

The daytime session on Saturday was taken up with seven excellent lectures by officers of the Noah's Ark Society and a concluding 'question and answer' session. Some fairly tough questions were aimed at the panel and interesting discussions took place ranging from such subjects as whether or not a cabinet is necessary for physical mediumship to the nature and source of the various energies used by spirit in the seance room. There were 68 people in attendance, all looking forward with excitement to the evening seance – they were not to be disappointed.

Before the seance we were briefed by Robin Foy, chairman of the Noah's Ark Society, on the dos and don'ts pertaining to physical seances. The society's number one concern is for the safety and protection of its mediums and it gives an excellent booklet to its members covering safety and other essential considerations when sitting for physical phenomena.

The seance room was double-checked for cleanliness and all sitters were searched – handbags, torches and cameras etc. were not allowed. It should be pointed out that although materialisation was not expected, full precautions were taken to the standard demanded for a materialisation seance – just in case.

The medium was again Stewart Alexander and he was bound securely (checked by Judith Seaman MSNU and Hylton Thompson) into a strong armchair. A cabinet was not used and because of the large number of sitters, they were arranged in two concentric circles of 24 and 44, Stewart being part of the inner one. Many of the sitters were inexperienced, so the lights were turned off for a 'dummy run' to ensure that everybody could withstand the totally dark conditions. There were no problems and the seance commenced with an opening prayer.

White Feather commenced with an introductory talk explaining that this was only the second physical seance experienced by his medium, in over 20 years, which was outside of the love and security of his own circle (the first occasion having been the dedication seance for the Scole Cellar) – there were a large number of sitters, and the conditions were very different. However, if we the sitters could create harmonious conditions the spirit world would do its utmost to achieve success. He ended his eloquent address by saying that while the young boy Christopher endeavoured to reunite the two worlds, they would try to gather energies both from the medium and from the circles for use in the experiment to obtain physical phenomena.

Christopher – affectionately known to his circle as 'shuffle-bottom' (and he did) – brought remarkably accurate evidence to several sitters interspersed with humorous banter and even a nursery-rhyme recital. At one point he asked for a lady with a yellow jumper and silver hair (remember it was absolutely dark). There was no response until a lady in the outer circle admitted to having a yellow jumper. Asked what colour her hair was the lady said she liked to think of it as blonde. Amid the inevitable laughter, Christopher, insisting that it was silver, asked us to put the lights on – which we did. I think it safe to say that the majority took the same view as Christopher! A personal message then ensued which the lady later confirmed to be extremely evidential.

Eventually a very modest spirit gentleman introducing himself as 'Jack' intervened and spoke of a plan which was being orchestrated in his world. There was great concern in the spirit world at the declining interest in Spiritualism and they were going to make every effort to re-establish physical mediumship and prove conclusively once and for all to the human race that there is no death. He asked for support from all those who sat in circles and from those who had influence in the 'movement'. There would be no more pussy-footing around from his side – only serious work.

At this point Christopher expressed dissatisfaction with the drumsticks which were provided for him. He requested one of the sitters whom he called 'Uncle Ray' to put the lights on and get his personal sticks out of the cupboard. This completed, and the lights out, Christopher asked for one of the three trumpets to be removed and then proceeded to lead two of the sitters nearest to the medium 'on a merry dance' as they were asked to adjust the positions of the remaining two trumpets in almost every conceivable direction until he was fully satisfied. Christopher then asked for music to be played, and eventually for the sitters to sing. The drumsticks began to beat loudly on the table, a handbell rang noisily at such a rate of vibration that it would be virtually impossible for a human hand to shake it fast enough – it was more like an electric bell – and then it happened.

One of the metal trumpets (identified by luminous rings on their bases) began moving slowly across the floor and almost appeared to investigate one of the microphones (which made the writer nervous as it was a special design newly purchased by him for the occasion). It then took off and made several revolutions of the room – just clearing the heads of the sitters. It began to swing in time with the singing, almost as if conducting a choir (actually the singing was quite good). Then, increasing its speed, it began to describe a perfect circle in the vertical plane at such speed that it looked like a continuous ring some six feet in diameter. The other trumpet then joined in and two luminous vertical circles were thus formed, one at each side of the medium. The movements would periodically change into arcs, the trumpets then swinging independently, rather like pendulums, in time to the singing.

This sophisticated form of levitation phenomena is often referred to as telekinesis which infers control by the mind. In this particular case the control was so precise and the energy expenditure so substantial that it could only be attributed to direct spirit control. Perhaps psycho-kinesis or dynamic levitation would be a more appropriate name.

At one time spirit had the drumsticks beating, the bell ringing and both trumpets flying like two enormous Catherine wheels all simultaneously. This continued for a while until – and most of us assumed that Christopher was responsible for this – one of the trumpets came out of orbit and was beaten mercilessly and continuously against what we assumed – and hoped – was the floor, for some time. The overall noise at this time reached a climax and had to be heard to be believed (bear in mind that we were also still attempting to sing as instructed by Christopher).

Suddenly, one of the drumsticks struck a small stool with such force that the stool almost fell over and the drumstick came to rest against the leg of an adjoining chair.

To cut a long story short, the trumpet was written off. Flattened completely at its wide end and badly bent and twisted at its narrow end, we had surely witnessed its 'last trump'. A small table on which the bell and drumsticks had originally rested was on its side with the bell beside it. The drumsticks were eventually recovered from various points in the room. Christopher was asked what he had done to the trumpet but he refused to accept the blame. The meeting was closed in prayer by the society's president, Alan Crossley. Reinspection of the medium's chair and bindings revealed no change. PS. One wonders if the Noah's Ark Society has public liability insurance to cover sitters who suffer injury from low-flying projectiles.

## OF CELLAR SITTINGS AND SEMINARS

BACK AT STREET Farmhouse, Scole, we had often joked about the fact that since the farmhouse was extremely old, it might have a ghost. Certainly the Scole Inn next door is strongly reputed to be haunted. After we settled into the property, we were soon to discover that many a true word *can* be said in jest. Only the house does not come with *a* ghost – but at least three that we are aware of. First of all, we have a phantom dog we have nicknamed 'Rufus'. He is extremely large and, with his shaggy grey hair, appears to perhaps be an Irish wolfhound. Both Sandra and I and other visitors have spotted him on several occasions and he has been heard to run the length of the house upstairs. Once, when the NAS were holding a committee meeting in the lounge at Scole, and with our own dogs well out of the way, there was a burst of audible growling heard in the room by every single one of the committee members. The tone of the noise was such that it was obvious it came from a very large dog and sounded as if it came from within the room, it was so loud.

We have a very shy-looking dairy maid (Street Farm was once a working dairy farm) decked in clothes from another century and complete with bonnet, who has been seen by us and by various visitors peeping out from the short corridor between the kitchen and the dining room. We believe, from information about her given to us by members of the spirit team who work with the Scole Experimental Group, that her name may be 'Dot' and that she is possibly responsible for some of the small things that regularly go missing from the house without explanation.

Finally, the farmhouse stands in its own grounds, and there is a long gravel driveway up to the house from the public road. On several occasions in daylight, our third 'resident ghost' has been spotted walking up the driveway past the house towards the back door. He always wears a flat cap and farm working clothes, probably from the 1930s era, and appears quite normal and solid as he is seen walking past the lounge window. In the early days we were always caught out – assuming that he was heading for the back door and about to knock on it. We would rush to the back door to see who was calling on us but, in the half-minute or so it took us to get there and open the door, the farm worker had simply disappeared. A few of the NAS committee members have been caught out in the same way.

The house itself contains a couple of mysteries. When fitting a carpet to one of the staircases, we discovered that the bottom stair has a hidden button which activates a powerful spring to reveal a secret compartment. Today the compartment is empty but who knows what treasures it once held? A walk-in cupboard between the kitchen and lounge hides the now bricked-up entrance to a secret passage; the lintel and stone surround to its doorway are still clearly visible as are the modern breeze-blocks that have been used to seal it. Furthermore, our living in the house itself is the fulfilment of a prediction given to Sandra by a clairvoyant medium many years ago, and long before she knew me, or was ever involved with physical phenomena. The medium told Sandra that she would one day live in a special house where she would enjoy riches beyond price and that there was a particular room in the house that would be blessed. There was also a large 'S' over the house which she could see. Well – here we are! Street Farmhouse begins with an 'S', and so does Scole. We live next door to the Scole Inn, which has a large sign over our wall, which begins with an 'S'.

In addition, we *do* have a special room (the cellar) where we have indeed experienced (and still do) spiritual riches beyond price, as a result of various experimental sittings for physical phenomena given by Lincoln and Stewart Alexander for members of the Noah's Ark Society. Currently we experience wonderful phenomena there every week, much of which is quite unique in the world today. Just as predicted to Sandra all those years ago – the special room *was* blessed by Stewart's guide, White Feather.

Sunday 5 April saw the second AGM of the society come and go with no surprises – all the officers retained their positions. I continued as chairman of the society and editor of the newsletter.

The cellar at Scole was now good and ready for the proposed experimental sittings we intended to undertake, and there were certainly several interesting seances which took place there. First, however, there was the spring residential seminar of the society, which took place at Gaunts House, near Wimborne in Dorset. The house was in a beautiful setting, the weather glorious, and our 130 delegates were thoroughly looked after by the host, Sir Richard Glynn. The seminar followed broadly the same format as the one in Leicester but, on this occasion, it incorporated two seances for all the delegates to participate in – one each by Lincoln and Stewart Alexander.

Both were held in the vast cellars of Gaunts House and under test conditions. The first, on 15 May, was with medium Lincoln, who sat for 130 people with most of his circle present. The sitting provided an apport of an antique Celtic cross possibly made of bronze (later authenticated by the British Museum) for Welsh representative Freda Paget. There followed a display of levitation by two trumpets, some independent voice communication and the partial materialisation of a spirit entity. At the end of the seance it was discovered that the medium had been turned around 180 degrees on a heavy antique chair so that he faced the wall. Before the seance, and without the added weight of the medium, the chair had needed two people to lift it in order to carry it into the seance room.

During the Saturday seance of the following night, all the delegates witnessed an amazing display of 'synchronised aerobatics' by the two trumpets, with drumsticks beating time on a table and a handbell ringing loudly at the same time. On both evenings the mediums were fully restrained with cable ties, straps and ropes – and the Saturday seance also produced a wealth of personal evidence through Stewart in trance, some of it from sitters' 'dead' relatives themselves.

It was at this seminar, too, that one of the members, Mrs Brenda Walker, kindly presented the society with a beautiful banner for display at their future functions, which she had hand embroidered.

The Gaunts House event was followed up by a five-page insert about the Noah's Ark Society and that recent seminar in the 13 June edition of *Psychic News*. This was paid for by the society and was superbly edited by Tony Ortzen, it being the last major job in his capacity as the paper's editor. It was designed to boost the society's membership and was not found wanting in that respect; following the insert and the following week's headlines on the society, there was a massive surge of interest in the NAS. At its height, the society could then boast over 600 associate members and more than 150 member circles in countries all over the world.

After many false starts, we had finally managed to negotiate with the Arthur Findlay College, Stansted Hall, to run a full week's course on physical mediumship there in January 1993. A measure of the popularity of the Noah's Ark Society at that time could be gauged from the fact that this course would be restricted to no more than 100 delegates. We sent out the booking forms on a first-come, first-served basis with the June 1992 newsletter. Within 48 hours of the booking forms being sent out the response was so great that we had filled the course, with enough applications left over to fill a second week!

The first of the Noah's Ark Society experimental sittings for members took place in the Scole cellar on 30 May with Lincoln as the medium. The sitting is best described in the words of two members who attended the event – Larry Dean and Celia Pennifold:

> When everybody was seated, Lincoln was strapped securely into his chair, which was standing in front of the cabinet. The lights were turned off, and we all started to sing 'Shenandoah'. It was not long before Lincoln's young spirit guide Charlie made his presence known to everyone through the independent voice. Then the fun started, with the trumpets rising high into the air and darting about. Robin Foy made a remark as to how amazing it was that the trumpets managed to miss the string of cowbells hanging down from the cellar ceiling and of course, immediately after that, the bells were hit time and time again by the trumpet with great gusto!
>
> A luminous gelatinous 'muppet' of the type used by anglers – it resembled a toy octopus – caused great hilarity when it was lifted up into the air for all to see as it danced there, and it was then projected with great force to the back row of sitters. Charlie asked

for its return and it was duly thrown back to take a further part in the unfolding spectacle. This was repeated several times, with Charlie on occasions catching it in mid-air. The muppet was also brought round the circle for the sitters to see the moving, materialised fingers of a child holding it.

One of the aluminium trumpets was very lively and moved with precision, hopping around the floor when it was not being levitated. A handbell rose to a great height and rang so fast that it sounded like an electric bell; in fact it gave quite a new meaning to the expression 'ringing in the ears' – it was actually quite deafening!

The swishing of curtains and blasts of cold air signified that several materialised forms were coming out of the cabinet, and many people felt their hands being held, or experienced touches. One sitter's face was caressed, and then firm hands were placed on his head and held there for a while. A lady sitter felt a hand running down her arm and over her palm, and noted that this materialised hand was solid and real, being warm to the touch.

Robin Foy was invited by spirit to take hold of the levitated trumpet and pull it hard. Despite his best efforts, he could make no impression on the firm spirit grasp. There was great commotion at one time when Sandra Foy was levitated on her chair. Robin very foolishly, and sitting with his back to the wall, made a remark that he doubted if spirit could move *him* – no doubt everyone knows that Robin is no lightweight, at 18 stones. The next instant, spirit had taken up the challenge! He felt two arms behind him lift up the chair (since his back was directly to the wall, it would appear that the spirit 'arms' must have come out of the wall to get enough purchase in order to lift chair and sitter) and Robin's surprised voice could be heard to emanate from higher and higher in the room as he soared up into the air! Luckily, he was not dropped down on top of the other sitters, but just moved forward into a space. A very tall lady next to him was then lifted, too. As a finale, the whole four-foot square hardboard sheet on the floor in the middle of the circle, complete with toys and minerals, was lifted uniformly two feet into the air with its contents unspilled. Water was also splashed onto several sitters.

There were several wonderful messages in independent voice given to sitters and we were even invited to ask questions. One particular communicator materialised and went to a lady in the front row, to give her comfort. As the lady's chin was cupped

> lovingly by materialised hands and her face gently caressed, the clear and perfect voice of 'Daphne' was heard, giving the lady consolation and upliftment. She also received healing on her legs from materialised hands.
>
> At one time there seemed to be *at least* three to four materialisations moving about at once and sitters in different areas of the cellar were being touched simultaneously. As the seance drew to a close, the medium and his chair were levitated backwards into the cabinet and there was a final flurry of activity.

Next on the list for the society was another one-day seminar, which was held at the Cardiff Spiritualist Church on Saturday 1 August. Organised by the NAS representative for Wales, Freda Paget, it was attended by over 100 people, many of whom had travelled from all parts of the UK. The previous evening, a number of us attended a private physical seance in the home of a local member of the society, which Stewart Alexander had consented to give. Despite the crush with so many people in the room, the seance was most successful, with the usual and now-familiar physical phenomena occurring. The seminar proved to be yet another winner for the society but Stewart really had to earn his keep on the day, with his lecture being the prelude to yet another experimental sitting, attended by all the delegates. The weather was extremely hot and humid and, although we had considered the seance of the previous evening to be filled to capacity with people, to my dying day I shall never know how we managed to pack over 100 people, seated in three concentric circles, into that tiny room. Most of the day, sitting on the rostrum, my mind had been preoccupied with what I considered to be an insoluble problem but, in the event, I need not have worried. The right number of chairs *just* fitted in – and without a shoe-horn being needed either.

This sitting took place in an atmosphere resembling that of a Turkish bath but, despite the soaring temperature and discomfort, the phenomena did not suffer – they included levitation of the trumpets and direct voice, as well as the thumping of a drum in perfect time with the lively singing of the sitters. Many evidential facts and messages were also delivered through an entranced Stewart.

Regular experimental seances were held for members in the Scole cellar throughout the summer of 1992. Some five of these used Lincoln as the medium and two were given by Stewart Alexander who, owing to his business commitments, was unable to attend as often as Lincoln.

One of these cellar sittings by Lincoln on Sunday 9 August was attended by Tim Haigh, the newly appointed editor of *Psychic News,* who featured his visit in that newspaper. I quote a few of his comments:

> We all took our seats. The medium entered and sat down on a heavy wooden chair in front of a cabinet.
>
> On the arms and legs of the chair were leather straps. I and another sitter were asked to fasten him in and examine the bonds very carefully. Although I am no expert escapologist, in my opinion he was securely bound.
>
> The lights went out. In complete darkness we had 15 minutes of singing to raise power, at the end of which time the curtains of the cabinet were heard distinctly to open.
>
> More singing followed and then, as we were half-way through 'She'll Be Coming Round the Mountain', footsteps were heard and someone recognised the distinctive presence of Charlie, the young spirit boy who acts as one of the medium's controls.
>
> Suddenly, a trumpet covered in luminous tape which had been placed on a board in front of the medium, rose up and started flying round the room at great speed.
>
> Several times it seemed to pass within an inch of my face. I felt myself leaning back in my chair to avoid being hit.
>
> But the trumpet did not seem to want to leave me alone. It floated over and started patting me on the cheek, much to my own and everybody else's amusement when I told them what was happening. Then it took off again, but eventually came back and rested on my lap.
>
> A voice told me to grab it and give a good yank. I took hold of the trumpet and pulled for all I was worth, but I could scarcely move the hollow aluminium tube.
>
> Charlie eventually shouted, 'Oi – that's enough!' after a particularly forceful tug from me, and the trumpet eventually came to rest on the floor. The guide asked for the instrument to be removed and it was placed out of the way.
>
> Charlie announced that he was going to try and deepen his voice. Robin explained this was because, although the guide seemed to be a young boy, he was in fact a fully grown adult in the spirit world. Apparently, although Charlie enjoyed coming back

as a small child, he liked occasionally to show people he was, in reality, a mature man. His voice now noticeably deeper, he told the circle, 'I've got to go now as the proper stuff is going to start'.

We waited for about five minutes and then perhaps the most remarkable phenomenon of the sitting occurred. The luminous plaque, which had been lying on a wooden board in front of the medium, rose into the air.

In the weak light it gave off, a 'face' could quite clearly be seen. After a short time, it floated to within eight inches or so of my own. I found myself looking into features which, if I am going to be honest, were a cross between the countenance of a dead body and an Egyptian mummy. Strangely though, I found it not the least bit disturbing.

Next, I was asked to move my chair to the right as far as I could, and the person on my left to move hers to the left, so that a woman behind could be reached.

I felt someone brush past and stand behind me. Two hands were placed on my shoulders and I was given a friendly pat. Interestingly, the hands were not only fleshy, but extremely hot. The woman was given a personal message of comfort by the spirit being – he never announced who he was – and she was almost overcome with emotion. I subsequently learned she was suffering from a chronic illness. The figure again brushed past me as he made his way back to the cabinet.

After a short interval, Daphne, one of Lincoln's main controls, spoke to the circle. She explained that if the sitters could see her, they might be somewhat repelled. Although the materialisations were progressing satisfactorily, she said, the forms were still relatively crude in terms of appearance. 'Efforts are being made,' she continued, 'to reproduce the hairs on the back of a man's hand, for instance, but it is not always easy.' Returning to the cabinet, Daphne bade everybody farewell.

Charlie made a last brief appearance and said in his distinct Cockney accent, 'That's yer lot.' He then rapped five times on the wooden board – the sign the sitting was to end – and a prayer of thanks was offered.

When Lincoln regained consciousness, the lights were turned up. His chair had been moved back about a yard into the cabinet, the curtains of which were now open. He was half naked – his T-shirt had been removed – and his wrists and ankles were no longer restrained by the straps. It seemed to take him five minutes to regain enough strength in his legs to be able to stand up and walk out of the room.

For me, the next cellar sitting with Lincoln, which took place on Sunday 30 August, was one of the most memorable sittings of my life. It was during that seance that my own father materialised and came to speak to me. His arms were quite solid as we embraced and then ensued a two-way intimate conversation during which we spoke of many things known only to the two of us and nobody else present at the sitting. His voice was instantly recognisable to me in its tone and style, as he spoke of his concern for my health, and made me promise that I would visit a doctor at the earliest opportunity. This subsequent medical examination revealed that my blood pressure was unacceptably high (hypertension) and appropriate treatment was given. (The same problem had in part been the cause of my mother's tragic illness which, for 20 years before her passing, had reduced her to a shell of her former self.) Those few minutes of conversation with my 'dead' father gave me an experience that was intensely emotional and it suddenly seemed to me that my quest 'in pursuit of physical mediumship' which I had now been involved in for nearly 19 years had at this moment shown itself to be justified and worthwhile.

One of Lincoln's guides, either Felix or Magnus, then asked me to attend the Hove circle as soon as possible, as they 'had things to discuss'. Almost as an afterthought, I was then invited to 'bring Mrs Foy too'.

Nine days later, Sandra and I were happy to attend a sitting of the Swift circle at Hove. It was a pretty intimate affair, as two of the regular five sitters were away on holiday at the time, but it was a memorable sitting nevertheless. I was given much advice on matters regarding the Noah's Ark Society, and had a prolonged communication with a materialised spirit who introduced himself as Lord Louis Mountbatten, and indicated his intention to help in any way he could on behalf of the society in the future. Several of Lincoln's guides and helpers also materialised during the course of the seance. They spoke of the possibility that Sandra and I might be able to develop a joint physical mediumship should we choose so to do and a short experiment was conducted to demonstrate that independent voice could be manifested in Sandra's presence, using her own psychic energy.

More importantly for us, we were told that, with one exception, *all* of our sitters in the home circle we were then running at Scole were not right for the development of the particular physical phenomena which the spirit world had in mind for us. We should therefore retain only one sitter in our circle and replace the rest (the gentleman concerned was named but, in the event, owing to domestic problems, he was in any case unable to continue with the circle).

This pronouncement by Lincoln's spirit guides was to make a momentous difference to our group which, at the time of this sitting, had just been ambling along for some time. It was subject to the same problem we had encountered so many times before over the years. For some reason which it was difficult for us to actually put our finger on, the total and vital harmony between sitters had not grown to the necessary degree for development of good physical phenomena to take place. The circle in its present format had become stale and we agreed with Lincoln's guides that we must now do something about it. This decision led directly to the start of the Scole Experimental Group and turned out to be the best decision we ever made, following the specific advice from spirit we had been given at Hove.

# STANSTED ON THE HORIZON

During September 1992, it had been decided by the NAS committee that we needed to bring the monthly newsletter up-to-date, with a more professional format. We therefore purchased a computer and a desktop publishing software package so that I could typeset the publication every month and give it a new image. As far as computers were concerned, I had no knowledge whatsoever of their uses and operation, and it was rather daunting for me to face and address the need to teach myself how to use the computer, laser printer and scanner which now sat on my desk before me. It was a real DIY job but I never realised then just how much I would come to rely on the technology. To remove the computer I now possess would be like cutting off my right arm.

I started by practising on the September edition of the NAS newsletter, in which I typeset a few of the articles. Member Marion Hancock, with her vast amount of journalistic experience and excellent knowledge of the history of physical mediumship, gained largely through reading the second-hand books on the subject that passed through her psychic bookshop, had for some time been helping me out with typing and she now took over the 'Lest We Should Forget' slot about physical mediums of the past which had previously been written by Stewart Alexander.

Stewart, at the same time, went on to greater things. Alan Crossley had been forced to retire as president of the NAS through ill health and, in September, Stewart Alexander became president – a post which he has held ever since.

The following month, I typeset the whole of the newsletter and this continued until I retired from the committee in 1994. To further improve the publication, from November 1992 onwards, we had it professionally printed, and I incorporated a photograph of physical phenomena or of a past physical medium on the cover each month.

It occurred to me that perhaps, over the years, the Noah's Ark Society newsletters may become collectable items but in any case, between them, they formed a remarkable history of physical mediumship past and present. With the backing of the committee, I therefore commissioned a number of custom-designed newsletter binders, so that members could keep their various issues in a decent condition. The timing of these was aimed to make them available during the Stansted week of the NAS the following year. The design, of which I was very proud, was striking and very attractive, with gold lettering on blue pvc.

On 29 September – during the week that my son started university at Bradford – Sandra and I were once again privileged to attend Stewart Alexander's home circle, where we witnessed some excellent physical phenomena and had numerous personal communications through trumpet direct voice and through Stewart's trance. Four days later, on 3 October in the Scole cellar, Stewart gave an experimental sitting for members at which Tim Haigh was present and Tim subsequently covered the seance on the front page of the issue of *Psychic News* of 17 October. The headline read 'Shirt removed in physical seance', and Tim went on to say:

> Physical medium Stewart Alexander had his shirt removed at a seance earlier this month ... even though he was wearing a pullover at the time, and had been securely bound to a chair. This display of phenomena was part of an impressive evening of trance control witnessed by over 30 sitters.
>
> Held in the specially built seance room in the home of the chairman of the Noah's Ark Society, Robin Foy, trumpets were seen to levitate, bells heard to ring, and hands appeared to 'materialise'.
>
> Mr Alexander, president of the society, went very quickly into the trance state after two sitters tied him to a chair. The lights were lowered and an opening prayer said. Luminous strips of fluorescent tape were clearly visible around two aluminium trumpets on a table in front of Mr Alexander. He also had tape on his knees.
>
> Almost immediately, White Feather, guide of the medium, began to speak. He welcomed everyone and assured us that

conditions were good. 'We shall do our utmost to try and blend our two worlds together as one. In a little while the boy known as Christopher will come and talk. His will not be an easy task for he will try and reunite you with your loved ones,' he announced.

He went on to say that physical manifestation would be attempted in the second half of the sitting. He stressed, however, if successful it would not be for entertainment purposes, but rather 'to show how close our two worlds are when we have a good medium and conditions are right'.

A gurgling sound filled the air followed by a little boy's voice which announced, 'I'm in now'. This was Christopher, control of Mr Alexander's home circle. To relieve the tension, he sang two nursery rhymes, but altered the wording. Everybody laughed. 'I'm going to try something. Is anybody squeamish?' Silence reigned! He said he wanted to demonstrate the type of control he had over his medium as many people, so he understood, believed the trance state was either self-delusion or faked.

The lights were turned up. Christopher asked one of the sitters to pick up a pair of pliers on a small table in the centre of the circle and pinch 'a nice bit of skin' on the medium's arm. During this rather disturbing procedure, Mr Alexander's face remained impassive. I was asked to do the same, but although I twisted and pulled as hard as I could, the medium appeared to feel no pain. A further sitter repeated the experiment with the same result.

With the lights once again lowered, Christopher explained that in the medium's home circle there were, on average, 500 people wanting to communicate, but that evening there seemed to be 'about 5,000'.

After a number of personal messages, another voice spoke. It turned out to be 'Jack', a regular communicator at Mr Alexander's home circle. 'There are so many people wanting to speak,' he said. 'I want everyone to know that what is taking place in the spiritualist movement at the moment, is only a forerunner of things to come. What I am emphasising is the fact we all survive the change called death. Isn't it wonderful when, from time to time, in seance rooms up and down the country, relations over here are able to communicate with those on your side. We are doing everything possible to try and break through as quickly as we can. The important thing is to have confidence in the spirit world,' he added.

Sitters were instructed to sing as various types of phenomena were to be attempted. Music was also played. It seemed to have the desired effect. Two trumpets, placed in front of the medium, rose into the air. Covered with luminous tape, they began to make patterns in the darkness.

Several people were tapped good-naturedly on the head. A bell was rung and a small table rattled rather violently. Drumsticks were heard distinctly to rap out a tune.

But it was the trumpets that were the most impressive at this point. Their height, distance from the medium – who was still clearly seated as luminous strips attached to his person indicated – and trajectory of flight, made the possibility of fraud distinctly unlikely. I felt a whoosh of air as something flew past. The sitter on my right announced the medium's shirt had landed on her lap. Delicate touches of fingers followed. They were warm, fleshlike, but felt not fully formed. Was this partial materialisation? Certainly no footsteps could be heard andI could sense no physical form in front of me.

After the phenomena ceased, more evidential trance followed. Frank Smith wanted to speak to Diane, who confirmed her presence.'I don't know if you remember me when you were a little girl? Can you remember falling badly on your face?'

Diane said she could, but it was clear she couldn't place the communicator who told her he was a friend of her grandfather, Harry. A soft woman's voice took his place. She said she was called 'Elsie' and asked to speak to Rose, who replied at once, immediately recognising the communicator.

'Fancy this, fancy this,' laughed Elsie. 'We had some lovely times, didn't we?' Told she had been sent loving thoughts after her passing, Elsie replied that she knew and was very grateful. Afterwards, I learned that her surname had been 'Walton' and she was, in life, a staunch Church of England supporter. She appeared keen to share her newly acquired knowledge that the spiritualist view of death was the correct one after all!

Christopher then returned and invited questions: How old are you? 'I was six and a bit when I passed.' When did you pass over? 'I have been asked this many times, but I never tell anybody. The reason is, Christopher might not be my real name, and every mum and dad who have lost a little boy might think it's me!'

> Can you see us (the sitters)? 'No, I can't right now. Sometimes I can and sometimes I can't. Sometimes I can't hear myself talk either.'
>
> Do you see us as we are physically or spiritually? 'When I see you, it is physically.' Are you continually striving to improve communication from the 'other side'? 'Yes, of course.' Do you feel you are succeeding? 'We know we are. From what I understand over here, there is a great big effort going on to try and bring physical mediumship back. There are circles all over the place starting to do well. This is just a beginning.'
>
> Where is Stewart now? 'He is standing beside his body.' Is he conscious? 'No.' Why do so many circles have a child guide? (This question was answered by Jack.) 'The reason is, most adults love children. At a physical seance, it is very important that people, who are often nervous, are made to feel at ease. Children know how to relax adults. If a child says something funny, it often seems a lot more amusing than if an adult had said it.'
>
> White Feather then closed the proceedings. The lights were turned on and Stewart was seen still clearly bound to the chair, but minus his shirt. 'Did you get anything?' he asked.

The next major event in the calendar of the Noah's Ark Society was the weekend residential seminar we held at the North Cheshire College, Warrington, from 13 to 15 November. This particular seminar had been organised by the NAS general secretary, Elisabeth Wheeler, and followed the same pattern as the previous residential seminars of the society. A presentation was made to Alan Crossley to mark his retirement as president, and a full agenda of lectures and talks by both committee members and invited guests ensured that this was yet another example of a wonderfully successful NAS seminar. Stewart Alexander acted as medium of the day during the experimental sitting for physical phenomena which took place on the Saturday evening in the theatre complex of the college, with all the delegates participating. Everybody at that sitting heard the voices of Stewart's guides as they opened and conducted the proceedings. Some of those present received personal communications from loved ones who had passed. The hand of one of the delegates was gently touched. Spirit lights in various forms were witnessed by most who were present, and the marked changes in temperature were somewhat dramatic for those sitting in the immediate vicinity of the medium. All had the opportunity to see the illuminated trumpets dance to the music, to hear the bell ringing and the drumsticks beating time to the music. A few of the sitters were invited to place their hands on the medium while one of the trumpets was manipulated by the spirit operators. These sitters were able to confirm that the medium remained deeply entranced and securely bound when the phenomena took place. It was later discovered that the medium's jumper had been removed and thrown to one side, although he remained bound to his chair.

Meanwhile, our home circle at Scole had been re-formed. There was a lady member of the Ark living close to us in Norfolk, who had indicated when she joined the society that she would like to sit in a physical circle. We arranged a meeting, and the long and short of it was that she started to sit with us on a regular basis. Until we met her, Sandra and I had continued to sit alone each week throughout September, to keep the circle going – and now we were three.

At the Warrington seminar, we discussed the state of the Scole circle and its lack of sitters with one of the members who was present and, despite the fact that he lived 75 miles away, he indicated that he might be interested in sitting every other week. Another lady who lived close to him also asked if she might become a member of the circle, too. Both sat with us for the first time on 23 November and joined the circle as regulars thereafter. Then we were five!

In the December issue of the newsletter, I introduced a new free facility into the publication, which I headed 'Circles Seeking Sitters'. The idea was that the member physical circles within the Ark could advertise free for new sitters to their circles. We knew from the early days of the society that several individual members would love the chance to join a circle and in the past we had actually been able, on occasions, to put enough members in touch with one another to form their own new circle. Having added this feature to the newsletter, we then took advantage of it ourselves and advertised for more sitters. The ad was spotted and answered by a Norfolk couple who were members of the Ark, and they first sat with us on 4 January 1993.

This gave us our full complement of sitters and, with the very special harmony we managed to build up between us over the months ahead, we had a solid foundation for what was to become the Scole Experimental Group, with its truly wonderful and unique phenomena.

However, there were more important things to think about in January 1993 – the Noah's Ark Society was about to hold its first full week's residential seminar on physical mediumship and its phenomena, at the Arthur Findlay College, Stansted Hall, Essex, from 22 to 29 January. Considered by many to be the 'Mecca' of modern spiritualism, the hall is a delightful place, and the society had filled every single bed in the place within 48 hours of announcing the event the previous year. All the 100 delegates were members of the Ark, and what a successful week that was.

Having been organised by the vice-president and publicity officer of the society, the only cloud on the horizon that week was the sad loss of Gordon Higginson, himself a physical medium, also president of the Spiritualists National Union and principal of the Arthur Findlay College. His funeral took place during our Stansted week and was attended by some of the delegates who knew him well.

During the week, in addition to two experimental sittings (both successful) for physical phenomena given by the NAS president, Stewart Alexander, we were also privileged to witness a demonstration of psychic surgery by Stephen Turoff and an experimental sitting for psychic photography, conducted by one of the guest speakers, Lionel Owen. Other speakers included medium Ivy Scott – over 90 years old and still going strong – and Wilfred Watts, who spoke of their experiences of physical mediumship over the years. Tom Harrison once again recounted his vivid memories of his mother's remarkable materialisation mediumship.

Daily workshops for psychic photography and EVP (I ran this one) were held. The results of the EVP one was quite amazing; by the end of the week, *all* participants were able to receive EVP messages themselves. Committee members of the Ark worked very hard to make the week the runaway success that it proved to be, and I am sure that most, like Sandra and me, on returning home, fell into an exhausted but happy state of slumber.

During a Scole cellar sitting on 27 February, with Stewart Alexander as medium and 35 other sitters, his guides undertook a unique experiment, in the hope that all participants would leave the seance afterwards with no doubts whatsoever in their minds that they had witnessed genuine physical phenomena.

The sitting started with the usual phenomena – the jangling of the seance room bells; the movement around the room of two trumpets, travelling in synchronised harmony to points of the room fully 15 feet away from the medium; the playful prodding of sitters by the same trumpets, which also tapped sitters lightly on the head, or caressed them gently and lovingly about the face or hands. (This happened to me and was quite an emotional experience.)

Following a noisy interlude, when Christopher proceeded to beat a set of drumsticks vehemently on the seance room table, declaring that 'it needed repairing', another of Stewart's guides, Walter Stinson, told the sitters that they were about to produce phenomena under conditions where everybody in the room was controlled and restrained to the point that nobody could move without the others knowing.

Walter instructed the sitters in the inner of the two concentric circles to hold hands, with the two ladies on either side of the medium putting their spare hand on the medium's knee nearest to them – and each placing their outside foot on the medium's foot nearest to them.

Finally, sitters in the outside circle put their hands on the shoulders of those in front of them who were sitting in the inside circle. This also included those behind the medium, and they controlled Stewart in this way, too. In fact, *absolutely everybody* in the seance room was thus fully controlled, so that it would be known immediately if anybody moved from their seat. In addition, the medium was securely tied into his chair in the usual way.

Under these stringent test conditions, we were all treated to a further display of synchronised movement by the two trumpets which continued to move away from the medium by up to 15 feet. While this was going on the two sitters next to the medium reported the movement of ribbon-like trails of ectoplasm across their arms, as the trumpets flew and hovered around the room.

As 1993 wore on, I continued to give talks and lectures about the NAS, its work and about physical mediumship as a whole. The society boosted its image and membership with a one-day seminar and publicity meeting (without a seance) which we held at Roehampton on 28 March. The third AGM of the NAS took place at the Sleep Inn, on 25 April, and ran true to form in that all committee members and officers were returned without contest.

Bram Rogers, secretary, companion and friend to Leslie Flint for 42 years, suddenly passed to spirit without warning on 4 May. It was a shock for most of us; I had known Bram personally for almost 20 years and he always seemed to epitomise good health. He was a man who was very charming, witty, warm and friendly – and his love of life was mirrored in his almost impish sense of humour. It was a great blow to Leslie, who was now over 80 years old himself – considerably older than Bram – and it was a blow from which I believe he never recovered. Later that year, however, Leslie, whose own physical mediumship had ceased by this time, was able to be physically reunited with his friend through Lincoln's mediumship. It was a crumb of comfort for him in his grief.

On 30 May, the society held a special experiment in the Scole cellar, at the instigation of Lincoln's guides. It involved the two physical mediums, Lincoln and Stewart Alexander, sitting together and being used simultaneously in trance by their respective guides – each medium accompanied by their complete home circle, and with both groups surrounded by an outer circle consisting of NAS committee members.

The Swift circle and committee members started the session off by singing but this did not suit Stewart's circle too well, and he had difficulty in 'going off' into trance, although this was eventually achieved. I was sitting in the corner, to the right of the cabinet, near Lincoln, and soon heard his chair being moved. It was discovered afterwards that he was still tied but that the chair had been turned around by 180 degrees, to face the wall.

Following this, I felt an icy blast from the cabinet, and its curtains were wrapped around me. Stewart's brother, Mike, was sitting on the other side of the cabinet. A materialised spirit, who emerged therefrom, touched his hands, then caressed his face and arms before speaking to him in the independent voice. Although Mike was relatively unknown to the medium, he received some excellent personal evidence from the materialisation which he had waited many years to get – and he admitted afterwards that had this come through Stewart, it would not have been convincing because Stewart was aware of the matter which was discussed.

I was then touched myself – being stroked on the hands and arms by a materialisation (possibly Felix, one of Lincoln's guides). Charlie, then fully materialised, made himself known. Two trumpets shot up into the air and moved around the room, occasionally ringing the bells which hung from the ceiling, and a luminous fisherman's 'muppet' was thrown around the room. Charlie then came up to me, and showed me his child's fingers silhouetted against the muppet.

The two trumpets already in the air were joined by a trumpet from Stewart's end of the room and all three danced around in a synchronised way. Lincoln's guide, Daphne, sang along to one of the songs in a clear independent voice, as Christopher came through Stewart, and conducted some friendly banter with Charlie.

Several sitters in the inner circle were greeted and touched by materialised figures. My wife Sandra – in the outer circle to my right – was breathing heavily and was obviously being used as a third medium on this occasion, as I felt an icy blanket of air from Sandra's direction creep over my knees towards the cabinet.

A spirit who identified himself as Lord Louis Mountbatten then spoke to me in the independent voice, confirming what he had earlier said, that he and two more from his family hoped to act as a guiding force for the Noah's Ark Society. He stated that he would bring something for me to establish his true identity and goodwill, and a memorial medallion was then apported into the seance room and dropped on to the floor in front of me. I believe that Sandra's energy was partially used in the production of this apport, as she was clearly tugged hard at the solar plexus when it arrived.

The medallion was shiny and appeared to be in 'proof' condition. On one side it bore the likeness of Lord Louis, with the years of his birth and death and on the other, the Mountbatten Royal Crest (Photographs of this medallion appear in the plate section).

This very special sitting was concluded when one of the Swift circle guides spoke through Stewart and White Feather spoke through Lincoln in a sort of 'exchange visit'. John Austin's wife, Gerry, who had recently passed into the spirit world herself, spoke to us and to John in the independent voice – her voice and mannerisms being intently recognisable.

The next week, I spent a considerable time researching the medallion apport which I had received, and ringing round the country's mints and coin dealers to identify it. I finally managed to discover that it had been commissioned by Broadlands, Lord Louis' home in Hampshire, following his death and was quite rare. Only 250 copies in total had been struck in cupro-nickel by the Tower Mint in 1979 and it had subsequently been sold to the public for the price of £4.99 per copy.

# THE RISE OF THE SCOLE EXPERIMENTAL GROUP

THE EARLY SIGNS of development within the new Scole circle were certainly encouraging. At one of the very first sittings with the new personnel, we were singing the tune 'Bring Me Sunshine' – the well-known signature tune of the comedy duo, Morecambe and Wise – when everybody heard a number of loud sets of clicks, continuing for some time, which sounded exactly like the clockwork false teeth that Eric Morecambe had used so often in his act during his lifetime.

On 26 April 1993, with only five of the regular seven sitters present, the trumpet was knocked off the table for the very first time. It fell three feet on to the leg of one sitter and from there down on to the floor. Two days later, when just Sandra and I sat together, a trance message indicated that we might expect a really rapid development of the phenomena when the circle was back to full strength.

The following week when we sat with six sitters, the trumpet fell over again. This time it appeared to be more controlled, and rested on the lap of one of the sitters. The room was full of clicks, raps, whistles and whispers. Some sitters were able to see quick flashes of tiny spirit lights; there were also several noises indicating movement on a shelf at the rear of the cellar. The tape of the sitting, when played back afterwards, was found to contain several instances of EVP, but there was constant interference with the recording, as if caused by static, until, that is, the trumpet fell over. From that moment on, and somewhat evidentially, the 'static' ceased. It is quite possible that the effect was due to a build-up of energy, and other circles have since told us that they have experienced similar effects on their own recordings. Perhaps it was the earliest sign that spiritual energy of some sort (as opposed to ectoplasm) was involved in the production of the physical phenomena in our home circle.

The summer moved on with no significant increase in the encouraging phenomena we had seen so far, but everybody was assuming that physical mediumship would develop with me, or Sandra, or both of us jointly as mediums. It was not to be, but nothing was changed in the circle till after the July/August 1993 weekend residential seminar of the Noah's Ark Society which I organised myself at Roehampton in south-west London.

As with all the other residential seminars of the Ark to date, the first one in the London area passed without a hitch, and was further enhanced by the addition of a couple of guest speakers. It was customary for all residential events to include an experimental seance and this one, with Stewart Alexander as the medium, was held in the theatre of the college (this being large enough to accommodate all the delegates, and relatively easy to black out). The sitting was excellent, with much trumpet and physical phenomena – with personal relatives and friends of the delegates able, on several occasions, to speak directly to their loved ones through the trumpets. Sometimes the spirit voice would come simultaneously through two trumpets at the same time – these being in different parts of the room, thus creating a sort of 'stereo' effect. The only confusion was caused by the fact that one of the delegates, without realising it, had gone into the sitting with a bunch of keys attached to his waist. These rattled constantly and the sound was occasionally mistaken for phenomena. A warning to others who sit in physical circles to *always* remove loose and noisy objects from their person *before* sitting!

With the Roehampton event behind us, we really got down to some serious sitting in our Scole home circle. I cannot remember quite how the decision was taken to implement changes but all the members decided democratically to change the focus of the circle from sitting specifically for Sandra and I. We threw the whole thing open for the spirit world to do whatever *they* wanted in the circle. We stated categorically that we did not care who the medium or mediums were. Nor did we care what the final phenomena we developed might be. We promised to provide the right conditions for physical mediumship and its phenomena to develop – to consult the spirit people every step of the way – and to leave the rest up to them.

Maybe this was the declaration the spirit team were waiting for, because from that point onwards there was no looking back. Two of the other sitters in the group were jointly taken into trance when we sat and, with just three of us present at the Monday sitting of 4 October, we received our first apport – a Churchill crown – as, we were told, 'a sign of greater things to come'. The apport was brought by the guide 'Manu', who is now always the first guide to speak whenever we hold an experimental sitting.

Rather appropriately, a few weeks later, on Remembrance Day, when all the sitters attended the Scole circle, we had seven apports – one for each member of the group – two small silver lockets, a silver thimble, a silver chain bracelet, a St Christopher medallion, an ornate miniature spoon inscribed on the reverse in French and a tiny gold medallion with unusual hieroglyphics which could be Inca in origin. Even more appropriately, the group consisted of four lady sitters and three men. Among the seven apports were four that were more suitable for ladies, and three that were more appropriate for men.

There was something of a lull in the Scole phenomena during the period that Sandra and I organised, and took part in, the November residential weekend seminar of the Noah's Ark Society at Cober Hill near Scarborough in Yorkshire. All went according to plan, with Stewart Alexander giving a demonstration of deep trance mediumship on the Friday night. Larry Dean and Celia Pennifold adequately described the Saturday night sitting we all enjoyed:

> The medium for the evening seance was Lincoln, who was giving his first public seance for over a year, and once everybody was seated in two big concentric circles, he was strapped into his chair in the usual manner. The bonds were thoroughly checked by two people. The red light was turned out and the sitting opened in prayer. Singing by the assembled company commenced, and after a number of songs, we all became aware that we could hear another voice singing louder and higher than the rest of us. It was, of course, Maria, one of Lincoln's regular communicators, singing from the spirit side of life in the independent voice.

The next person to make themselves known was one of the medium's guides known as Felix. Although there was some infiltration of light, he described the conditions as 'adequate'. He spoke for quite a lengthy period of time, answering questions and giving the odd piece of pertinent advice – often showing knowledge of the identity of the questioner just by the sound of their voice. He also placed his solid hands on Sandra Foy's neck and head to give her healing.

Next could be heard the voice of the child guide, Charlie, who was proclaiming that he thought Felix would never finish speaking! Charlie manipulated the trumpet and levitated it briefly – but he soon seemed to be worn out by the effort, judging from his choice remarks! He then went round touching various sitters, whilst his head could often be seen against the light as he moved around the room.

We were both fortunate, because Charlie greeted us by name, and Celia had the added pleasure of feeling Charlie's little fingers being placed in her hand. One sitter asked Charlie to push up her glasses for her because they were sliding down her nose, and Charlie was quick to oblige. He also gave a short demonstration of his skills in manipulating the electric keyboard which was lying on the floor in the middle of the room, with a further demonstration of his ability to change his own voice from that of a child to that of an older person (which in reality he is in his own world, having grown up in spirit).

When Charlie had finished speaking, the wonderful, clear and precise voice of Lincoln's guide, Daphne, gave us a talk as an introduction to the communicators who were to follow – pointing out that as the messages would be of a personal nature, and intended only for each particular recipient, they should not be discussed after the sitting. Suffice to say that these messages, which came through in the independent voice, provided some wonderful and very emotional evidence for each of those who received them. One appeared by way of an apported message, contained on tissue-like paper, but printed in tiny dots.

When the communicators had finished, Daphne spoke again, and in particular answered some questions put to her by Joe Cooper, who was curious about her earthly existence. Finally, he was fortunate enough to receive an apport of a picture of a fairy on a piece of light wood. This was particularly interesting in that Joe

> was the author of a book on the subject – *The Case of the Cottingley Fairies* – and two of the spirit guides had earlier expressed their view that the existence of fairies, or rather, nature spirits/elementals, was fact and not fiction.
>
> Once the sitting had ended the lights were put back on, and it was found that Lincoln's bonds were still intact – but a jumper and shirt that he had been wearing earlier when the seance started, with the bonds passing through the jumper, had been removed and thrown into the centre of the room. However, the cardigan that had been *on top* of the jumper and shirt was still in place on the medium.

When we returned home after the Cober Hill seminar, the phenomena in our home circle at Scole really took off with a vengeance. On 13 December, for instance, with all seven sitters present, Manu, speaking through one of the mediums who was in deep trance, opened the proceedings as usual, with two other guides, Patrick (a one-time Irish priest in his lifetime), and Raji (a lovable ex-military character from India) speaking to us at length through the other medium who was *also* in a deep trance state. A string of cowbells, that were hanging from the ceiling above my head, rang merrily, and spirit lights of a spectacular variety (like shooting stars) were seen by all.

The trumpet levitated, moving up to the ceiling and circumnavigating the room. In all, it stayed aloft for a full eight minutes. We were told that it was being manipulated by two young spirit people who were located on our central table and that it was the ultimate aim of spirit to make them, and other spirit visitors, visible to us in the near future.

On this occasion, the movements of the trumpets seemed exceptionally skilled to us and we were told by one of the guides that there was *no ectoplasm* involved in this amazing physical phenomenon that was unfolding before us. The guide went on to inform us that a new method of producing physical phenomena was being successfully pioneered by the spirit team working with our group. Instead of ectoplasm, they had brand new technology which utilised *only* energy – this being a blend of energy from three specific sources; firstly, spiritual energy, which they brought with them from the spirit world; secondly, energy that was taken from the sitters and, lastly, energy that was drawn from 'columns' or 'reservoirs' of natural 'earth' energy which exist in certain geographical locations of our world.

While we talked to the guides, the trumpet moved gracefully all over the room, including through the legs of not only the chairs, but also one of the medium's legs. It finally glided up in the air again, to place itself accurately (and softly) in an upright position on the table, where it started to rapidly rotate and rattle.

It was therefore with an exceedingly light heart that most of the Scole group members trooped down to Hove the following evening to attend the special annual Christmas Tree Seance of the Swift circle.

We were all full of anticipation as we assembled on the south coast, clutching our wrapped Christmas presents of toys and sweets etc., which we hoped would be enjoyed by the spirit children who traditionally attend these special Christmas seances. As the room was prepared, our presents, plus some sweets and a number of balloons were placed under the decorative Christmas tree.

We were not to be disappointed. What followed proved to be one and three-quarter hours of mellifluous mayhem, as the various guides and spirit children came to converse excitedly in the independent voice, while the children ripped open the presents and played with them. At the same time, chocolates were taken off the tree by the children, who unwrapped them before generously distributing them to the various sitters, also simultaneously playing with the balloons, which they proceeded to knock about the room with gusto.

After Lincoln (who sat under test conditions) had gone into trance, a burst of singing from the assembled sitters brought forth a lady's independent voice, singing beautifully along with us by way of an overture to the rest of the phenomena.

There were several excited spirit children who came to speak to us before opening their presents. One little girl introduced herself as 'Ruby', telling us she had been three years old when she 'died'. She chose a doll in a basket for her present, which had been under the tree. More children, including an 'Edith', 'Becky' and 'Thomas' came to chat, picking out their presents, which they then opened and played with. Toy cars whizzed around the room; rattles were noisily shaken and toy trumpets were loudly blown.

One little girl brought an apport of a black tie, which belonged to nobody present. First it was placed on the lap of one of the sitters, and then she proceeded, with much giggling, to tie it to my left ankle, and to the ankle of the lady sitting on my right. As the lights went up afterwards, we discovered ourselves well and truly joined together.

Several of the guides from the Swift circle put in an appearance that evening. There was Charlie of course, who seemed pleased with the chocolate Father Christmas bought especially for him, and then he, Bapu and Felix walked around the room, lovingly touching all the sitters with their solid materialised hands – each individual displaying totally different characteristics of size and feel in the hands that they offered.

John Austin's wife Gerry spoke to him, while circle guides, Daphne and Portrai, conversed with the rest of us. Several sweets were apported through the narrow end of the levitated trumpet and confetti was sprinkled by Daphne over two of the sitters who had just got married, since she was unable to attend their wedding in person.

When the lights went up afterwards, the room looked like a battleground with toys and paper everywhere. What a night that proved to be!

In the meantime, however, the phenomena at the Scole circle were becoming more and more spectacular by the week, with constant loud raps and thumps on the cellar walls, chairs, table – everywhere. The spirit lights performed passable imitations of shooting stars in dramatic fashion and then settled down to explore the cellar leisurely and completely. Sitters were told that it was necessary, when working only with energy, for the spirit team to construct a 'canopy' of energy overhead, under which all the work would take place. Such a 'canopy' had now been perfected and could be erected in seconds by the spirit team in future. We were about to start a new year and 1994 was to prove a year of massive change for all the Scole sitters, as we realised just how important and significant the work within the group was becoming.

The first sitting of the year, on 3 January, yielded seven more apports and a profusion of phenomena: the ringing of bells, levitation of trumpet and other objects including the central table, raps (some sounding as powerful and loud as if the table was being struck by drumsticks), taps, thumps and spirit lights, sitters being sprinkled by water and chairs being moved about as though spirit people were sitting on them. That night, we seemed to have the lot! This sitting certainly set the pace for the rest of the year.

The following week we were instructed by the spirit team at Scole to keep the group and its exciting phenomena 'under wraps' for the time being. We were to close the circle with immediate effect, allowing no visitors until such a time as guests were sanctioned directly by spirit. Because the work at Scole was so important, so different and so new, we were asked never to make comparisons with the work of past physical mediums, whose phenomena had been produced by ectoplasm, instead of the energy which was now being utilised in our group. To enable us to move away totally from the old and classic ways, we were also to remove the trumpet and replace it for the time being with a cardboard tube with luminous tape around its ends so its position could be seen as it levitated and moved around the room. Several other objects were also provided by us for the spirits to experiment with – we had been told they wished to undertake experiments in levitation – such as a cube ball, balsa-wood cube, silver-foil-covered box, fisherman's luminous 'muppet' and a ping pong ball.

Over the next few weeks, all of these objects levitated and moved around the room in a controlled manner, often hovering in mid-air in front of one of the sitters and 'nodding' in response to their comments – while the bells in the room rang merrily. There were amazing displays of spirit lights dancing and moving about the cellar at speed; on one occasion, no less than 19 lights fell from the ceiling, one after the other, into the table, and shortly afterwards, the same number, one after the other, shot out of the table into the air. All the time that this wonderful phenomenon was going on, our spirit guides from the 'team' spoke to us via the mediums, who were constantly in an entranced state – giving a full commentary on what was going on, what they intended to do next and why, and explaining the technical points and mechanics of the phenomena, which was extremely helpful as we continued enthusiastically to help spirit pioneer their brand new methods.

The spirit lights continued to develop, becoming larger, brighter and more versatile. Gradually they started to touch sitters on a regular basis, sometimes feeling like a fluttering butterfly as they alighted on sitters' hands (or heads if they happened to be bald!), and at other times appearing quite solid, like a chopstick, drumstick or marble. We were told that they consisted of pure energy, which could be manifested in many forms.

When we appeared to have a quieter sitting early in February, and I commented that the team must have 'forgotten the formula for levitation', a couple of seconds later the table (which was quite heavy) levitated off the floor and shot at speed across the circle – followed by the sound of heavy drumsticks drumming on it (there were no material drumsticks in the room) created by solidified energy.

On 14 February, St Valentine's Day, we had seven more apports at Scole. The day before, Sandra and I had been invited to another physical circle we had never previously visited, in order to advise and assess their progress. This turned out to be quite an amazing sitting. None of the sitters went into trance and it seemed that phenomena here were also being produced by the use of energy. Soon after the sitting started, an 'energy' voice from mid-air bade us all 'Good evening and welcome'. At this circle, they were accustomed to having a tea-break in the middle of the proceedings, and when it was time for this, a man's 'energy' voice told us to 'Have a good break'!

During the second half of that sitting, the table rushed around the room – at one stage, trying to climb right up on to my lap. I was touched several times by solidified spirit hands, which felt quite warm and normal. Sandra's face was stroked by similar hands, and one sitter had his glasses taken off and placed on the central table, some feet away from him. A lady was pulled to her feet by a tall, fully materialised spirit figure during our rousing rendering of the 'Anniversary Waltz' and he then proceeded to dance with her to the music. Another sitter had his leg lifted on to the table by a materialised form, who then gave him reflexology. There were more 'energy' voices throughout the sitting, and numerous souls conversed with us directly on a whole variety of subjects. The event, which had been a fascinating insight into another circle, lasted about four hours, including the tea-break, but showed us that ours was not the only group whose physical phenomena were being achieved by the spirit people using energy alone.

The next week, on 21 February following the instructions of the spirit team at Scole, we put on a special sitting for one of our guides, Patrick McKenna. As a one-off sitting, we provided the requested cabinet in the cellar, in which one of the mediums sat. Speaking through the trance state of the medium, Patrick soon made himself known, and the phenomena began with a number of spirit lights. However, it was obvious that they were much brighter than before.

There was a certain amount of rapping as usual but the main observation was that the lights were developing in front of our eyes into luminous patches. These became more prevalent, growing and receding in size and brightness. For the first time, the surface of the table was illuminated as the lights passed over it. The smaller of the lights started to emit 'beams', like torchlight, as they moved around the group, and from time to time 'sheets' of light, some two to three feet square, flared up for a few seconds in different places, giving brilliant illumination as they did so.

However, the picture was not yet complete, as the phenomena seemed to work up to climax. Patrick told us to look towards the cabinet, as he wanted to show us something. Four or five times in total, a small light shone a beam on to the fully materialised figure of Patrick himself. We all saw his head and shoulders, and one sitter was able to see him clearly right down to his waist.

Earlier in the evening, Patrick had explained that the new mechanics which the spirit team were using in our group involve quantum physics, and that results are achieved by the manipulation of atoms and molecules. The team wished to experiment in this field to see what could be achieved. We were also told that in the near future, we would be partaking in some experiments for psychic photography.

# SPIRIT PHOTOGRAPHIC EXPERIMENTS AT SCOLE

HAVING TOLD US that we would shortly be involved in a phase of psychic photography, the spirit team at Scole lost no time in getting the photographic experiments off the ground. Just a week after the initial announcement, on 28 February we introduced a 35mm camera into the dark cellar, loaded with a conventional 24-frame colour film. This was put on a chair at the side of one of the sitters, so that she could pick it up and use it in the dark room when instructed to do so. (I hasten to add that there was *no* flash on the camera and *no* normal source of light in the room.)

After the guide Manu had come through to speak to us, both sets of bells suspended from the ceiling rang profusely, heralding the arrival of Patrick, who confirmed that it was the intention of the spirit helpers to see what could be achieved with psychic photography. He spoke of the 'materialisation' we had witnessed at the previous sitting and explained that, although his image had appeared real and solid to us at the time it was not actually so. The image had actually been 'projected' from the small spirit lights, giving a hologram sort of effect. From now on, we would be seeing these projections regularly – at any time, and in any part of the room. Since this type of phenomena was brand new, and previously non-existent to our world or to the spirit world, I took the liberty of inventing suitable terminology for it. From now on this kind of phenomenon would be known as 'Visible Projected Phenomena', with each instance of it being described as a 'Visible Projected Image', or VPI for short.

Spirit lights started to fly and dance about the room and the guides Patrick and Raji informed us that the spirit team would try and project images into the camera for us. At this point the sitter with the camera was told that, at her own pace, she could take pictures as she wished. She then took 'snaps', trying to aim the camera towards the spirit lights. After a few shots, she put the camera down on the spare seat next to her, where it proceeded to continue to take its own snapshots, much to our amusement, winding itself on after each shot had been taken. The last five frames on the film were used up in this way, but for the very last photograph, a spirit light sat right in front of the lens and posed as the picture was taken.

Needless to say, when the film was developed the next day, we could not believe our eyes. In fact our first reaction to it was that we must have been given the wrong film by mistake. It *was* our film though and there were no less than 11 amazing images on it. One of these was of the spirit light which had obligingly posed in front of the camera for us, but the rest were totally unconnected and the subjects of the photographs varied greatly. There was a copy of a 1940s photograph of St Paul's Cathedral in the Blitz, and the second frame was of the same photograph sideways on. Another showed a wrecked bus after a night of wartime bombing in Coventry or London, with a further shot of this, too – also sideways on. The sixth image showed the front page of the *Daily Mirror,* dated 16 December 1936. The seventh showed a group of soldiers from the First World War. There were three more showing groups of people, but the pictures were unclear and blurred. A final photograph, also unclear, seemed to show a bride with head-dress. We were subsequently informed by our spirit helpers that all of these initial photographs were actually copies of photographs that currently existed somewhere in the world but that they would eventually be bringing originals for us.

Since the sitting with the first 'photographic' results had taken up almost three hours, we started a little earlier the following week, this time providing *two* 35mm SLR cameras, duly loaded with conventional colour film. The sitting was an extremely noisy one, because we had placed a new tambourine in the cellar and spirit took to it immediately. It was levitated and beaten like a drum, in time to the music we were playing. There was indeed much spirit activity all evening, with the now customary spirit lights, and footsteps being heard around the room most of the night. Two of the guides tried to explain the photographs we had received the previous week and told us that, although they would not be working specifically on the photography at this particular sitting, they would do so again in a couple of weeks. It was, however, during these sessions that we were introduced to yet another new form of phenomenon, which the team spent the major part of the sitting perfecting. This we termed the 'Extended Voice'. It involved the instantaneous extension of a medium's vocal chords to any point in the room and even, on some occasions, into the fabric of the walls. Our medium could be speaking normally in trance, with his voice obviously coming from his own mouth, when suddenly, the voice appeared to be refracted or diverted to come from elsewhere, with dramatic effect.

There was a further VPI that evening, showing the head and shoulders of a male spirit person who seemed to be looking at me. This was shown twice, and appeared to be fully three-dimensional. It was not possible from the brief glimpses that we got to positively identify the spirit entity. The lights developed further during the evening to beam on to the sitters, lighting up parts of the room, plus our feet, hands and knees from time to time. We were also asked to provide some paper and a pencil or pen for the next sitting.

On 14 March the phenomena developed even further. After a while, we were told by Raji that they were building up for something special and that, to achieve it, the spirit team would have to lower the temperature considerably. This was done as promised and the level of coldness was extremely noticeable. We then had a short communication from a spirit who represented himself to us as simply Paxton. We subsequently discovered that he was a very evolved soul but, at the time, he explained to us that he was not normally able to communicate with those on earth direct – his communications would possibly be passed on by guides such as Patrick or Raji – but that a definite decision had been taken by the Council of Communion, of which he was a member, for him to communicate direct with the Scole group occasionally, because of the importance of our work with physical phenomena. He further explained that the Council of Communion is a group of higher souls who oversee and control the work of the Scole group and similar groups working with energy in the same way; also having a high degree of control regarding intercommunication between the earth plane and the spirit world where groups such as ours were concerned.

When the sitting finished, it was discovered that among the various other forms of physical phenomena we had experienced that evening, there had also been a definite attempt to write with the pencil on the blank piece of paper. The drawing, about two inches by one-and-a-half inches, appeared to depict the letter 'P' – perhaps this had something to do with 'Paxton'.

On 21 March we had two apports almost as soon as the experimental session started. These were both old pennies and were dated 1936 and 1940, representing the years of two of the first 11 photographs (St Paul's, 1940 and the 1936 *Daily Mirror*). The lights and levitations were particularly extensive; for instance, the central table levitated to a height of about four feet and stayed in that position for a few minutes (we could tell its height from the tabs on its top surface), before rising to ceiling height, where it stayed for a good five minutes prior to its gently descending again.

One of the cameras at that sitting started to take its own snapshots again, and duly wound itself on. There were just three pictures this time, almost identical and showing – as we later discovered – a picture of the 'canopy' of energy erected by the spirit people over our group while we were working. Sitters were touched by the solid spirit lights on several occasions and more work was done on the psychic 'scribblings'. This time, a square and two semi-circles had been drawn on the paper.

The following Saturday, Stewart Alexander gave a cellar sitting at Scole for members of the Noah's Ark Society where, for a brief period, he was able to demonstrate ectoplasmic phenomena once more. With 31 sitters in total, the two trumpets flew around the cellar – from the ceiling to the floor, and from one end of the cellar to the other, sometimes with a trumpet simultaneously at each end of the room. A communicator spoke through one of them to a relative who was present.

Although Stewart had been feeling 'under par' during the previous week, the sitting was excellent, with White Feather, Christopher and Walter Stinson communicating extensively. Walter picked out a lady of his choice, and asked her if she would like to 'feel the hand of a man who has been dead for 80 years'. The lady sat next to Stewart temporarily and held one of his hands as instructed by Walter to ensure he stayed where he was. Stewart's other hand was held by the sitter on his other side, and the lady next to him was touched several times by Walter's materialised hand, as he explained that he dipped his etheric hand into the ectoplasm before touching the sitter.

The sitting was quite remarkable, however, in that Stewart's spirit helpers allowed the sitters to see a mass of ectoplasm around his face in red light. After a long period of crackling and rustling as the ectoplasm built up, the light was put on for about three or four seconds on no less than three occasions, to the delight of the sitters, most of whom had never seen ectoplasm before.

Just 48 hours later, during the customary Monday sitting of the Scole group, we had the psychic photography back with a vengeance. With two SLR 35mm cameras present, Sandra was asked to pick one of them up and aim it at the table. She was instructed to take a picture and wind the film on every time one of the spirit guides said 'Now!' – until the film was used up. The other camera was independently levitated and moved around the cellar by spirit, who themselves took photographs and wound the film on. When the films were developed, each of them again contained 11 different images. Some were people, some were places but all seemed unconnected; they were much clearer than on the first occasion we had obtained 'photographs' in this way.

During this same session, the central table levitated to the ceiling in a split second, and remained out of our sight for about ten minutes. One of the guides joked that they had taken it up through the ceiling into our library above. He also told us that they would be trying to obtain solid projections that week, and two of the sitters later felt solid hands on their shoulders, whose fingers were fully animated. A number of Solid Projected Images we obtained included two or three faces in mid-air. One life-sized image was of a man with a bowed head, and another clearly showed a miniature head on the central table. A fair amount of time during the course of this sitting was also devoted to improving and perfecting communication via the extended voice phenomenon.

The Scole group sitting of 4 April yielded even more exciting developments. It was obvious that solid figures were moving round the room and we were all touched in turn (or occasionally simultaneously) by definite, animated spirit hands, which I recall felt very cold, at times – almost wet. One sitter had his hand actually shaken and was able to feel some form of clothing at the wrist. A child's hands were heard to clap loudly from various parts of the room, and audible kisses were blown, which we returned. Soon afterwards, there was the sound of paper being ripped off the clipboard and thrown. It was later discovered that the name 'Sammy' was written in childish block capitals on a piece of paper. Patrick confirmed that a child had been present and explained that he had that night been allowed to be in charge of the phenomena. He told us that we had gone forward amazingly fast and what spirit themselves had thought would take months or even years of development had actually happened in just a few weeks.

On 11 April we were constantly aware of the solid physical presence of a number of spirit children. We asked them to leave us their names and, at the end of the sitting, we found that seven separate children's signatures and drawings had been left for us on the paper we provided. It was at this sitting, too, that a Chinese guide called Hoo walked around the room. He could be heard clearly as he shuffled round with short steps on the carpet. We could even hear the creaking of his shoe leather. He touched a couple of the sitters, then stopped in front of Sandra. Leaning over her, he took her hand and lifted it up, saying, 'You will see me soon!'

There was great sadness the following week when we learned that Leslie Flint had passed away on 16 April. There was a feeling that this was the end of a very special era but we knew that he would now be reunited with his many friends and guides who had gone before him to the spirit world. In an official capacity as chairman of the Noah's Ark Society of which Leslie was an honorary vice-president (as well as in a personal capacity), Sandra and I attended his cremation at Brighton on 21 April. The crematorium was packed for the short service and we went back to his home afterwards as a mark of respect. Leslie had been one of the 'greats' where physical mediumship was concerned, and many of those people at his funeral had been personal friends and eager sitters over the years.

We had attended the service with a friend of ours who was sitting in a physical circle we had recently assessed, where they had solid materialised spirit forms walking around the group. By this time, we had solid spirit people walking around in the Scole group and, in addition, we were standing talking to Lincoln, who had been getting materialised forms through his own mediumship for some time. We must have been quite a rare and unique group as we stood together talking, representatives of three separate groups who were all enjoying regular contact with materialised spirit beings. None of us then was allowing too much publicity of our work in the field of physical phenomena.

Suddenly a stranger walked up to us and introduced himself, saying that he understood I was from the Noah's Ark Society. He told us that he had spent many years sitting with Leslie, who had become a dear friend, but that for over 20 years, he had been searching fruitlessly for a circle where they had materialisation. He said that he understood such phenomena were very rare and asked whether I had heard of anybody inside or outside the Ark who had ever developed materialisation. I mumbled some sort of noncommittal response, but was not at liberty to divulge what any of us there was getting. If only he knew ... He was speaking to members of three separate circles who were regularly getting the phenomena he was looking for. I still smile when I think of that moment.

Throughout 1994 and 1995, the development within the Scole group has accelerated and psychic photography has become one of the important aspects of our work. Towards the end of 1994, we started to put out some flat Polaroid films in the dark room, which we developed through a blacked-out Polaroid camera afterwards. We frequently obtained some wonderful colour films of energy this way but the best was yet to come when we started to get wonderful results on *unopened* (still in its plastic tub) colour and black and white 35mm Polaroid slide films. In this category, we have now amassed over 150 wonderful slides of original photographs direct from the spirit world. I do not propose to go too deeply into this later photographic work here, as it will be covered in my next book, and interested parties can keep up to date with our work through the *Spiritual Scientist* bulletin (details on page 331). Suffice to say that our current photographic experiments are producing really mind-boggling results, which are totally unique in the world today.

On 6–8 May, we were involved in the Noah's Ark Society 1994 residential weekend seminar and AGM at the Hove Excelsior Hotel, near Brighton. Sadly, it was to prove the last seminar that Sandra and I would attend as committee members of that society, because spirit had other plans for us, and would soon be asking for a complete commitment from us to the work that we were undertaking within the Scole group.

Our swansong within the Ark was to be a sitting of Stewart Alexander's home circle which we were invited to attend on 28 June. As always, we were welcomed by Stewart's circle leader, Ray Lister, and his wife June. Ray always travelled with Stewart when he gave his sittings and looked after him whenever he was in the trance state. Ray was also a committee member of the Noah's Ark Society, and his help in blacking out the rooms where seances were to be held was invaluable at all the society seminars. This particular seance, at Stewart's home circle, turned out to be a really excellent one. White Feather opened the proceedings. Then young Christopher came next, referring to how well our Scole group was doing, and he told us that he visits our group from time to time to see what's going on.

Walter Stinson acted as Stewart's main guide of the evening. He too confirmed the importance of the Scole group, and stressed that the group must come before anything else. Following an aerobatic display by the two trumpets, Sandra's mother and father spoke to her through one of them, while my own father spoke to me through the other trumpet, saying that he had met Leslie Flint in the spirit world (which was quite evidential for me as he had never met him in life – a fact that the medium was unaware of). My father was surprised that Leslie was 'an ordinary bloke'. He had somehow expected him to be sort of mystical.

During the sitting, we twice saw visible ectoplasm in red light around the medium's chin and chest area. The appearance of this substance was preceded by the now familiar noise of crackling, such as would be produced by aluminium foil or cellophane paper as the ectoplasm built up, and this noise continued for some time. Following this display, and in red light, Sandra's father was able to transfigure Stewart so that both Sandra and I could recognise and identify him.

There were a number of written spirit messages discovered at the end of the sitting. Sandra had a personal one from her mother and father and we had a joint one from one of the guides at Scole, thanking us for our work.

# THE NEW SPIRITUAL SCIENCE FOUNDATION

OVER THE WEEKS and months ahead, the Scole group's work continued to develop and expand. Early in July, we put on a 'special night' for our guide Raji, during which he instructed us in meditation techniques. He also told us that healing would play a large part in the work of the group and that he would bring something to help us in this direction. We discovered afterwards that a quantity of 'holy ash' with healing properties had been apported during the sitting, in addition to an Indian medal and some uniform buttons. Even more striking was the other apport – an incense stick – which in addition to being apported, was also lit by psychic means.

On 11 July 1994, there was an apport of an original copy of the *Daily Express,* dated Monday, 28 May 1945. Considering it was so old, it was in almost mint condition, but although kept away from air and light since then, it is *now* showing the usual signs of deterioration associated with all newspapers, due to the chemical impurities in the mechanically produced pulp used for the manufacture of newsprint. After all, it *is* 50 years old! I was told by Manu that it came from one of my helpers and I would understand the reason for it being given to us. On the front was a photograph of the then prime minister, Winston Churchill.

It was in the course of this sitting that Paxton came to talk to us, and to instruct us in the ways of Spiritual Science. We were told that Spiritual Science is the science of life and the afterlife. He also explained as fully as possible the direction they were working towards with the new spiritual energy technology in our group. It was requested that we should start a quarterly bulletin to be known as the *Spiritual Scientist,* to keep scientists and interested parties informed of events and phenomena within the Scole group. Simultaneously, we were to create an organisation called the 'New Spiritual Science Foundation' which would, in the fullness of time, act as an umbrella organisation for people and groups of like mind who were working in the new way, with energy-based phenomena. At the millenium (the year 2000), we were to drop the word 'new' from the title of the foundation.

Each and every member of the Scole Experimental Group was asked to give their lives wholly and totally to the important work which was being undertaken there and it quickly became obvious that, with the growing workload, there would not be enough time to spare to continue our high-profile involvement on the committee of the Noah's Ark Society. Over its first four years, the society had already successfully completed the job it was set up to do – to bring back physical mediumship and its phenomena permanently. Sandra and I had thoroughly enjoyed that experience – very emotional for me, since I had *personally* founded the society – but we knew that with the competent 'crew' the Ark now had on its 'bridge', our presence on the committee was no longer vital to its success and we would therefore be leaving it in good hands. It was the right time now for Sandra and me to retire from one project in order to undertake another and we reluctantly announced our retirement as officers and committee members of the NAS from the end of August 1994. I continued, however, to edit the September issue of the Noah's Ark newsletter, which meant that after creating the publication, I had edited 50 issues before retiring.

Paxton went on to cover the use of energy for the production of physical phenomena in more depth. There are four main differences between this method and the more traditional ectoplasmic methods. Firstly, the use of energy is much safer for the medium, although trance is still necessary in the early stages of development. Secondly, the time factor plays a big part – development of phenomena using the new spiritual energy technology is much quicker than by the more traditional methods. Thirdly, the variety of physical phenomena that can be produced through the use of energy is much greater and finally, although the energies would still be focused through our trance mediums, the other sitters would play more part in providing the bulk of the energy for spirit's use. So the whole thing is more of a group effort than an individual effort by a medium or mediums.

We were allowed to ask just two questions: *Question 1*: Why is it, when these energies have always been around, that they can only now be used for physical phenomena? *Answer*: Because it is only now that a suitable set of people have come together to facilitate that use. *Question 2*: Is the Council of Communion the same as, or part of, the White Brotherhood? *Answer*: Yes and No. Our Council of Communion is 13 in number. In the spirit world, there are many, many councils dealing with all sorts of matters, including communication, phenomena and healing. The White Brotherhood is the name given to one of these councils but not our council.

Over the next few sittings of the Scole group, in addition to Patrick and Raji, another prominent spirit helper began to make herself better known to us. This was Mrs Emily Bradshaw. With her no-nonsense approach and impeccable English, Mrs Bradshaw seemed to be more involved with bringing extremely evidential personal evidence for the sitters during her earlier visits to us but she has since become one of the mainstays of the group from the spirit side of life. Today, she is one of only two guides and helpers that speak to us *every* week (the other being Manu, who speaks through the same medium). The other regular helpers, although always there in the background, do not always speak during the course of a sitting.

Towards the end of August, I had been asked by a medium who ran a spiritual and psychic centre in Felixstowe, Suffolk, to undertake a weekend residential seminar for him on physical mediumship and its phenomena. He was aware of my previous work within the NAS, and felt it would be an interesting experience for the people who regularly attended his centre to learn more about this important aspect of mediumship. I agreed to run such an event and a date was set for a seminar from 4 to 6 November. I hoped that an experimental sitting for physical phenomena might be arranged for the Saturday night, 5 November and was delighted when Stewart Alexander, president of the NAS, agreed to be the medium.

It occurred to me also that it would be an interesting experiment if the spirit team at Scole would agree to allow a demonstration of trance mediumship only by one or both of the Scole group mediums on the previous evening for the Felixstowe delegates and, consequently, with the mediums' consent, the Scole spirit team were asked for their reaction during one of the regular group sittings. Nobody was more surprised than I when they not only agreed to such a demonstration, but also told us they would be prepared to try an experimental sitting to see if we could obtain physical phenomena in the new way, with energy.

It would be necessary for us to work up gradually towards having a large number of participants sitting with us and our first single visitor (we had no say in the matter!) would shortly be named and invited (through us) by the spirit team to sit with the Scole group. In addition, we would have to undertake at least one experimental sitting away from the Scole cellar prior to the event, to ensure that phenomena could be produced outside of the cellar.

Paxton, now also proffering the Christian name John for himself, came to talk to us at the end of August, and asked if we could produce a broadsheet for visitors and participants in experimental sittings to read, so that we could let them know the feelings they might experience during a sitting of the Scole group. For instance, with the new energy phenomena, there may be a feeling of slight nausea within visitors, which might be accompanied by some dizziness. There could also be a gentle 'pulling' sensation from various parts of the body and possible 'heaviness' of the limbs. All visitors and sitters must be assured, however, that should they be touched by the energies during a sitting (an everyday happening for members of the Scole group), they would not come to any harm. It was also possible that sitting in the Scole group might cause visitors to experience a certain measure of clairvoyance and clairaudience for themselves while sitting there and we were asked not to encourage visitors to seek this experience specifically.

At this same sitting, one of the Scole group members asked whether spirit might allow lighted conditions during experimental sessions. Patrick answered by saying that they were intending to bring their own spirit lighting for sittings and were actively working towards this end. Had lighting been introduced into the circle at an early stage, however, the development of phenomena would have been significantly slowed down and the spirit team had felt that, at this stage, the phenomena were more important than having lighted conditions.

Early in September, it was confirmed that our first visitor was to be the medium who ran the spiritual centre at Felixstowe and it was duly arranged that he would be present for a special sitting on 4 October. Throughout the month of September, the team practised for the visitors, bringing more and more examples of physical phenomena – spirit lights, apports, the ringing of bells, raps and taps, etc. All of the sitters in the Scole group were regularly being touched by solid rods of energy (often in response to *mental* request), and we could hear the staccato drumming of 'nonexistent' drumsticks and chopsticks.

The plans of the spirit team to work with unopened 35mm films and Polaroid films, and with the glass domes, had been shelved for a while until our experimental 'visitor' phase was completed, as the team's whole attention was focused on the coming experiments. On 23 September, the group sat upstairs at Scole in the library and were not disappointed by the phenomena. Without a doubt, it *would* be possible for excellent physical phenomena to take place for our Scole group away from the cellar that we were now so used to and comfortable in.

During the sitting of 26 September, the group was told that a famous medium of the past was present and wanted to wish us luck for our forthcoming 'public' debut. She would bring us something to confirm her identity, from a period of her life that was not too happy. This turned out to be an apport of an original copy of the *Daily Mail* newspaper, dated Saturday, 1 April 1944. Like the newspaper apport that we had a few weeks earlier, this was in almost mint condition. It carried an article and photographs on the conviction and subsequent imprisonment of Helen Duncan, under the ancient Witchcraft Act.

The sitting with our first visitor went very well, and he received an apport of a brass elephant on a plinth to take away with him. There was plenty of the usual interesting physical phenomena for him to see and hear, and to reflect on afterwards. Mrs Bradshaw provided him with some personal evidence of survival during the evening too. We had been instructed to put a 35mm film in the room for this sitting (without a camera), and when it was developed, it revealed a red image, consisting of three different shades of red on a green background. Since the film had not been exposed to light during the course of the sitting, this simple result was extremely impressive.

On 10 October, we had our first results on a couple of flat Polaroid films that had been left face down on the table in the blacked-out room during the sitting. One showed a column of coloured smoky energy and the other showed two definite shapes on a greeny-yellow background. A 35mm film, placed unopened on the table in its light-proof plastic tub, showed results on four separate frames.

Four days later, we were permitted to have two visitors; these were the husband and wife of two of the sitters. One sitter had her birthday on this occasion and was brought a lovely apport of a silver and obsidian bracelet. The physical phenomena were superb and prolific, as they were the next week when we had six visitors sitting with us.

The final dry-run practice for the planned Felixstowe experiment took place in the Scole cellar on 28 October. This time, we had 16 visitors, making 23 sitters in total – about half of the sitters we expected at Felixstowe. Despite the fact that two members of the Scole group were feeling a little 'under par', it was an extremely good sitting, with lots of physical phenomena, which went on for two-and-a-quarter hours. Some of the visitors this time had never before sat in a physical circle and must have been a little apprehensive. Patrick came to chat for a while after Manu's initial greeting, and he went on to explain to the visitors the nature of the spirit world's new energy technology and resultant phenomena.

On 4 November, we undertook a unique experimental sitting at Felixstowe. This time there were 39 sitters in all, including the Scole group themselves. Staff and helpers at the centre had worked very hard at blacking out the area selected for the sitting, in order to make it suitable for such an experiment, and a trial period with the lights off proved it to be just as dark as the Scole cellar itself.

All the sitters were generally enthusiastic, and happily joined in by singing or humming the first two tunes played, until Manu came through as usual, and assured everybody that he had plenty of energy to work with during his 'blending' exercise. Patrick followed hot on his heels, and was in excellent form with his ready witticisms, which made everybody laugh and relax. Again, there were a number of people present who had never before had any experience of physical phenomena, but they all warmed to Patrick straight away, and responded positively to his 'double act' with Mrs Bradshaw.

The sitting lasted for over two hours and during this time there was almost constant activity by the spirit team. Spirit lights started up shortly after Patrick came through, and continued throughout the experiment, performing their usual aerobatic and 'firework' display. At one point, the lights danced up and down on the table, giving off a 'contact' rap as they touched the table's surface. As if that were not enough, one light repeatedly and visibly penetrated a Pyrex basin standing on the table before passing through the solid table itself, and emerging once more from underneath. The whole 'penetration' phenomena took no more than a split second each time it occurred.

A set of hanging bells rang frequently – on the first occasion, heralding Patrick's initial words. Mrs Bradshaw also introduced herself to the sitters and was in top form throughout, giving a number of evidential messages to the assembled company. Raji soon made his presence known and, speaking through his medium, had all the participants in stitches. There was much audible rapping on the table, walls and ceiling. In response to a request from one of the Scole group, the raps became so loud as to be almost deafening.

After the event, sitters soon discovered that the Pyrex bowl contained a quantity of apported ash with its inherent healing properties. Subsequent information revealed that this had come from the funeral pyre of an Indian 'holy man' (although I wish we had known that *before* we tasted it!) and its presence fulfilled the promise previously given by Raji that a further supply of this ash would be given to us. There was also an apport of an unusual silver necklace, possibly of African origin.

Overall, this private weekend seminar proved to be rather historic, because it also included Stewart Alexander's successful experimental sitting for physical phenomena on the Saturday evening, with results produced by the use of ectoplasm. Never before, anywhere in the world, had traditional spirit world technology, producing excellent physical phenomena by the use of ectoplasm, been seen in the same place, and at the same time as phenomena produced through the new, energy-based spirit technology.

The Felixstowe seminar was a one-off situation. If any of us at Scole had considered that it might herald the regular inclusion of visitors into the group, we would have been mistaken. The phenomena we had at that point, although prolific, had not moved far enough forward for the spirit team to consider its demonstration in a wholesale manner. We were still being asked to keep our results as quiet and as low-key as possible, because the team were aware that if we had too much publicity before the phenomena was sufficiently advanced, we would be inundated with requests for sittings – a fact that has always gone hand in hand with psychic phenomena of a physical nature. In the past, Leslie Flint had often related how he had at times been plagued by strangers arriving at his door without prior notice from all over the world, hoping for a sitting – even, on occasions, in the middle of the night.

It was hoped that news of the amazing physical phenomena at Scole would seep out slowly but, on 7 November, Paxton told the group that the 'cat was well and truly out of the bag' now and that, following several council meetings and discussions in the spirit world, the powers that be had reluctantly come to the conclusion that the intended bulletin would have to come out sooner than was originally anticipated. It was therefore with this in mind that our first December 1994 issue of the *Spiritual Scientist* – the bulletin that we had been asked by the spirit team to create and publish on a quarterly basis – was limited in its initial complimentary circulation, going only to those who it was felt would be interested in, and benefit from, the revolutionary new work. The publication is now in its second year and, as it inevitably grows in its readership, is attracting a tremendous amount of attention from eminent scientists and researchers (as well as the general public) with its comprehensive reports of the Scole group sittings. It is no longer necessary to limit the circulation and subscribers are now to be found in many countries throughout the world. In fact, so successful has it been (subscription rates are kept to a minimum level) that the initial photocopied 15–page version has already been replaced by a professionally printed magazine in glossy format.

The *Spiritual Scientist* is the official voice of the New Spiritual Science Foundation and will eventually include news, views and opinions of other groups who are working with the energy-based spirit technology in the same way as ourselves, as well as information and regular updates on the foundation itself.

Towards the end of November, the group underwent a period of consolidation, and entered into the start of a new phase, with truly scientific experiments. We were instructed to introduce the glass domes into the centre of the group, as they intended to start working with them on a permanent basis. The spirit team now wished to experiment with sustainable spirit lighting (as opposed to the mobile spirit lights we already had), which would be a regular feature of our sittings and the large dome would play a major part in this work. In addition, there were other pieces of scientific equipment which we would be required to build and provide from time to time. The first of these, which was created by a member of the Scole group to specific instructions, was a device which had two square metal plates mounted in wooden blocks about four feet apart. The blocks were connected by about four feet of wooden dowelling, which had a very low wattage torch bulb mounted midway between the two end plates. This was connected by means of a single electrical wire from the bulb to each of the two plates, but no circuit was created, as the plates were so far apart. The intention of the experiment is that, using energy only, the spirit team will at some stage be able to light up the bulb.

Some of the regular trance communicators – guides and helpers such as Patrick and Raji – stood back a little from now on, speaking to us less frequently in order to allow certain spirit scientists from the team to converse with us, so that we could be given running commentaries on the experiments they were undertaking. Usually when this happened, they would go on to demonstrate to us the exact effect they had just described.

Throughout December, the 'photographic department' of the spirit team came into its own, and we began to experience fantastic breakthroughs with the photography. Using 35mm Polaroid films which had never been opened, but remained throughout within their light-proof plastic tubs on the central table of the Scole group, we have had wonderful 35mm slides on many occasions, which have depicted a whole series of different and original subjects. We were able to develop the films immediately an experimental session was completed, using special Polaroid equipment, under test conditions, in full view of all those present. Over the months ahead, we received over 150 of these amazing slides, some showing 'areas of communication' within the spirit world itself, in both black and white and colour.

With Christmas coming up, we asked the spirit team if we should consider the possibility of a special sitting at this festive time. This led to their suggesting that we might celebrate a 'festival of light', rather than have a traditional 'Christmas' sitting – it seems that our spirit team of helpers prefer that everything we do in connection with our work in the field of physical phenomena is tackled in an entirely new way – and we went ahead with this special sitting on 27 December. It was a lovely occasion, with dozens of candles lit in the cellar and plenty of physical phenomena to match the festive mood.

1995 proved to be a very exciting year for the Scole group. We sat twice every week, and I can honestly say (hand on heart!) that since we started to get excellent physical phenomena ourselves at Scole, we have *never* had a totally blank sitting. We were getting close to the time when we would be cooperating regularly with scientists and researchers and organising frequent half-day seminars for members of the public to learn about the new phenomenon, and indeed, to witness it for themselves.

Members of the Scole Experimental Group experienced 83 different applications of physical phenomena in just 23 months, and this number rose almost every week. The ongoing phenomena included such items as: apports, ringing of bells, mobile spirit lights, levitation, spirit photographic imagery, breezes, temperature variation in the cellar, the sprinkling of water on sitters, spirit writing, sustained spirit lights in glass dome (in different colours), solid spirit entities constantly present during sittings and walking about at will touching sitters, SVOs (self-luminous Sustained Visible Objects), brought about by the spirit team from the spirit world for us to observe, solid spirit entities showing themselves to us in the spiritual light from the dome, spirit lights passing through such solid objects as the central table and sitters bodies, the heavy central table dancing the 'cancan' and 'energy voices' from spirit speaking to us directly from mid-air or from the solid spirit person themselves.

So far, the list of phenomena obtained is colossal, but we know that it only represents the tip of the iceberg. Much more is to come in the months and years ahead, as the Scole Experimental Group and the New Spiritual Science Foundation continue with their historic work – a true partnership between our world and the spirit world. I feel extremely privileged to be a part of this unique working group and believe I have finally caught up with the physical mediumship and the physical phenomena which I have been pursuing all these years.

# MY FRIEND WINSTON

AT THE VERY beginning of this book, in my Foreword, I mentioned that my long-running quest to obtain for myself the regular production and demonstration of sustained and repeatable physical phenomena has ultimately proved to be extremely successful and, along with other members of the Scole Experimental Group, I am now able to enjoy and experience these spirit-world wonders every week.

I also explained that three people over the last 22 years have, by and large, provided for me the necessary inspiration, motivation, leadership and dogged determination for my efforts to succeed in the end. The roles of Leslie Flint and my wife I have already dealt with, but there is one very special spirit person without whose help I doubt that the whole exercise would have succeeded. I refer to Winston Leonard Spencer Churchill, who has many times shown himself to be an excellent friend and motivator.

The connection starts very early on in the story, when I was sitting in my first physical circle – that of Elmer Browne, in Leicester. During 1974, in the course of my part-time second job of navigating locum doctors around the Birmingham area, I was one day listening to the radio calls coming from the locum HQ while the doctor I was travelling with was in someone's home attending to a patient. Suddenly, an urgent call came in for us. Some way across town from our present position, a man had collapsed with a suspected heart attack. When the doctor got back to the car, it was my job to navigate him to the next patient by the quickest route possible, following the A to Z street map which I had, and I would normally tell the doctor, 'Go left here ... Go right here ...' or, 'Straight on here ...' etc. It was doubly difficult at night times, because in the dark, it was nigh on impossible to spot the house numbers. Even with a powerful torch such as we carried, it slowed us down considerably, having to pick out the numbers with the torch from the car.

On this occasion, there was a further complication in that the shortest route to the patient's house involved intersecting the long road in which he lived approximately in the middle, and I had no idea whether the patient's house would be to the left or the right, which could have resulted in further delays. I had just made up my mind to say to the doctor, 'Go right', when I clearly heard the voice of Winston Churchill (which of course, I recognised immediately) tell me to turn left, where I would find the patient's house about 400 yards on the right-hand side. I felt we had nothing to lose and consequently followed the instructions given by the voice. Needless to say, the patient's house was exactly where I had been told it would be. The doctor's help was urgently needed there, and the man's life was saved. I often wonder what he would have thought if I could have suggested to him that his life had been saved by a discarnate Winston.

Since this was the first time I had ever had any sort of communication from someone who had been famous in their lifetime, I racked my brains for many months afterwards, wondering if I had imagined it or, perhaps even, if I might be going a little insane. I certainly did not tell anyone else at that stage of my unusual experience. I just could not figure out why someone like that would be interested in me, or what I was doing, but in the end the episode passed, and faded into the mists of time. Until, that is, I started to visit numerous mental mediums for private sittings.

Some mediums would tell me that a politician was trying to communicate – others a war correspondent. It seemed that Winston was very careful and very inventive in those early days to try to prove his presence to me. Some mediums mentioned a 'Leonard', others a 'Mr Spencer'. I was told that he was representing himself as an author on more than one occasion, or even as an artist. In his lifetime, Winston was all of these things, and more. Finally, at a private sitting I had with clairaudient medium Doris Stokes (not so famous at that time) at the SAGB on 27 April 1976, he finally gave three of his four names by way of positive identification. The conversation went something like this:

*Doris Stokes* Does the name 'Spencer' mean anything to you?

*Me* Yes.

*Doris* I asked the man to give me the rest of his name, and he says he doesn't think he should give it in case it rings any bells. And I don't know the man – [to me] I don't even know you, dear, do I?

*Me* No.

*Doris* [to the communicator] Well, if you don't want to tell me lovey, I can't push it.

Shortly afterwards, Doris returned again to the subject of this communicator:

*Doris* That name – that Spencer something. I think it's Spencer Churchill. Winston Spencer Churchill!

*Me* Yes.

From the very start of the Romford circle, Winston frequently came to speak to us via the trance state of the medium John. Even more evidential was the fact that he also started to speak regularly through me, using my own trance, and has for many years continued to do so. When we visited Leslie Flint for a seance, Winston was often there to speak to us, and when the Romford circle achieved the independent voice, Winston was one of the prime movers in our achieving that success as well as constantly being one of the main independent voice communicators.

There was one occasion when Sandra and I had visited Chartwell, Winston's home in Kent, and not mentioned that fact to anybody else in the circle. While there, we had noticed the feelings we often experienced when a spirit person came close to us but, above all, we had been surprised to notice in his study a carving of the 'praying hands'. It seemed to signify an interest in things spiritual and we had no prior knowledge of the fact that in his lifetime, Winnie might have been interested in spiritual matters. A couple of days later, we went for a sitting with Leslie Flint along with the rest of our circle.

Winston came as usual to speak to us, and told Sandra and me: 'I believe you were somewhat surprised the other day!' What wonderful evidence that was for us, since nobody else knew we had been there, let alone of our surprise at the 'praying hands' in his study.

Over the years, there have been many instances when Winston has managed to say a word or two in independent or trumpet direct voice at the various circles we have held. So much evidence of his presence has been amassed, that there is no longer a question of us ever doubting that he is frequently with us. It is significant, therefore, that the very first controlled phenomenon we obtained in our current group – the Scole Experimental Group – was an apport of a Churchill crown, or that he should see fit more recently to bring us an apport of a 1945 newspaper, featuring his photograph on the front page.

When Winston first spoke to us regularly, we knew little of his private and personal background but a clear picture has emerged gradually which leaves us in no doubt as to the fact that he was a very psychic man in his lifetime. His great grandmother on his mother's side was half Native American, and Winston had a difficult childhood, constantly seeking love and approval from his parents. He was a sensitive child and was, I believe, guided psychically throughout his life. Could it be sheer coincidence that following his capture by the Boers (as a war correspondent) and during his subsequent escape, he should choose to go for help to the *only house for 30 miles* or so that would not hand him back to his captors? I do not think so.

There is ample evidence to suggest that Winston himself was able to develop a form of automatic writing, and there is little doubt that many of his speeches were inspired. Throughout the last war, it is a fact that he was constantly obtaining spiritual guidance that would be helpful in his wartime leadership. Along with other prominent wartime personalities, he would often visit spiritualist mediums for a sitting. One of his favourites was 'battling' Bertha Harris, and he would often visit her with colleagues such as De Gaulle, parking his car in the blackout a couple of streets away from Bertha's home and then walking there.

One might ask if Winston ever had an interest in physical mediumship and I believe that should be answered with an emphatic *yes*. I recently uncovered a reference in a best-selling book by author H. Dennis Bradley (*The Wisdom of the Gods,* 1925) of a seance which took place in his home Dorincourt in Kingston Vale near London on Wednesday, 22 April 1925.

I should perhaps explain that Dennis Bradley had brought the famous trumpet and independent direct-voice medium George Valiantine over to England from America which was Valiantine's home. This was the second visit which Bradley had organised for Valiantine to England, the sittings on the first occasion being chronicled in Bradley's previous book, *Towards the Stars.*

Following his first contacts with Valiantine and his mediumship, Bradley and his wife had gone on to develop direct and independent-voice mediumship themselves at their home and were also able to get several other forms of physical phenomena.

I am convinced that Winston sat in his first physical phenomena seance at Dorincourt on 22 April 1925, at which time he was chancellor of the exchequer. I have verified with the Churchill Archives at Churchill College, Cambridge, that he would have been in London at the time, as he presented a budget a few days later. If I am correct in my theory, it would also explain why Winston was aware from an early date that a second world war was a distinct possibility and was warning of it way before most of the other English politicians believed such a war possible. I am still attempting to obtain some documentary proof that Winston did, in fact, attend this sitting with Valiantine for physical phenomena, but it is proving a difficult task as no personal diaries of Winston's have survived for this period and, in any case, he was obviously shy of publicity in this particular connection.

However, for what it is worth, I quote here from *The Wisdom of the Gods* Chapter 58:

> It had been arranged some few weeks back that this evening should be reserved for a certain gentleman and statesman who must remain anonymous. I can only say that he is one of the few really great men of intellect in Britain. He has occupied one of the highest positions in the State, but there are political reasons why his name should not be mentioned.
>
> We all dined quietly before the sitting, and there were present Valiantine, my wife, myself, and the anonymous gentleman, whose first experience of a seance this was.

The conditions appeared to be quite good, as after the first record had been completed upon the gramophone Dr Barnett [a spirit helper] came through and spoke.

Bert Everett spoke in his shrill tones; Kokum spoke, and also Pat O'Brien, who stayed for some little time, addressing each of the quartette. Bobby Worrall spoke with us and referred to Pat's [Bradley's young son] doings during the daytime.

The first of the personal spirits which manifested was that of George Curzon [Lord Curzon of Kedleston], using the luminous trumpet. He spoke on two or three occasions to the anonymous sitter and to me. He referred to certain well-known characters in the political arena whom he wished to be informed that he [Lord Curzon] was *alive*. During the conversation he was insistent upon the point of the possibility of a coming catastrophe, which would be likely to have a terrible effect upon our civilisation, saying: 'You must use every endeavour to stop those wars. Tell the ——— Tell ———' [The names, which Bradley was unable to publish, were, of course, volunteered].

Lord Curzon referred to his last illness, and he then volunteered the name of Dr John Everidge, and made a reference to an operation which had been performed on him.

The reference to Dr John Everidge I omitted to record in my notes at the time, although the name was, of course, heard by the four of us. My attention was drawn to this important omission by the spirit of Lord Northcliffe, speaking in his own voice at a seance held on the following Friday, and this extraordinary incident is recorded in Chapter 61.

I asked the anonymous sitter, who knew Lord Curzon quite well, if he knew whether Dr John Everidge had attended Lord Curzon. He replied that he did not know, and added that he had never heard of Dr Everidge. Neither had any of us.

A little later, using the luminous trumpet, another spirit addressed the anonymous sitter. This voice spoke to him in tones which vibrated with emotion. It was the spirit of a very near relative. The sitter could not hear what was said very distinctly – he is a trifle hard of hearing – but he continued the conversation throughout with delicate sympathy. [From personal experience, it is often difficult to distinguish clearly what is said by direct voices speaking out of a trumpet, whatever the state of one's hearing, as the instrument tends to muffle the voice to a certain extent and this would particularly apply to someone present at their first seance.] Personal messages of love were given through, and although little of what might be termed an evidential character was volunteered, the correct date of the passing over of this spirit was given. This was an evidential point. Using the luminous trumpet, the spirit voice spoke on several occasions, but at times, apparently, it found it difficult to sustain the power. After *she* had gone, the voice of Dr Barnett came through, and confirmed her actual relationship. [This is likely to have been the voice of Jennie, Lady Randolph Churchill, and Winston's mother, to whom he had been very close. She died on 29 June 1921, which was less than four years prior to this seance.]

Later, speaking in the independent voice, Annie [Bradley's 'dead' sister] spoke to me and my wife. She said that it had been a little difficult for the previous spirit which had spoken to materialise her voice, as it was the first time she had attempted to do so.

At the close Dr Barnett spoke to us all for some considerable time. He discussed with us various subjects, but in particular dealt with a catastrophe which was likely to happen in the forthcoming years. Speaking in very determined tones to the anonymous sitter, he said that unless a great wave of spirituality should sweep over the world, the next war, which would be waged from the air, would destroy our civilisation. He said that the crucial years were from this very moment until 1927, and he impressed upon us the urgent necessity of spreading spirituality as the only possible means of averting this disaster. [Since there is no time in the spirit world, in my experience it is one of the most difficult things for spirit entities to impart to us correctly when they make predictions concerning events of the future. While the predictions themselves are invariably correct, the timing attributed to those events by spirit communicators is often wrong.]

What historic implications this seance report by H. Dennis Bradley has! Remember it was written in 1925 and the Second World War did not raise its head for another 14 years. If it *was* Winston who was present at that seance (and in my own mind, I am sure that is the case), then he was the subject of a dramatic warning from the spirit world, and was therefore in a better position than most to know that a second world war would happen.

He would have been further encouraged to believe such a warning by having a one-to-one evidential conversation with his 'dead' mother, and would have been convinced of the reality of her identity by her reference to personal information known only to the two of them. Likewise the communication from Lord Curzon, who Winston knew well. He would have recognised the voice and mannerisms beyond a shadow of a doubt and realised the value of the warning that was being imparted to him.

It is possible that Pat Bradley, the young son of Dennis, is still alive today, albeit at an advanced age. He would know the true identity of the 'anonymous sitter' mentioned in his father's book as, perhaps, would other members of the Bradley family. It is also possible that descendants of George Valiantine, the American medium, would be able to verify my theory as to the fact that Winston was present at Dorincourt in 1925. I would be delighted to hear from any reader who can shed further light on the matter.

I have not forgotten Winston's promise to us many years ago, when he spoke in the independent voice at our Romford circle. He told us that it was his eventual intention to dictate a book to us in this manner and Jock, one of the spirit helpers at Romford, told us during a sitting that he had already seen this book in its entirety in the spirit world. I am still of the firm belief that when it is possible for him to do so through the Scole group, Winston will dictate such a book to us. When that happens, I shall be proud to arrange for its publication.

Printed in Great Britain
by Amazon

61652416R00200